D1755514

The Equity Derivatives Handbook

The Equity Derivatives Handbook

Edited by
John Watson

Published by
Euromoney Publications
in association with
Bankers Trust
The Chase Manhattan Bank N.A.
Intercapital Equity Derivatives Ltd
Merrill Lynch
Paribas Capital Markets
S.G. Warburg

Published by
Euromoney Publications PLC
Nestor House, Playhouse Yard
London EC4V 5EX

Copyright © 1993 Euromoney
Publications PLC
ISBN 1 85564 199 2

All rights reserved. No part of this book may be reproduced or used in any form (graphic, electronic or mechanical, including photocopying, recording, taping or information storage and retrieval systems) without permission by the publisher.

The views and opinions expressed in the book are solely those of the authors and need not necessarily reflect those of the institutions which have acted as co-publishers or contributors to the book. Although Euromoney has made every effort to ensure the complete accuracy of the text, neither it nor any co-publisher or contributor can accept any legal responsibility whatsoever for consequences that may arise from errors or omissions or any opinions or advice given.

Typeset by PW Graphics Ltd.
Printed in England by
Jolly & Barber Ltd, Rugby

Contents

	vii	Preamble
Chapter 1	1	A conceptual background to equity derivatives
	2	What is an equity derivative?
	2	Historical perspective
	4	Needs of end-users
	6	The financial product life cycle
	7	Differences between derivatives and other financial products
	9	A common sense explanation of derivatives
	15	Brief description of market segments
	19	Problems
Chapter 2	21	The uses of equity derivatives for investors
	21	Investor profiles
	29	Survey of market development
	33	Investor uses of equity derivatives
	51	Conclusion
Chapter 3	53	The issuer's perspective
	53	Comparison with the fixed income derivatives market
	54	Equity derivative securities
	63	Summary
Chapter 4	65	Equity-index-linked derivatives
	65	Overview of the market
	67	The instruments
	69	Advantages of EIL derivatives
	72	EIL swaps
	85	EIL notes
	89	Over-the-counter EIL options and warrants

Chapter 5	**95**	Case studies
	95	Using swaps during a manager search
	96	Swaps to gain foreign exchange exposure
	96	Swaps to reallocate assets without booking bond losses
	96	Swaps to diversify a family trust
	97	Using caps and floors to protect equity gains
	98	Earning equity returns without frequent marking to market
	100	Using index-linked deposits to gain global exposure
	100	Enhancing S&P 500 returns through fixed income management
Chapter 6	**103**	Exotic options
	104	Classes of exotic option
	105	Path-dependent options
	115	Options on more than one asset
	116	Currency-linked options
	118	Compound options
	118	Regional options
	118	Review
Chapter 7	**121**	Pricing and mathematics
	121	Conventions
	122	Traditional product pricing
	127	Theoretical option pricing
	137	Concerns
	137	Conclusions
Chapter 8	**139**	Regulatory and documentation overview
	139	Background to the UK regulatory environment
	142	The regulatory system
	150	The future
	151	Taxation of derivatives
	152	The United Kingdom
	157	The United States
	159	France
	162	The ISDA confirmation for OTC equity index option deals
	171	Appendix
Chapter 9	**179**	Long-term implications
	179	Introduction
	180	Impact on other financial markets
	181	Impact on the equity market
	190	Likely evolution of the derivatives market
	193	Conclusion
Chapter 10	**195**	Glossary

Preamble

It is often said that those who can do, do and those who can't, teach.

Within this cynical statement there is perhaps an unfortunate element of truth. In the ever-competitive financial markets anyone who has discovered a new way to make money may have a reason to broadcast the result. At the same time, he has an even better reason to keep it secret.

It is often forgotten that, quite apart from their need to compete, all those who make a living from the financial markets have a vested interest in promoting the health and standards of the market as a whole. We should not forget the need to expand and improve the quality of the cake in our preoccupation with the size of our own slice.

No one seriously expects any publication to provide a DIY guide to a sure and safe way to make a fortune. Market practitioners are going to keep their most proprietary techniques under wraps until they find their way into the public domain by other means. But, with the extremely rapid pace of development in the equity derivative market, the non-proprietary area is already large and rapidly expanding. The quality and continued growth of the market requires that this area be properly understood and the understanding widely disseminated. This way, standards of professionalism among market professionals, and thus the confidence of end users may be raised.

I believe that it is at least partly in this spirit that so many of the market's most prestigious firms and leading practitioners, who are otherwise in fierce competition, have co-operated in sponsoring and contributing material for this book. I am pleased to feel that the result is a handbook which consolidates the present state of evolution in the non-proprietary technology of the equity derivatives market and presents it in a form which is both comprehensive and yet accessible even to non-specialists.

John Watson
July 1993

A conceptual background to equity derivatives

John Watson

Westminster Equity Limited

It is no exaggeration to say that there has recently been an explosion of interest in equity derivatives. This interest has not all been positive; on the contrary, there has been a very mixed press.

At one extreme, derivatives, including equity derivatives, are seen as potential saviours of the profitability of the securities industry. Some major houses now report as much as one-third of net income from derivatives, with an increasingly significant amount from equity derivatives. At the other extreme, derivatives are, for some, inseparably associated with risk. Like nuclear energy, they are considered powerful but dangerous – "another Chernobyl waiting to happen".

Their detractors suspect equity derivatives of exerting a malign influence on underlying markets. The most explicit case is where the Japanese authorities, until recently, blamed derivative-related trading for their stock market's dramatic fall.

Some supporters see derivatives as capable of producing almost magical results – the financial counterpart of the Gulf War military technology. Cynics suspect them as yet another gimmicky method for avaricious investment bankers to part unwary investors from their money. No doubt the latter hope to see derivatives go the way of so many market fads and disappear into obscurity.

Nothing more poignantly captures the mixture of fear and respect with which this market is regarded than what we might call the "myth of the rocket scientist". Derivative market practitioners are frequently referred to as "rocket scientists" – not least by colleagues in other fields of the securities industry.

Whatever the meaning behind the myth, it is clear that being a rocket scientist is no guarantee of competence, nor a necessary qualification for success, in this industry sector. The myth has helped cloak the industry in mystery and has undoubtedly deterred many "non-rocket scientists" from entering the field.

It is fair to say that mathematical fluency will make certain aspects of the business more readily accessible, but those without a strong mathematical background should not be intimidated into avoiding it as a specialisation. The subject is now beginning to break out of its specialist bounds into the area of financial general knowledge. It is increasingly difficult to justify senior management responsibility in the banking industry without at least a general understanding of derivatives in today's markets.

The time is therefore ripe to attempt to counteract some of the myths and to make the subject more obviously approachable to the non-mathematically literate generalist. In attempting this we will try to show why, like them or not, derivatives have an established and growing importance. Derivatives are here to stay and, as one major market figure has been known to comment – "they are too important to be left to a bunch of geeks" . The lid has been lifted on equity derivatives and, for better or worse, like the lid of Pandora's box, it will never be put back on.

What is an equity derivative?

An equity derivative can be defined as a traded financial instrument (security), the value of which can be derived from that of a share or group of shares (the "underlying" security).

An understanding of equity derivatives will require some understanding of the general nature of traded financial instruments as well as an understanding of the general nature of derivatives. In fact some theories of share valuation analyse shares as derivatives (a share being seen as a call option on the value of a company), in which case it could be argued that the understanding of shares requires an understanding of derivatives rather than the other way round. As a method of introducing the basics we will explore some of the more important senses in which the concepts of derivative and underlying are more mutually dependent than the terms imply.

Historical perspective

The image of derivatives as something ultra modern and highly complex – the rightful domain of the "rocket scientist" – is highly misleading in one major respect. It understates both the time and extent to which many of the fundamental concepts involved have already been in existence and in everyday use in "simple" stock trading or investment.

Ancient history

In one sense the history of derivatives is as long as the history of trade itself. It may be said that a logical condition for a trade of any kind to take place is the prior existence of a firm offer or firm bid. A firm offer of stock is a free call on the stock, given by the offeror to the offeree. The fact that the call may only be of very short duration is irrelevant. Logically there must be a period of time during which the call option comes into existence prior to the trade. In the same way a firm bid is a free put option.

Anyone who feels that such options could have no value or practical significance should consider the process of broking a market, which can be understood as acquiring such free options from end-users and "selling" them to other end-users for immediate exercise. The establishment of traditional broking businesses in their various forms is adequate testimony to the practical significance of such options. Hence the claim that the history of options is as long as the history of trade itself, or even marginally longer!

It could also be said that forward transactions came to exist as soon as trade came to be settled on credit rather than for cash. In fact any credit extended for interest can be said to be a derivative (a contract for future delivery of cash). In this sense a loan is a simple purchase or sale for cash of a derivative (the future delivery of cash). At this level, the concept of a derivative is neither as alien nor as new as it first appears.

There is one more important sense in which derivatives can be said to have been around before their recent condensation into a commodity product or identifiable market sector. Stock portfolio managers have frequently been divided into cyclical or counter-cyclical categories. The behaviour of the former is characterised by a tendency to reduce market exposure at low (and increase at high) market levels. This may be an accidental consequence of having limits on the amount of "pain" which it is possible to tolerate in a weak market while being allowed to "gamble with profits" in a strong market. The counter-cyclical manager's behaviour is exactly opposite.

It has been pointed out that, in following these policies, fund managers are (perhaps unwittingly) shadowing the adjustments which a market professional would make in dynamically hedging an option position. In buying at high and selling at low market levels, the cyclical manager (of a long stock portfolio) shadows the hedge strategy of a seller of a call option on the portfolio. This can be explained as follows:

A hedge is, by definition, a position equal but opposite to that being hedged. The cyclical manager's position is equal but opposite to a short call position, so the net result of his policy is to replicate holding a (long) call option on his portfolio. Similarly the counter-cyclical manager, by buying low and selling high, shadows the hedge strategy of the holder of a long put position and so replicates being short of a put on his portfolio. (Fuller explanations of the process of delta hedging an option position are given later in this chapter and in Chapter Seven.) The same phenomenon can be expressed in terms of trending or mean reversion. A stock trader who believes the market is trending will sell as the market goes down and buy as it goes up. If he believes it is mean reverting he will do the opposite. The trend-following trader also therefore replicates holding a call and the mean reversion trader replicates a short put position.

This raises important questions for the traditional manager. First, could a cyclical (counter-cyclical) manager not more simply, cheaply and effectively execute his strategy by buying (selling) a call on the market or sector of the market? Secondly, does the (cyclical or counter-cyclical) portfolio manager not need to understand the behaviour of options and their corresponding delta hedges in order to understand even the behaviour of his existing portfolio as managed under his existing strategy? Even the fund manager who thinks he has no interest in derivatives or who is not allowed to deal in them may, from a study of derivatives, have a great deal to learn about the likely behaviour of his portfolio.

Finally, there is one most fundamental and crucial sense in which derivatives have been around as long as the underlying market. We shall return to this later as it can only be explained in the light of put/call parity, which is discussed later in this chapter.

Modern history

Some claim that the existence of derivatives as a product type distinct from that in the underlying market can be traced back to the 18th century where forward agreements were concluded for trading commodities in Japan. But these are not derivatives in the modern sense of the word since they were not treated as instruments separately tradable in their own right. However, several familiar products which have been around for some time are really derivatives, although they are not generally recognised as such. Any basket or portfolio of stock is a derivative in that it can be traded as a unit and its price varies with that of the underlying shares. A stock loan is a derivative because when the stock is sold the resulting position can be considered as a security (which costs the net of the sale proceeds and the margin), the value of which is a function of the price of the underlying. Any purchase or sale of stock on margin or partially paid is a derivative and can be seen as exactly analogous to stock index futures.

The history of equity derivatives (which would be recognised as such today) really has two distinct starting points. The first was the establishment in Chicago of trade in stock options – initially OTC and subsequently on the CBOT exchange in 1973. The second, which is really the beginning of the recent explosion of interest, can be traced to the establishment of the OTC market in equity derivatives as recently as 1987. The predecessor of this was not the Chicago-originated markets in stock futures and options but the markets in swaps and long-term options in foreign exchange and interest rate products which had developed during the early to mid-1980s in the "global" market centres of London, New York and Tokyo.

There was a growing awareness that the skills and techniques involved in these markets were specific neither to particular underlying product types nor to swaps alone. As a result, the swaps market in interest rate and foreign exchange products grew quickly to embrace, first, options on the same products, then swaps and options on other products including equities and commodities. The equity derivative market today can, with the diversity and maturity of its products, be identified most easily as the offspring of the swaps market.

Why equity derivatives?
It sometimes appears to outsiders that derivative markets exist only to create profits for market intermediaries. However desirable a state of affairs that might be to market intermediaries themselves, it ought to be clear enough that it would provide no basis for the continued existence and development of the market in the long term. It should go without saying that the existence of a market in equity derivatives must, at least in the long term, be contingent on its products satisfying, at an acceptable cost, the real needs of end-users. The question is, what are those needs and how does the market satisfy them?

Needs of end-users

Execution considerations
Many of the end-user needs addressed by derivatives can be grouped under the pedestrian but none the less important heading of efficiency of execution.

Liquidity/speed of execution
The advent of derivative products, and particularly of exchange-traded stock index futures, has made possible portfolio restructuring on a scale, and at a speed and cost, previously unimaginable.

When immediate, large-scale portfolio adjustments are necessary, the way is blocked for any investors who are forced to make them by buying or selling physical stock. The selection of stocks to trade will often in itself be a decision of great complexity, which can be made at speed perhaps only by adopting a brutal and arbitrary approach. Furthermore, the attempt to trade stock in size for any but the most liquid issues incurs significant negative market impact.

Transaction costs
No matter how favourable a deal the investor may have cut with his broker, he will never be able to undercut the cost of gaining exposure to the equivalent market

through futures. Exchange-traded equity index futures in all major markets have lower commission rates, lower bid/offer spreads and frequently more liquidity, than the underlying markets. To deal in physical stock where futures would be an acceptable substitute can involve paying a premium equivalent to many times the transaction costs of dealing in futures.

The logical needs of end-users of options
In the case of options, it is possible to set out some general rules for their use. These can be summarised neatly by saying that an option purchase is an instrument of uncertainty while an option sale is an instrument of indifference. In other words, the natural buyer of an option is someone with an identified need for protection against future uncertain events. The natural seller of an option is someone who is indifferent to the outcome of future uncertain events.

Uncertainty – the natural option buyer
One first step for any market end-user in setting policy objectives is the identification of tolerance levels or "thresholds of pain". Taking a very simple example, an equity investor may need to "guarantee" that the value of a fund at maturity will not be less than the original amount invested. Where such a tolerance level has been established it can be satisfied by the purchase of an option. For example, a call option will protect a buyer of the underlying against high values in a rising market and a put option will protect a seller of the underlying against low prices in a falling market.

The existence of tolerance thresholds above which a buyer cannot afford to buy, or below which a seller cannot afford to sell, thus logically implies a need to buy options.

Indifference – the option seller
Another first step for the policy formulating end-user is the identification of areas of indifference. An equity investor may, for example, have maximum and minimum limits within which he must maintain his investment in one market as a percentage of a global equity portfolio. Say he must keep a minimum of 10 per cent and a maximum of 20 per cent of his portfolio invested in German stock. Within this range, he may be indifferent to the extent of say 6 per cent. He may wish to avoid the 10–13 per cent and 17–20 per cent ranges, but may be completely indifferent to his location in the 13–17 per cent range. In this case, he can sell an option which effectively gives the option buyer the right to determine his exact exposure to the German market as a percentage of his total exposure within this range.

Anyone who has identified an area of indifference such as this can be said to have a real need to sell options in the sense that he owns something which to him has no value (his indifference) but for which others may be prepared to pay.

Expressing views
The traditional view of an equity investor might tend to have been expressed in terms of a particular stock, sector or market being undervalued or overvalued. While holding and restructuring physical stock portfolios is inefficient, it does provide a means of expressing these views, especially where the type of view taking might be described as stock picking.

But views may be more complex, in which case they are less easily expressed through adjustments to a physical stock portfolio. Time horizons and price limits, maximum, minimum or average prices might be incorporated. For example, the view that the average level of the Nikkei 225 Stock Index during the second half of 1993 will be between 22,000 and 25,000 cannot be simply or efficiently expressed by a strategy of holding physical stock. It could, however, be very well expressed by a derivative position (the purchase of a forward Asian call on the Nikkei struck at 22,000 and capped at 25,000).

There is a two-way relationship between the existence of views and the existence of the products through which to express such views effectively. The formation of more sophisticated views by market end-users produces demand for new derivative products, but the existence of those new derivative products stimulates other end-users to formulate views they would not previously have had. A cynic may draw a comparison with *The Road to Wigan Pier*, in which George Orwell asked a coal miner how long he had lived with the problem of having no bath at home. After a pause for reflection the miner replied, "Since you mentioned it".

There are undoubtedly cases in which market intermediaries talk the need for a product into existence, and such needs may be well be, in some sense, completely artificial. But we would suggest that the widening range of available derivatives and the increasing sophistication of market end-users, which is partly its result and partly its cause, will be one of the major forces shaping the development of the equity and equity derivative markets during the next several years.

The needs of end-users and the means of fulfilling them through the use of derivatives is examined in detail in Chapters Two and Three.

The financial product life cycle

Markets in financial products, including derivatives, evolve according to a recognisable process. Understanding the derivatives market involves knowing which stage in this process the various sectors of the market have reached. This knowledge makes it possible to predict market developments as the products evolve naturally from one stage to the next.

It is possible to sub-divide them indefinitely, but the main stages are: the arbitraged stage; the traded stage; and the brokered stage.

The arbitraged stage

At this first stage in the product life cycle, there are few transactions and very few participants. Profit margins can be high but each transaction is structured individually. There is no transparency in pricing. Documentation may be complex as terms needed to reflect previously unseen conditions must be negotiated individually.

The participating institutions in the market tend to be the major integrated global banks or investment banks. The individuals involved will be either arbitrageurs or proprietary traders who act rather like in-house managers of the house capital. Or they may be origination people who design and engineer transactions so that their component parts are laid off with third parties and none of the risk (or only that part of it which is the stock-in-trade of one of its existing trading books) remains in house.

The traded stage

A traded market is characterised by the emergence of market-makers prepared to quote prices – particularly two-way prices on a reasonable spread. This presupposes a certain degree of understanding among market professionals about the definition and pricing of transactions, although the understanding may be shared by very few. The market at this stage is the rightful preserve of houses with the culture and systems to manage, and the appetite to commit capital to, the running of extensive risk books. Such market-makers will normally number only two or three, who will try to make prices only to end-users. If the number increases then it will not be long before inter-dealer trade and active broking develops.

The brokered stage
At this stage the product has become "commoditised". Standard terms have evolved for the definition and pricing of transactions. These may even be embodied in agreements between industry groups. Turnover is high and there are many market participants, although margins are low. Pricing becomes more transparent. It becomes possible, even for houses with no particular appetite for the product, to commit capital and to play a significant part in the business. Inter-dealer brokers who allow market-makers to trade anonymously between themselves will finally develop. The natural ultimate fate for the heavily brokered product is to become exchange traded.

A common game played by many houses is to show prices to the market, as if making a market, but with the intention of acting as broker. In fact many of the most active market-making houses are themselves among the most active brokers, although the two functions are normally carried out by different (sales as opposed to trading) staff.

As financial products evolve through these stages, so the number and types both of people and of institutions handling them change fairly predictably. As the power of technology develops and the skills involved become more widely dispersed, so the speed of this evolutionary process is accelerating constantly. It is a question of whether this process will continue indefinitely, with a constant flow of new arbitrage products to fill the spaces vacated by the products passing on to the next stage. It feels as if exchanges, as the ultimate repositories of all products, have a guaranteed future, whereas market arbitrageurs, market-makers and brokers all depend on the continuity of this flow for survival.

Differences between derivatives and other financial products

As a sub-species of the genus "financial product", derivatives are subject to their general life cycle. They also show some important distinguishing characteristics.

First, because of their price relationship with the underlying, derivatives can be hedged or synthesised by taking positions in the underlying. A buyer of an option who does not wish to hold it to maturity does not need to find a seller. He can effectively unwind the position by hedging it. A derivative market-maker may therefore be a "manufacturer" rather than simply a "wholesaler" of derivatives.

The process of "manufacturing" derivative positions necessarily involves a more integrated approach to financial instruments than has hitherto characterised financial intermediaries. This has far-reaching practical implications. For example, the manager of an equity derivative book must quantify and neutralise not only his equity-related exposures but also, for example, his exposures to interest rates and foreign exchange.

Secondly, the relationship between derivatives and their underlying markets is quite unlike that between one underlying market and another. For example, it is common enough for a salesman of one "underlying" financial product (say bonds) to know nothing about another (say commodities). It is often unnecessary, since the clients for one underlying product may have little interest in another, and there is little likelihood that the client will buy one underlying product as an alternative to the other. On the other hand, the same clients (and the same staff at those clients) may well be responsible for dealing in both the underlying product and its derivatives. And, while it is very unlikely that a stock transaction could be replaced by a commodity or other underlying financial product type, it may quite appropriately be replaced by an equity derivative transaction.

Comparison of equity with non-equity derivatives
At this stage in the development of the market, there are many differences in detail but little essential difference between equity and non-equity derivatives. The equity derivative business has more in common with other derivative businesses than with the underlying equity markets.

It is sometimes said that understanding the general nature of derivatives is more essential to an appreciation of equity derivatives than is understanding the underlying equity market. Some would go so far as to say that too much familiarity with the underlying equity markets can obscure an understanding of the equity derivative markets.

It would be dangerous to interpret this as meaning that there are no significant differences between equity and non-equity derivative markets. There are several differences which have contributed to the individual history of the market and to the present state of its development. Perhaps the most crucial is the liquidity of the underlying. People who are familiar with the foreign exchange, bond and liquid futures markets may have something of a rude awakening in applying derivatives technology evolved in those markets to the equity market. Ignoring ticketing costs, transaction costs in those markets may be measured in single figures of basis points, whereas with single stocks, trading costs may reach three figures (ie, 1 per cent) quite easily.

A confusing factor is that the process of exchange trading is sometimes thought to overcome the effect of the market bid/offer leading to a gross underestimate of the costs of stock trading. This in turn leads to considerable distortion of the net volatility which can be captured in delta hedging compared with the market volatility measured on a daily close/close basis.

Even the bid/offer spread (estimated in the Japanese market example below at 1.5 per cent) can grossly understate this effect since it reflects the average minimum touch for TSE (Tokyo Stock Exchange) stocks as a whole. Dealing in size in individual stocks can incur a bid/offer of anything from 0.25 per cent to 5 per cent and up. This means that the spread of capturable volatility around the daily close/close volatility varies enor-mously from stock to stock. Anyone unable to overcome this problem, and failing to take it into account, is in severe danger of having his fingers burnt in pricing equity, particularly single stock, options.

Using the Japanese stock market as an example, round trip dealing costs (for a reasonable size ¥25 million trade) would typically add up as follows:

- Sales tax   = 0.3 per cent
- Commission 1.0 per cent × 2 = 2.0 per cent
- Bid/offer spread   = 1.5 per cent
- Total   = 3.8 per cent

It is thus as easy to understate the differences between equity and non-equity derivatives as to overstate them. It is useful to understand how some of the points of contrast between the underlying instruments are more apparent than real.

Take the difference between a stock and a bond. The most obvious apparent difference is that a stock is not "repaid" by the issuer. But this did not stop the active development of the market in "perpetual" bonds where principal is not repaid. Furthermore, an active sub-section of the bond market has developed to trade bonds where the borrower is in default and where, in consequence, the principal may never be repaid or where any repayment may be partial and at an uncertain date.

Another obvious point of difference between stocks and bonds seems to be the degree of uncertainty of their dividend (or interest or coupon payment). But this has not prevented the active development of the floating rate note where only the next due interest payment is determined.

These considerations lead to the conclusion that it is more appropriate to view different underlying instruments themselves, and hence their derivatives, as being at different points on the same continuum, rather than as generically distinct.

Other derivative markets

Major derivative markets exist for both interest rates and foreign exchange, with commodity derivatives some way behind. Recent attempts to introduce derivatives on property have so far met with little success, but new market sectors reputedly under development include derivatives on credit risk. In theory it is possible to have a derivative on anything which has a price. In practice the development of a derivatives market is constrained by the underlying, and particularly by its liquidity, transaction costs and the possibilities for shorting it.

A common sense explanation of derivatives

At this stage in the development of the market, derivatives can be divided into two simple categories. The first category involves the concept of the time value of money – futures, swaps and long dated forwards (all of which may be referred to as forwards). The second category is that of options which involves, in addition to the concept of time value, the concept of probability. More or less all derivatives traded at present are combinations of, or variations on, these two basic derivative types. The fundamental concepts behind both forwards and options are in essence very simple.

Nature of a forward

A forward purchase of a commodity can be seen as a normal ("spot") purchase with the purchase price being borrowed by the buyer from the seller until the settlement date, while the seller retains the commodity purchased until repayment of the "loan". Interest on the loan is built into the price of the forward and the "fair value" of the forward is the spot price plus the cost of interest until settlement. Complications such as

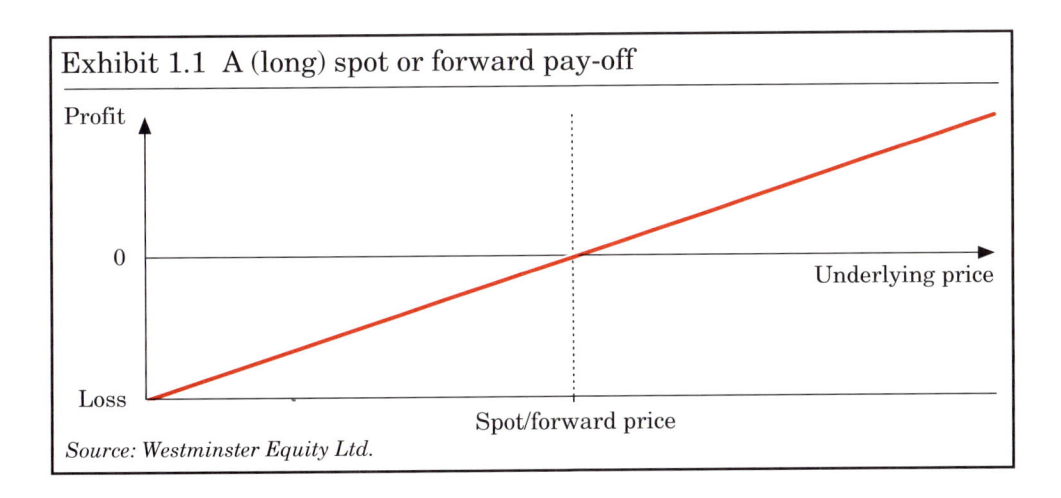

Exhibit 1.1 A (long) spot or forward pay-off

Source: Westminster Equity Ltd.

economic as opposed to physical delivery or margining on futures obscure, but do not alter, this simple basic nature of a forward.

Futures can be defined simply as exchange-traded forwards, and swaps can be defined simply as series of forwards. The simple nature of swaps is disguised by the fact that (ignoring exchange of principal) the forwards in the series are all executed at the same rate. Variations on the basic swap such as forward swap, amortising swap and zero coupon swap are mostly straightforward elaborations on this theme.

Given that, at maturity, the value of a forward will by definition be equal to that of the spot, there is no difference between the exposure to the price of the underlying afforded by a forward or spot position. The same pay-off diagram (Exhibit 1.1) can thus be used to illustrate both spot and forward transactions.

Forward hedging/arbitrage
It is easy enough to see how a forward position can be hedged and arbitrage profits made where there are sufficiently large price anomalies. For example, if the forward price of a commodity rises sufficiently above the spot, then arbitrageurs will buy it spot and sell it forward, paying storage charges and interest until the forward delivery date. Similarly, a commodity which is sufficiently cheap on a forward basis can be arbitraged where it is possible to borrow the commodity. This is done quite simply by selling the commodity spot and buying it forward, with the spot sale being settled by

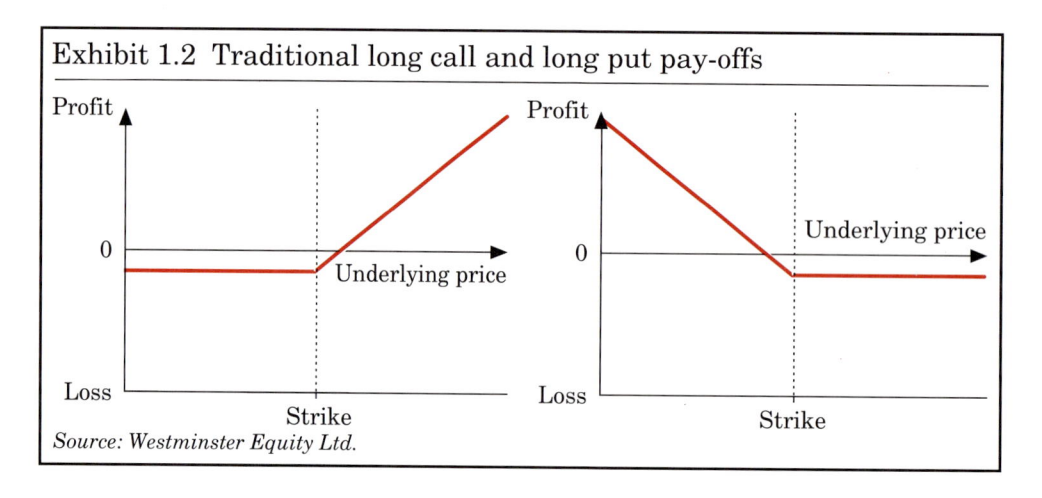

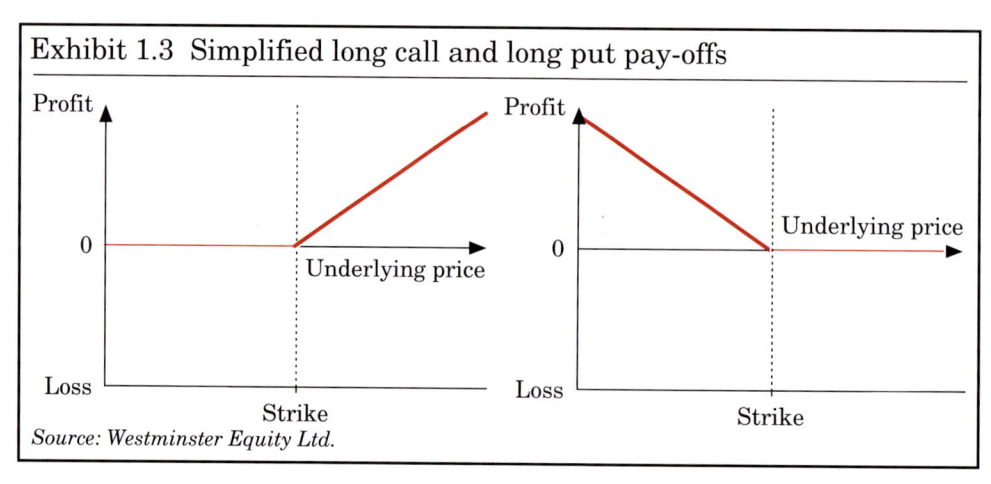

Exhibit 1.2 Traditional long call and long put pay-offs

Source: Westminster Equity Ltd.

Exhibit 1.3 Simplified long call and long put pay-offs

Source: Westminster Equity Ltd.

delivery of the borrowed commodity. Delivery of the forward purchase is used to repay the commodity loan. These types of arbitrage are commonly referred to as "cash/futures" or "cash and carry" arbitrage.

Nature of an option

Options are also in essence very simple. Probably the easiest way to see this simplicity is to look at their pay-off diagrams (Exhibits 1.2 and 1.3). These show that the pay-off of an option can be seen simply as one-half of that for a spot or forward transaction. Option pay-off diagrams usually incorporate the option price into the pay-off, but that simply obscures their essential simplicity to no great purpose.

The simple nature of options can be explained verbally by saying that a forward gives the obligation (which logically includes the right) to buy or sell the underlying, whereas an option gives the right without the obligation. Hence, for example, if I enter a forward purchase I am obliged to complete the purchase at the agreed price – even if the price of the underlying falls in the meantime forcing me effectively to take a loss (ie, by buying above the market price). If I buy a call option on the underlying I am not forced to buy and so need take no loss if the market price falls.

Put/call parity or put/call conversion

It follows directly from the above description of forwards and options that they can be combined (assuming for simplicity the same strike price and maturity) in the following ways.

A forward purchase (+ FWD) is equivalent to owning a call (+ CALL) and being short a put (− PUT):

$$+ \text{FWD} = + \text{CALL} - \text{PUT} \quad \text{(see Exhibit 1.4)}$$

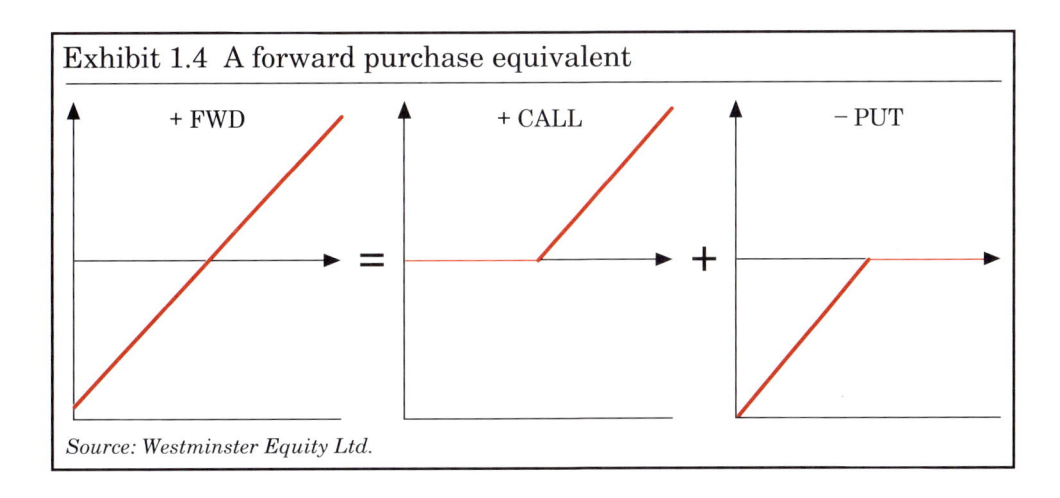

Exhibit 1.4 A forward purchase equivalent

Source: Westminster Equity Ltd.

A forward sale (− FWD) is equivalent to owning a put (+ PUT) and being short a call (− CALL):

$$- \text{FWD} = + \text{PUT} - \text{CALL} \quad \text{(see Exhibit 1.5)}$$

Either of these expressions can be rearranged to:

$$+ \text{CALL} - \text{FWD} = + \text{PUT} \quad \text{(see Exhibit 1.6)}$$

combining a long call position and a forward sale produces a long put position, or

$$+ \text{PUT} + \text{FWD} = + \text{CALL} \quad \text{(see Exhibit 1.7)}$$

combining a long put position with a forward purchase produces a long call position.

Exhibit 1.5 A forward sale equivalent

−FWD = +PUT + −CALL

Source: Westminster Equity Ltd.

Exhibit 1.6 A long put equivalent

+CALL − −FWD = +PUT

Source: Westminster Equity Ltd.

Exhibit 1.7 A long call equivalent

+PUT + +FWD = +CALL

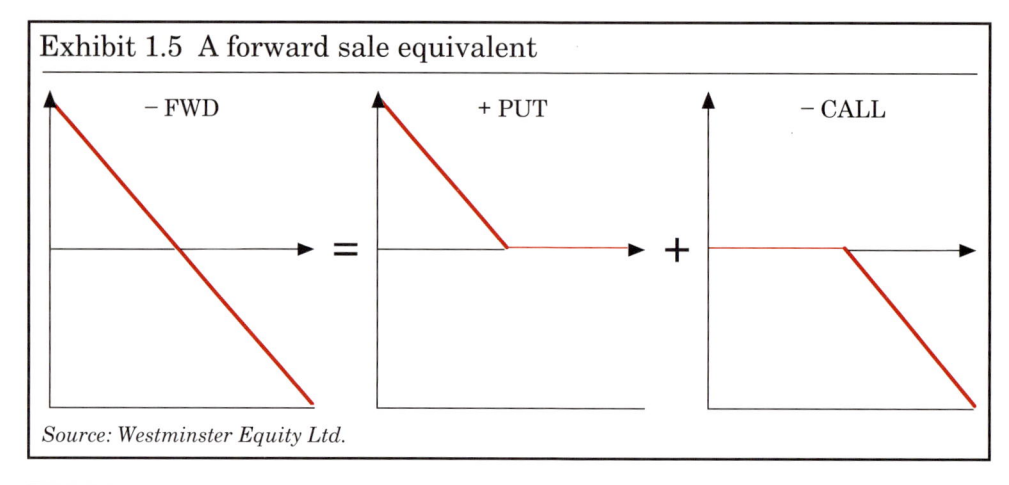

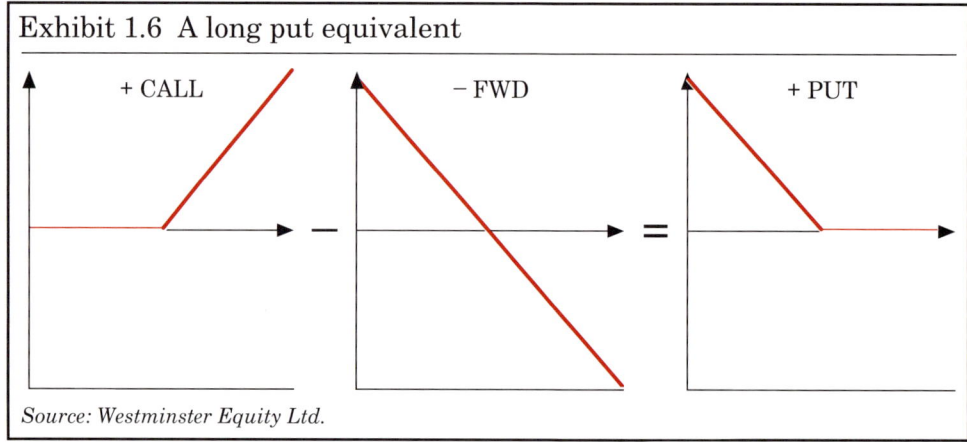

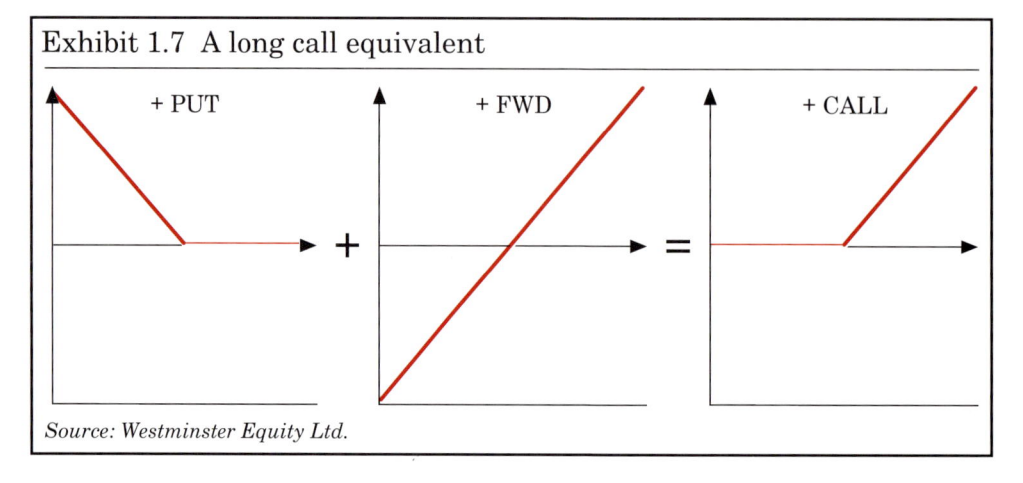

Source: Westminster Equity Ltd.

Common sense explanation of put/call parity

The rules of put/call parity are very simple and it is easy to see the relationships involved by means of pay-out diagrams. It is not so easy to understand their meaning in common sense terms. The relationship is so fundamental and illustrative of the essential nature of puts and calls that it is worthwhile to attempt a common sense understanding.

If I own a put on a stock, legally I have the right but not the obligation to sell the stock at a fixed price. Ignoring transaction costs and assuming options are at-the-money (ie, the strike price is equal to the market price), if the stock price at maturity of the put is below this fixed price it will always be rational to exercise – ie, sell the stock at the fixed price (and irrational not to). If the stock price is higher than the fixed price at maturity it will always be rational not to (and irrational to) exercise. This can be summarised in common sense terms by saying that at maturity a put owner will always sell (at the fixed price) if the stock price falls (and not otherwise).

In the same way, the owner of a call will always buy (at the fixed price) if the price rises. If a call owner also enters a forward transaction to sell the stock, then he is a seller regardless of the stock price move. If the price rises he therefore simultaneously buys (by exercising the call) and sells (by settling the forward), the stock at the same price. The net effect is that he does nothing in a rising market (just like the owner of the put). In a falling market he will sell the stock at the fixed price (by settling the forward), exactly as will the holder of the put.

In summary, the holder of a call who has also entered a short sale, will always be a seller in a falling market and will otherwise (net) do nothing. Which places him in exactly the same position as the holder of a put.

Conclusions on put/call parity
As mentioned above, forward and spot positions may be regarded as identical as far as pay-out is concerned. This means that one of the formulations above (+ FWD = + CALL − PUT) may be re-expressed as:

$$\text{long spot} = + \text{CALL} - \text{PUT}$$

In other words, owning a share is equivalent to owning a call and having sold short a put. The apparently simple entity – a (long position in) stock – can thus be broken down into two component entities; a (long) call and a (short) put. While analogies with "splitting the atom" might be too dramatic, it does seem meaningful to view a "cash position" as a composite rather than a simple entity. The advent of derivatives technology has made it possible to deal separately with the parts of that composite.

This gives the lie to much of the traditional debate about the relative advantages of derivatives and cash instruments. People who deal only in the cash markets are already dealing (albeit unconsciously) with derivatives. Its just a question of how aware they are of that fact and of the possibilities offered by it.

Option pricing, hedging and arbitrage
Pricing options
So far, this analysis of options has left out the question of price. The pricing of options has been the subject of many well-known technical papers. For many practical purposes, the theory can be assumed and does not require any understanding in depth. It is for each individual to find a level of understanding appropriate to his practical needs and intellectual curiosity. A fuller explanation of the concepts and theories involved is given in Chapter Eight. Here, we will restrict the explanation to a simple sketch in common sense terms.

The price of an option is the (present) value of its future pay-out. Since we cannot know how the market will move and thus what the exact pay-out will be, the first step is to assign probabilities to different levels of pay-out. This is done by assuming that the price of the underlying will move randomly but with an assumed volatility. Given the share price today and the volatility of the future share price movement, the probability of the price of the share being within any given price range at any future point in time can be calculated.

Exhibit 1.8 Option premium

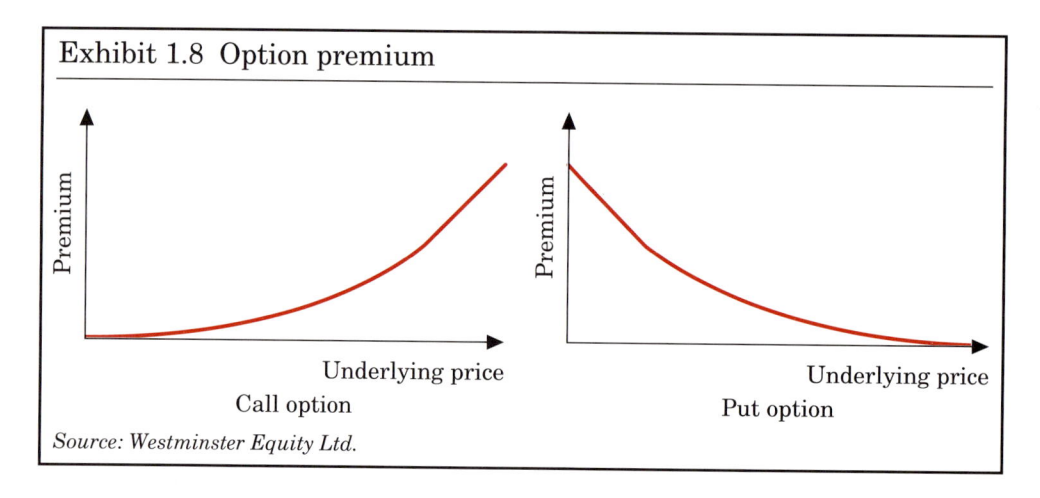

[Two graphs showing Premium vs Underlying price: Call option (upward curving) and Put option (downward curving)]

Source: Westminster Equity Ltd.

Hence a probability can be assigned to the pay-out resulting from the share price being in a given range at maturity of the option. The higher the volatility the greater the probability of higher pay-outs. The value of each pay-out is the amount of that pay-out multiplied by its probability. The value of the total pay-out of the option is therefore the sum of the values of these individual pay-outs, and the fair price for the option is the present value of this total.

Clearly the longer an option has to run, the higher the probability that the price of the underlying will rise to reach any given level. Also the closer to (or further in) the money, the higher the probability that the price will rise to reach any given level. Ignoring interest rates, given the maturity and strike price of an option and the volatility of the underlying, the "fair value" of the option can be "derived" from the price of the underlying (see Exhibit 1.8).

Option hedging
Once the fair value of an option can be calculated for all points in time and all levels of underlying price, it is a relatively straightforward matter to calculate the hedge. Logically this is a question of calculating what position in the underlying will offset the impact of a change in value of the option. To non-mathematicians and those unfamiliar with the properties of option premium curves and their tangents, it may not be obvious that there is an answer to this.

Even to non-mathematicians it may seem reasonable that there could be found, by trial and error if necessary, a position in the underlying which, when taken together with the option, will give the lowest net change in value (of option plus underlying) for any given (up or down) move in price of the underlying. It is less intuitive that, the smaller the price changes, the disequilibrium between the impact of an up jump and that of a down jump will tend to disappear. This means that, for a very small price change, there is a position in the underlying which will neutralise the effect of a directional move in the market on the value of the option.

Mathematically, the solution is the tangent to the premium/price curve and is calculated as the first derivative of premium in terms of price – ie, by differentiating the premium function with respect to price (see Exhibit 1.9).

Option hedging and arbitrage
A common factor between the two basic derivative types is that from the value of the underlying the "fair value" of the derivative can be calculated. It is one thing to calculate "a fair value", but final proof of the calculation is whether this value can be locked

Exhibit 1.9 Option deltas

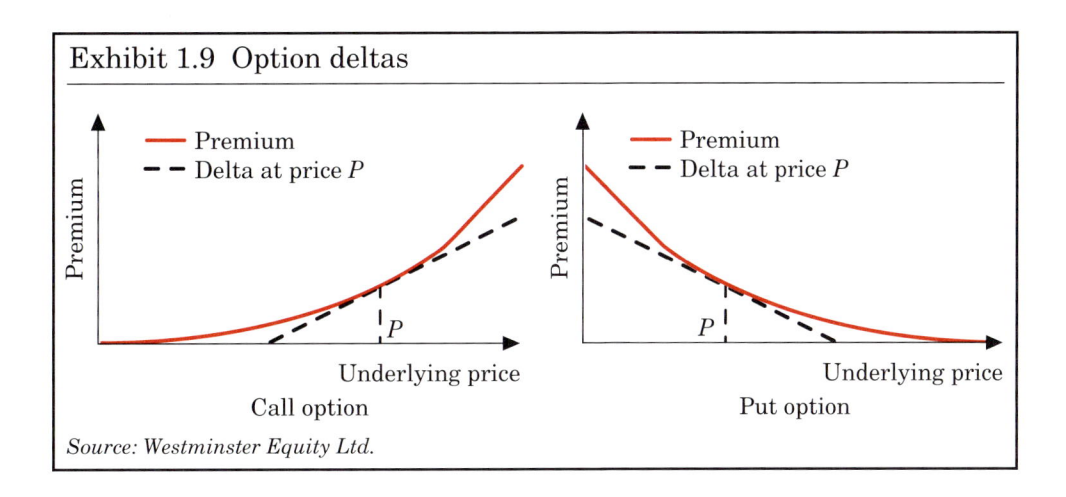

[Two charts: Call option and Put option, each showing Premium (solid red) and Delta at price P (dashed black) versus Underlying price, with point P marked.]

Source: Westminster Equity Ltd.

in by hedging. In the case of forwards it may well be possible actually to lock in the fair value. The so-called "cash and carry" or "cash/futures" stock futures arbitrage business is doing exactly that. But in the case of options it is only possible to lock in the fair value subject to the anticipated level of underlying price volatility actually being experienced during its life. The risk of variation in the final result due to the divergence of experienced from anticipated volatility, is an open risk which it is the prime function of the option risk manager to assume and manage.

With this qualification it can be said generally that derivative pricing may be confirmed by checking whether someone buying the derivative for that price would tend to recover the cost from the pay-out. The idea is that, by generating a sufficiently large number of synthetic price histories which are random but which conform to the volatility and interest rates assumed in the pricing, the mean of the outcomes (ie, cost minus pay-out) should be symmetrically distributed with an acceptable dispersion around zero. This process, often referred to as Monte Carlo simulation, does, however, demand extra care in its application to equity derivatives due to the particularities of transaction costs in the equity markets.

A more rigorous method of checking the pricing and hedge strategy can be employed by using a similar technique to Monte Carlo simulation, but assuming that the position is hedged dynamically with the hedge being rebalanced with underlying price moves according to synthetic price histories during the life of the option. Again, the pricing and hedge strategy will be confirmed by the approximation of the mean outcome (cost plus hedging P/L minus pay-out) to, and its dispersion around, zero. This technique has the additional advantage of giving invaluable information on the effect of such variables as rehedge time, price interval and hedge volatility on the efficiency of the hedge strategy.

Brief description of market segments

OTC markets
In general, exchanges only really trade derivative contracts which are the most standard or ("orthodox") and, usually, short term. Although many equity warrants and convertible bonds are exchange listed, the real markets in them are usually OTC. In particular, exchange-traded equity options and futures are generally short term with real liquidity being restricted to the "near" contract, which usually means a maximum

of three months. In addition, the only liquidity in exchange-traded options is in contracts where the strike is close to spot or the forward. Almost certainly, anyone who needs a long-term forward or option, or an option with a strike far from the money or with particular dates, will need to look outside the exchanges to the OTC markets.

In the OTC markets, varying degrees of standardisation of product (or "commoditisation") can be seen. Particularly in the field of forwards and at-the-money equity index options out to five years, two-way price "indications" are quoted on the screen by some brokers. On this basis it is easy to distinguish, at one extreme, a sub-section of the OTC market where reliable screen prices are quoted by a number of serious houses, and particularly by the brokers. This might be called the brokered OTC market. At the moment it includes "plain vanilla" options out to five years on major indices. At the other extreme, we might distinguish a "tailor made" section where there are no screen quotes. These include most "exotic" options (see Chapter Six) and especially those on unusual indices, baskets of stocks or individual stocks.

The process of commoditisation encroaches continually on the arbitrageurs' and market-makers' territory, forcing the bid/offer spread down and providing benchmarks for pricing less standard products.

Warrants and options

The distinction between options and warrants is frequently a source of unnecessary confusion. Speaking simply, it is possible to say that any warrant is an option but not all options are warrants. The additional defining characteristic of a warrant is tradability. But since anything for which there is a willing buyer and seller is by definition tradable, this should be restricted further to options which are designed as, rather than happen to be, tradable instruments. Being designed as tradable is of course no guarantee of actual liquidity, but at least it will remove some practical barriers to finding a potential buyer. The holder of an OTC option may, on the other hand, find that the only real potential buyer is the original seller, which may considerably widen the effective bid/offer he will incur in turning a position around.

The so-called "credit gridlock" – a futuristic nightmare of the markets seizing up due to credit constraints – is much exacerbated by the recent growth in the non-warrant sectors of the OTC market. The natural flow of product, from the OTC option to the exchange-traded sector, acts as a natural valve to release this pressure. A major question overshadowing the equity derivative market is whether this valve is capable of handling the build-up of pressure from the OTC sector.

Types of warrant

Simple equity (single stock) warrants
Although these are frequently issued as part of a package together with straight bonds ("host bonds"), they are plain vanilla calls on the shares of an individual company with one subtle difference. The seller of the call is the company into whose stock the warrants are exercisable and, on the warrants being exercised, the company will normally issue and deliver new shares. The shares after exercise will therefore be worth less than the shares before exercise. This means that simple option pricing models such as Black Scholes or binomial models need to be adjusted to apply to equity warrants. While it is quite possible to make such adjustments, many market participants have attempted to develop proprietary pricing systems which obviate the need for it.

Covered warrants

Covered warrants are call options issued by a third party (normally a bank or securities house) which are exercisable into existing shares of a company. From the above it can be seen that (forgetting credit and liquidity considerations) a covered warrant should always be worth more than an equity warrant with identical terms.

The warrant is said to be "covered" since the issuer covers his position by holding against it either a position in the underlying stock or an offsetting option position. In the first case, if the covered warrants are exercised, the issuer is able simply to deliver the stock he owns. He is therefore neutral to the market on the upside, but retains as a "profit" the premium received from selling the warrant. On the downside his position is unchanged (apart from having received the premium), and he retains the downside of a long stock position. The issuer of covered warrants against a long stock holding has thus carried out a classical call/put conversion.

In the second case, the offsetting option position held by the issuer will normally be an equity warrant or a convertible bond. Unless the position is an exactly offsetting equity warrant, the issuer will always be left with some element of mismatch in his book. In some cases covered warrants have been issued which are identical to the offsetting warrants in all but currency of denomination, which means that the issuer is effectively locking in an immediate arbitrage gain. The main reason for this has been demand from Swiss retail or quasi retail investors who put a high premium on investing in instruments denominated in their own currency.

Basket warrants

Basket warrants are a form of covered warrant where the underlying instrument is a basket of shares rather than an individual share. Normally the basket concerned will represent an identifiable sector of an individual country's market, or, less commonly, representatives of the same sector from the markets of a number of different countries.

Index warrants

Index Warrants are (either put or call) options on the value of a stock index. They effectively give the holder the right to buy (or sell) all of the stocks in the index exactly in accordance with their representation in the index. The issuer (seller) of the warrant is usually a bank or investment bank which hedges itself in the index futures or underlying stock. Occasionally market end-users (for example the government of Denmark) have been the issuers of such warrants in order to enhance the credit quality of the investment. Exercise of the option is naturally economic rather than by delivery of the underlying. Some index warrants have stock exchange listings but generally the real markets in them are OTC and sometimes confined to that provided by the original issuing bank.

These instruments are describe in detail in Chapter Four.

Other equity derivatives

Equity-index-linked notes

These hybrid instruments are normally tailor-made to address specific perceived investor demand and as such may display a great diversity of features. The standard product is a straight bond with an "embedded" equity-index option. The embedding of the option in the bond is achieved by netting the option's pay-out off the principal repayment of the note at maturity.

The typical issuer is a normal bond market end-user. The arranging bank or investment bank will normally neutralise the issuer to the equity exposure in the transaction through a swap while its own resulting exposure is dynamically hedged in the futures or underlying cash markets.

There is normally little or no secondary market trading in these issues. Frequently a whole issue will be privately placed with one institutional investor and the "public" appearance is maintained purely for cosmetic (league table) purposes.

The heyday of this type of product was the late 1980s when substantial quantities were sold mainly into the Japanese institutional investor market.

An important generation of related products are those which offer a minimum repayment (normally the principal amount of the note) at maturity. These instruments, and their warrant equivalent ("moneyback" warrants), have played an important role in bringing investors who are otherwise derivatives adverse into the options market.

Primes and scores

These American exchange-traded derivative instruments are basically simple options positions on single stocks. The score is equivalent to a simple (European style) call on the underlying stock. The prime is equivalent to a combination of a long position on the underlying share plus a short position on the (score) call. From put/call parity, this is equivalent to a short put position on the underlying stock. This is a practical example of splitting a cash instrument into its component (long call and short put) positions as discussed earlier in this chapter in the section on put/call parity.

The legal vehicle utilised in this process is the Americus trust which buys and holds the underlying shares and issues the primes and scores.

Similar types of product are traded on CBOE under the names of Leaps and Bounds.

Exchanges

The real markets for stock index futures and short-term and plain vanilla options on both indices and single stocks are the major exchanges. Some 14 exchanges trade options on a total of more than 800 shares in 8 countries world-wide (see Exhibit 1.10).

Stock indices have evolved as a means of monitoring the overall and sectoral performance of stock markets. Recognised stock indices are maintained by all significant stock exchanges and also by some independent agencies, notably Dow Jones, Financial Times and Morgan Stanley. In total about 1000 indices are compiled by some 50 exchanges and other agencies world-wide. For example, in Canada alone there are more than 80 indices maintained by the three major exchanges with FT and MS maintaining one each. The vast majority of these relate to particular sectors of a market distinguished according to industrial group, region or size of company.

Of these indices, exchange-traded derivatives have been developed on a total of 50 indices on nearly 30 exchanges as far afield as New Zealand and Helsinki. The total number of index derivative contracts traded now exceeds 60, of which about half are futures and half options. In almost all cases, the derivative is on an index which is meant to be representative of the whole market concerned rather than any particular sector. Derivatives on sub-sectors or baskets are found in the form of warrants and OTC options, but are not yet exchange traded.

Exchange-traded index options are rapidly invading territory which until recently (in the case of many European indices) was occupied by index warrants.

Exhibit 1.10 Option exchanges

Exchange	No. of shares with listed options
NYSE	50
Pacific SE	139
CBOT	200
Philadelphia SE	110
Montreal SE	27
Toronto SE	43
Vancouver SE	20
LTOM	70
Monep	22
Stockholm Options Market	17
SOFEX	13
DTB	14
Frankfurt SE	57
Australian SE	26

Problems

It would be inappropriate to end an introduction to equity derivatives without mentioning some of the problems. We have already touched on the recurring fear of a credit gridlock, the legal implications of which are explored in more detail in Chapter Eight.

One more potentially problematic question is that of regulation. How is the market regulated? Can it be regulated? Does it need to be regulated? These are major issues which need to be addressed and to which the answers are by no means clear. The markets we are dealing with are global and electronic. It is not possible to police flows of information, instructions, funds and securities by posting extra guards at the border. It is increasingly difficult to identify the businesses involved as operating within the jurisdiction of any sovereign state or other law-making body.

While we have pointed out that, in essence, the products are very simple, their appearance is frequently extremely complex and their essential simplicity may be very difficult to discern. Furthermore, the products are evolving constantly and so the net effect is for the sector increasingly to become comprehensible only to market practitioners. Much existing commercial law dates back to, and relies on precedents from, the 19th century or before. From that viewpoint, today's markets would look like a creation from the wilder realms of science fiction.

The expectation must be that the intellectual gap between potential regulators and market development will only increase with time. The nightmare of the regulator must be that the derivatives market may turn into a kind of financial Sarajevo, where there is some clear expectation that the authorities should do something but where they have no ability to co-ordinate any effective intervention. In the best case, the market may develop in a perfectly healthy way without intervention, and no doubt markets such as the Eurobond market could be cited as a precedent. It must be said, however, that bankers, left to their own devices, have not always acted in their own best interests and a note of caution may not be inappropriate in this instance.

Consider the following two, fairly self-evident statements. First, that much legislation in the financial field focuses on the rights of the equity investor to have adequate and accurate information on the basis of which to make a reasonable investment decision. Secondly, that a major part of the responsibility of the corporate treasurer in today's market is to minimise his company's exposures to extraneous factors – eg, interest rates, foreign exchange rates, commodity prices. The corporate treasurer's main means of achieving this objective is by taking positions in derivative products. Those positions may not be reflected adequately, or even at all, in publicly available information. If the corporate treasurer were 100 per cent successful, the effect might be to neutralise the company's exposures. If he overhedged, the result would be to reverse the exposures, which might mean that the logic of the investor's decision making could well be quite right but the result totally wrong.

If investors have a right to information about a company's economic position, they must surely have a right to know its positions in derivatives. In which case, some regulatory body has a duty to ensure that they receive it. Whether or not investors could reasonably be expected to absorb that information and weigh it in their investment decisions is another matter.

2

The uses of equity derivatives for investors

Nigel Morris-Jones and Ron Slivka

J. P. Morgan

Investor profiles

The following survey provides a brief overview of equity investors world-wide, broken down by type of investor, and focusing on the potential of equity derivatives for each category of user.

The investors described are in effect the end-users. Banks, brokers and money managers are excluded since they are mostly acting as financial intermediaries. As discretionary managers of pension fund portfolios, fund managers clearly play a major role in influencing the funds in their use of derivatives (a role which is not explicitly described in the following section). There are still areas of overlap even between those categories separately treated below: for example, insurance companies are partly managing the balance between their premiums and claims, but also (particularly in Switzerland) act as fund managers for pension fund money. Banks clearly play a vital role both as the providers of derivatives to investors, and as arrangers and distributors of retail-based products, as well as being depositaries, custodians and advisers for equity investors (eg, the big three Swiss banks control vast amounts of pension money). However, banks are not generally end-investors and hence their role is not emphasised in the following comments.

Corporate and public pension funds
The investment strategies of European pension fund managers vary distinctly from country to country and, despite the recent forces for convergence, still show the effect of domestic market culture and tradition. The US and UK have by far the largest share of global pension funds, dwarfing the European and Far East pension industry. The most noticeable feature of all is the UK's heavy weighting towards equities versus bonds, with pension funds having around 80 per cent of their assets in equities.

The main reason for the UK's preference is that of experience. In the 1970s and 1980s UK equities offered an average real return of 8.1 per cent against 0.8 per cent for bonds and, over longer periods, similar patterns prevail. If the UK, whether in or out of the ERM, were set credibly for an extended period of low inflation, the argument for bonds would grow stronger. For example long dated gilts yielding 9.5 per cent in a 3.5 per cent inflationary environment (Germany's average inflation over the past 25 years) give a competitive real return. However, this logic only becomes compelling if the UK equity dividend yield falls more in line with other markets. So far UK equities have managed to compete with bonds largely because of the high dividends demanded by institutional investors. Real dividend growth ran at an average rate of 5.7 per cent during the 1980s, in excess of the wage inflation rate, which is generally taken to be the minimum return needed for mature pension funds. This is again a cultural factor unique to the UK.

However, the UK's preference for equities cannot be entirely explained by its post-war inflationary history, since over a long period bonds have actually been a poor investment even in traditionally low inflation countries. For example the average real return to a Japanese investor of Japanese bonds was just 0.2 per cent in the years 1976 to 1990 against 10.9 per cent from Japanese equities. German bonds averaged a real return of 2.7 per cent against 9.5 per cent from equities and US bonds returned an average 0.6 per cent loss versus a 4.7 per cent positive yield from equities. These figures suggest that there are other factors to explain why European investors favour bonds over equities. One reason is that funded pension schemes have been almost exclusively an Anglo-Saxon practice, with the European approach being to fund pensions on a pay-as-you-go basis. This has led European investors to favour low risk, low return government bonds with the certainty of a fixed income. For example Dutch pension funds, by law, have to produce a 4 per cent minimum real return which, in the 2.5 per cent inflationary environment during the past decade, can be achieved in government bonds alone. Another factor is the maturity of pension funds in the UK. While these funds were in the growth stage during the 1970s and 1980s, with durations of 15–20 years the best way to protect capital value was in equities.

However, with the ageing of the UK population the cash flow profile will change. As outgoings rise relative to premium income there is an argument that pension funds should shift from equities more into bonds. In the meantime the European pension fund industry is likely to transfer more of its investments into equities because of the same demographic shifts. The practice of having the working population pay for the pensions of the retired is becoming increasingly onerous as the proportion of older people rises. This is true particularly in Germany, France, Belgium and Italy where the population growth has slowed. One solution has been for governments to increase greatly the tax incentives for personal pension plans, and for pension funds to begin to fund themselves for their future obligations. It is estimated that continental pension funds may grow from $675 billion in 1990 to $997 billion in 1995 and that because of the longer duration of these funded schemes equities should play a bigger part than before.

The main exceptions to the continental European pattern are Switzerland and the Netherlands. In the Netherlands there are some large pension funds with a weighting in equities of about 25 per cent, which is 10 per cent more than at the end of 1988. This will probably increase over the next few years, due mostly to competitive pressures to produce higher returns than the legal minimum, and also for market risk diversification reasons. The Swiss pension fund industry was restructured along Anglo-Saxon lines a few years ago by the passing of a law requiring all companies to either start their own scheme or join another larger one. Already the total volume of Swiss pension funds has reached about half that of the UK and the proportion is growing fast. However, unlike the UK, Switzerland does follow the continental pattern in keeping only 7–8 per cent in equities. In Germany there are only 70 companies operating pension schemes of any size, and the remainder, which have so far operated a book reserve system to pay pensions directly out of corporate profits, have over the past five years invested rapidly in *spezialfonds*. These are investment companies open only to legally incorporated entities, and are nearly all run by banks. Only a small proportion of *spezialfond* money is in equities (70 per cent being in bonds), but this is likely to rise as the level of non-domestic investment increases.

As far as the growth of international diversification in investment strategy is concerned, again the arguments are theoretically attractive but the circumstances are still too uncertain to cause radical changes. For example although Japan has increased its foreign holdings from 1 per cent to 16 per cent over the last 10 years, the US has risen from 1 per cent to only 5 per cent. It has been expected until recently that European pension fund managers will double their holdings in non-domestic major European stock markets, from $50 billion to $100 billion, in the belief that the EMS will eliminate exchange rate risks. In the UK the process was accelerated by the abolition of exchange rate controls in 1979 and, in the last decade, UK pension funds have increased their holdings of foreign securities from 7 per cent to 18 per cent. However, even without the exchange rate element there is an argument that the increasing internationalisation of trade and business removes the necessity for portfolio managers to seek diversification. Indeed stock markets have begun to move more in step with each other (New York is correlated 0.76 with European and Pacific Rim markets, up from 0.5 10 years ago) so that investment abroad does not bring as much reduction in risk as anticipated. Furthermore the overseas stocks most usually bought are the large familiar names which themselves have more international, and less domestic exposure. This is the counter argument to the traditional view that investors will increasingly diversify abroad and may partly explain the relatively slow progress achieved so far.

In summary, the forces for convergence are strong, as demographic influences cause more UK pension funds to go into gilts and simultaneously European pension funds to increase equity weightings. However, cultural background will continue to inform the actions of portfolio managers and convergence will depend to a large extent on the success of European integration.

Scope for derivatives

The various influences described above are leading to an increasing interest in the use of equity derivatives on the part of pension funds: European funds are moving into equities for the first time via derivatives; UK funds are looking to maximise cash yield from their portfolios by buying downside protection or using equity swaps; and all funds are seeking access to non-domestic markets via index call options or swaps. However, in most jurisdictions the pension funds are heavily regulated and, if not explicitly prohibited from using derivatives, there is sufficient confusion in the law to inhibit their use. For example in Germany some pension funds are held in the form of *spezialfonds* which, together with mutual funds, are subject to the KAG law (*Kapital Anlage Gesellschaften Gesetz*). This law restricts the use of derivatives to listed instruments and sets limits relative to total assets. It also requires not less than 50 per cent of assets to be invested in German securities.

Similarly a Swiss law sets the maximum foreign currency investments at 20 per cent, and total equity at 30 per cent. Even so Swiss pension funds are relatively free under the present law to use swaps and options in that they can buy and sell calls, and buy (but not sell) puts. However, they have been relatively inactive in listed and OTC derivatives. In France, Italy and Spain pension provision is mostly in the hands of the state, and occupational bodies. Corporate pension funds are few and of recent origins.

The UK pension funds are regulated mainly by the Investment Management

Regulatory Organisation (IMRO) but it was the 1990 Finance Act which specifically allowed them to use derivatives without losing their tax exemption. Unlike US funds UK pension funds do not need to mark assets to market but, since 1988, have been required to declare in their accounts if they cannot meet their discontinuance liabilities. In effect the main brake on derivatives is the problem of establishing the legal identity of the counterparty: most pension fund managers prefer to deal in their own name rather than reveal the underlying fund name, but this imposes the limit of the managers' own creditworthiness. Even so, some UK pension funds have been involved in the use of basket trading, futures and exchange-traded options from the early days.

US pension funds have been relatively slow in seizing the opportunities of equity derivatives, mostly because of the complexity of the tax and legal issues involved. In brief, pension plan sponsors need to comply with applicable state and federal laws (especially trust law), the Commodities Exchange Act (CEA) and, in the case of corporate pension plans, the Employee Retirement Income Security Act (ERISA). Also, FASB 1987 requires US pension funds to value their assets at market value once a year. In particular, plan sponsors subject to ERISA should avoid dealing with entities which are parties in interest (PIIs) – ie, buying options from a bank which already acts as its custodian, trustee or investment adviser. However, this problem can be solved relatively easily as the restriction does not apply to sister companies.

There is one further legal complication, in that sponsors must also comply with laws relating to futures and options by following the "safe harbour" guidelines established in July 1989 by the Commodity Futures Trading Commission (CFTC). This means that transactions have to meet certain criteria defining their individually tailored nature. The US tax treatment of derivatives has also been very convoluted and has only recently been simplified. It is clearly of paramount importance that tax-exempt entities should not jeopardise their status by entering into derivative transactions: the tax-exempt status of pension plans established under state or municipal law seems to be unquestionable, but that of corporate plans, endowments and foundations is more open to interpretation. This means that income from derivatives should not be taken as "unrelated business taxable income" (UBTI). Most funds now accept that the established UBTI exemptions in the Internal Revenue Code together with the changes proposed on 30 August 1991 cover almost all possible derivative structures, whether stand-alone or embedded.

Despite these obstacles, US pension funds are beginning to use derivatives – particularly futures. Indeed, in 1987 the Committee on Investment of Employee Benefit Assets (a standing committee of the Financial Executives' Institute representing some 6000 US and Canadian firms holding employee benefit assets totalling more than $300 billion) testified to Congress on the beneficial uses of financial futures in managing pension fund investment risk.

The other noteworthy trend among all pension funds of whatever nationality is the increasing use of indexation, passive tracking and the use of benchmarks to measure performance. The main performance measures in the UK are Combined Actuarial Performance Services (CAPS) and the WM Company, and these are now expanding their services into continental Europe, particularly Germany, Holland and Switzerland. Indexation is generally related to the major stock market indices plus the MSCI Europe and World Indices. More fund managers are taking a "quantitative" rather than "stock-picking" approach. For example, it is estimated that the proportion of funds under passive index management in the US will reach 30 per cent of pension money in 1993 – a proportion much higher than elsewhere.

Insurance companies

The main participants in the OTC equity derivative market so far have been insurance companies. This reflects the lighter burden of legal restrictions, and also the requirement to mark assets to market for annual accounts. Insurance companies' asset allocations are similar to those of pension funds with equities amounting to around 85 per cent of UK insurers' assets and 7–8 per cent of European insurers' – though the latter have higher proportions of non-domestic stocks than the pension funds. Continental and Scandinavian insurers are much more heavily involved in real estate, which has until recently offered a better hedge against inflation than the relatively small domestic stock markets. The same forces for convergence as in the pension fund market can be observed amongst insurance companies, with several UK insurance companies publicly increasing their holdings of gilts.

In general insurance companies in the UK, Switzerland and Scandinavia are free to use equity derivatives, the only constraint being that the activity should be related to their normal business, and provided that they are not mutuals. Continental insurers are more heavily regulated. For example German insurers abide by the VAG (*Versicherungs Anlage Gesetz*) guidelines which restrict use of listed or OTC options according to three different criteria, whether for hedging, as new investments, or for revenue enhancement.

Any reluctance shown by the insurers about the use of derivatives stems from a wariness of instruments which can be seen by shareholders as speculative. However, once a few insurers become convinced that derivatives have a valid function as hedging tools, the practice grows rapidly. For example, it took only one UK insurance company to declare in its 1991 annual report that it had bought index puts as protection for its portfolios to initiate similar activities by rival insurers. Among continental insurers the competitive use of defensive derivatives has yet to begin, but should be as rapid once it happens.

European insurance companies have concentrated on writing covered calls and short-term option strategies. Their sophistication is indicated by the success of the option exchanges. Since the DTB (*Deutsche Terminbörse*) was introduced in January 1990 volumes have increased many-fold and there are now a large number of regular participants, trading listed options with usually short maturities (three to nine months) and in relatively small sizes. Familiarity with the use of DTB options is leading to increasingly adventurous forays into the OTC market. A similar pattern has developed in Sweden, the UK and particularly France, where the MONEP is one of the most liquid markets outside the US.

The Japanese insurance companies have been major participants since the early days of the equity derivative market as buyers of Nikkei-linked bonds. These structures were designed to provide high coupons, since Japanese insurers are required to pay claims out of current income. The higher than market coupons resulted from the investor implicitly selling put options on the Nikkei 225 Index. If the Nikkei fell below the levels prevailing at the time (1988–90), investors would receive reduced principal amounts at redemption but could write these losses off against reserves; and of course after the spectacular bull market of the 1980s the insurance companies were sitting on huge unrealised capital gains, which both provided a cushion for any losses but also had led to the expectation of further market increases. The slide in the Japanese equity market of the last two years has put an end to this particular structure but has caused a second wave of transactions designed to "rescue" the insurance companies from the original position.

Corporations

Corporates have so far been involved in the equity derivative market mainly as issuers of equity-linked notes. In these structures the corporates' equity exposure is almost always completely neutralised with OTC derivative positions, so that the net result for the corporate is an obligation with an advantageous cost of funds. Chapter Three looks in more detail at these structures.

However, some corporates have positive cash balances, which exceed their seasonal cash flow requirements and which are invested in-house. This is mostly a feature of the continental European corporate sector because of the requirement for corporate pensions to be paid out of current income. The pay-as-you-go system of pension fund management probably causes corporates to maintain higher cash balances than they would otherwise require. Although these are to all intents and purposes pension funds, the cash is not officially ring-fenced and is available to general creditors in the event of a bankruptcy (depending on the exact jurisdiction). Of course some corporates delegate the management of these investments to outside fund managers but there are some notable exceptions: Siemens AG has publicly stated its intention of competing with the *Spezialfonds*, managed by specialist fund managers. In the US, corporate investment managers have become active users of derivatives, selling covered calls or executing costless collar strategies. They are also increasingly looking at derivatives to replace, as well as augment, the underlying assets.

Apart from using derivatives within their investment management process, corporates are also beginning to see the advantages of equity derivatives in other areas, most notably in M&A activity, management of their own outstanding shares, and creation of Employee Stock Ownership Programmes (ESOPs). British companies can hedge ESOP exposure by buying calls on their own stock and thus hedging their commitments more accurately than running an in-house delta position, as well as complying with the requirements of the Companies Act regarding ownership of their own stock.

Companies can also utilise equity derivatives to hedge or subsidise the cost of a stock repurchase programme. Some companies have sold slightly out-of-the-money put warrants on their own stock as a means of generating premium income. This premium serves as a subsidy in the event of a rise in the stock price during the course of the repurchase programme. Alternatively, should the stock price fall below the strike level during the course of the programme, the stock is simply put to the company. Sales of put warrants do not serve as a true hedge, but rather as a subsidy. Other companies have purchased calls on their own stock in order to create a direct hedge against an increase in the stock price. Generally, companies employing such strategies must have enough daily trading volume in their stock to allow the put purchaser (usually an OTC derivative market-maker) to hedge itself in the underlying stock.

Companies can also use OTC equity derivatives to hedge corporate exposures to a variety of equity performances. For example, some companies use equity swaps as a means of reducing or eliminating exposure to the equity of other companies which they own but may be restricted from selling. Similarly, corporations involved in stock purchases of other companies may use short-term OTC equity derivatives to hedge such exposures.

Mutual funds and unit trusts

The growth in the US mutual fund industry over the last 20 years has been dramatic. In 1972, less than $100 million of funds were invested with mutual funds. That number has grown to over $1 trillion and the number of mutual funds in the United States has grown from about 400 in 1972 to over 3100 by early-1991. The amount of equity funds under management as a percentage of the total funds under management has actually dropped since 1980 in response to the tremendous growth of the money market mutual funds. Approximately 30 per cent of the money in mutual funds comes from institutional sources.

Mutual funds are classified according to stated investment goals, types of investment and desired risk. Examples of such classifications include capital appreciation or current income, domestic investment or Pacific Rim investments, and large-cap stocks versus small-cap stocks. Large mutual fund advisers typically manage funds in a number of classes, although the finances of the separate funds are maintained separately.

US mutual funds are highly regulated at both the federal and the state levels. Laws governing mutual funds require exhaustive disclosure to the SEC, state regulators, and shareholders. Funds are required to provide a detailed prospectus to all potential investors. The prospectus must state the fund's investment objectives, investment methods, and desired level of risk. Specific investments are not subject to regulatory review so long as the fund is investing in accordance with its objectives as set forth in its prospectus as well as in compliance with the law. Of greatest importance to derivative applications is that most mutual funds take the view that they cannot use OTC equity derivative products unless their prospectus specifically mentions use of such products. Since most prospectuses were written before the development of the OTC equity derivative markets, many mutual funds believe that they are precluded from using these products. Changing the prospectus would require that the mutual fund management take a vote of the shareholders in the fund, an action they are typically not interested in undertaking. However, new funds with up-to-date prospectuses are generally including provisions enabling them to use derivatives.

In addition to maintaining compliance with the objectives and techniques mentioned in the prospectus, a US mutual fund is subject to a myriad of regulatory, tax and accounting requirements. Most important from the standpoint of equity derivatives are the accounting requirements. Mutual funds are required to calculate their net asset value (net asset value is the sum of cash, securities and accrued earnings minus all liabilities) on a daily basis. Illiquid investments can create difficulties for this requirement.

In summary, some US mutual funds have been significant buyers of medium-term notes or CDs with fixed income or currency derivatives embedded in them. Perhaps the most famous example of such notes are the inverse floaters. Equity-linked notes have been less common among the mutual funds.

European funds

Mutual funds in Europe are equally highly regulated, each country having a different regime. In general European mutual funds are allowed to buy only listed options. For example the German mutual funds are regulated by the KAG rules, which also apply to *Spezialfonds*. The interesting feature of the German mutual funds is their concentration in the hands of four or five major funds managers which are themselves subsidiaries of the leading banks, that act as custodians.

In France mutual funds account for the majority of French savings, and competitive pressures have made them very active participants in the MATIF and MONEP. They are regulated by the Commission des Operations de Bourse (COB) under a law known as the OPCVM: French mutual funds have to be managed by a French management company and operate through a French depositary which actually holds the assets. These depositaries are banks, insurance companies and other financial intermediaries, and because of their role in the structure usually control, and often own, the fund managers. There are effectively two forms of mutual fund: the FCP (*fond commun de placement*) is an investment vehicle in which the investor in effect buys participation certificates; and a SICAV (*société d'investissement à capital variable*) is a sole purpose linked company with a board of directors in which one can buy listed shares. The COB requires all funds in France to publish their net asset value on a weekly basis. They cannot trade OTC options, but can (and do) buy listed derivatives up to 10 per cent of total assets and they are empowered to enter into equity swaps. There are also two sorts of SICAV in France: one which distributes all its profits, which is tax-exempt; and the other, known as a *SICAV de capitalisation*, in which capital gains and dividends are reinvested in equities. The latter sort are taxed on dividends but exempted from withholding tax and capital gains tax. Belgium's equity SICAVs have also been exempted from the 25 per cent withholding tax and 10 per cent tax on interest income since 1990.

A similar system to that of the SICAVs is in place in Italy and Spain. In Italy mutual funds are governed by the "1983 law", and until recently were forbidden from entering any option transactions at all. The law is in the process of being changed so that Italian funds will be able to buy options, listed and OTC, and sell covered calls.

The first index funds appeared on the continent during 1991 in France (though they still account for less than 1 per cent of funds invested in French equity and bond mutual funds) and in January 1992 in Germany (based on DAX futures).

Hedge funds
Hedge funds have until recently been exclusively a US phenomenon, developing rapidly since the 1950s to the point where there are now about 400 in the US. The definition of the hedge fund has become wider over the years. They are mostly unregistered limited partnerships, that are equity-based, use leverage and shorting techniques, and where the general manager earns 20 per cent of the total return as an incentive fee in return for putting his own money at risk.

Returns have been generally much higher than from non-hedge funds, often running in excess of 30 per cent and sometimes exceeding 50 per cent net of fees. Investors need to be "qualified" (ie, have a $1 million net worth), and initially were wealthy individuals, though recently institutions have been getting involved. One other generally unifying feature of the market is the advanced technology and modern portfolio theory (MPT) employed by almost all funds, and this in particular has made some hedge funds intrepid users of derivatives. The basic positioning of most funds involves using a stock portfolio as collateral to borrow cash with which to buy more stocks. If a fund also shorts stocks to raise cash then the leverage effect can be very considerable. Derivatives are therefore used both to establish short stock positions (equity swaps and forwards) and also to take long positions by buying calls. Clearly spending all the invested amount on call premiums achieves a far higher leverage effect even than the traditional long/short structure.

Hedge funds have begun to migrate to Europe where margining requirements for stock borrowing are less rigorous than the 50 per cent imposed by Federal Reserve Regulation T. It is also possible in Europe to escape from the restriction that only 25 per cent of a hedge fund can be ERISA money. There are also some tax timing advantages for non-US investors in buying an offshore fund.

The other recent development is for hedge funds to become registered to allow the participation of ERISA pension funds, particularly now that ERISA allows the payment of performance fees.

Individuals

Banks and brokers aiming at distribution for the retail market and wealthy individuals have proved enthusiastic users of derivatives. There are many examples of financial instruments being sold to individuals in the branches of banks and building societies, by financial advisers and agents, and by private banking account officers. They are called by different names, usually descriptive of the guaranteed principal and equity element, but all are variations of the equity-linked note structure. We have so far seen UK building societies and insurance companies launch such products with many different acronyms, following on from the "GROIs" popular in Switzerland, and "BICs" and "GICs" in the US. In Italy these products have accounted for a large proportion of equity derivative business so far, and have been distributed by local agents representing some of the major banks. The last year has also seen the launch of several similar products (usually protected into the local currency) in the Nordic countries. In Belgium, France and Luxembourg derivative based SICAVs have begun, and particularly in France the new PEAs, allowed since September 1992, have proved fertile ground for equity derivative professionals.

Equity warrants have also traditionally been a retail-targeted product, and the best established example of this is the client base of the private Swiss banks, which have taken much of the Japanese equity warrant product as well as other more recent index warrants.

Survey of market development

Listed and OTC derivatives vs. stocks

The growth of listed derivatives in the US during the 1970s and 1980s forced a redefinition of the market-place for equity transactions. In this redefinition, allowances had to be made for equity strategies pursued in conjunction with equity derivatives or through derivatives only. By the mid-1980s stock index futures and stock index option markets of substantial size were added to the already well developed market for single stock options. The high volume of transactions in these new markets, together with the developing arbitrage linking them with the stock market, naturally prompted a re-evaluation of the constituents of the equity market. Nowhere is this better demonstrated than in the measurement of relative market share.

To conduct this exercise, three derivative classes are defined:

1 options – including listed single stock and index options;
2 futures – including all listed index futures;
3 OTC – including all unlisted, structured equity offerings such as swaps, collars and options.

The notional amount of stock controlled by futures or options contracts can be used to measure the approximate size of the equity market for a derivative class. For example, the dollar amount of stock represented by a single S&P 500 stock index futures contract is by definition $500 multiplied by the S&P 500 Index. This notional amount adjusted for volume and then accumulated in a year can be added to similar calculations for other index futures contracts to provide an estimated total annual notional volume. Similarly, the dollar size of stock represented by a single S&P 100 Index option is $100 multiplied by its strike price. By aggregating such calculations across existing contracts an estimated total annual notional dollar volume of transactions is calculated. These figures can now be used to compare the relative sizes of markets for equity transactions. A comparison of all derivatives classes with stock transactions for 1992 appears in Exhibit 2.1 for the two largest global markets – the US and Japan. All calculations are approximate and intended for guidance – there are no published statistics on OTC transactions and so the market share in this year was estimated.

In Japan the proportions of the equity transactions market represented by derivatives have recently come to resemble more closely those of US markets. In 1992 futures activity was double cash volumes. In the US similar measurements over prior years reveal that on average options, futures and stocks each represented approximately one-third of the market for equity transactions.

The primary value in such an exercise arises from the realisation that transactions in physical shares are not always the dominant form of stock activity. In some sense it could be argued that managers executing only in stocks are ignoring approximately two-thirds of the total equity market in the US and potentially more in Japan. A second value in comparing market shares arises from reflection on the nature of the relationships between the elements of this more broadly defined equity market. Listed options and futures do not exist apart from one another any more than stock and derivatives. All are linked at every interface of the market share diagram (Exhibit 2.1) by arbitrage that prevents excessive price disparities from arising in related markets.

Some forms of arbitrage are more visible than others. For example, stock index arbitrage, linking stocks with index futures was the focal point of the financial press in the US just prior to and following the 1987 market correction. In Japan, a similar focus

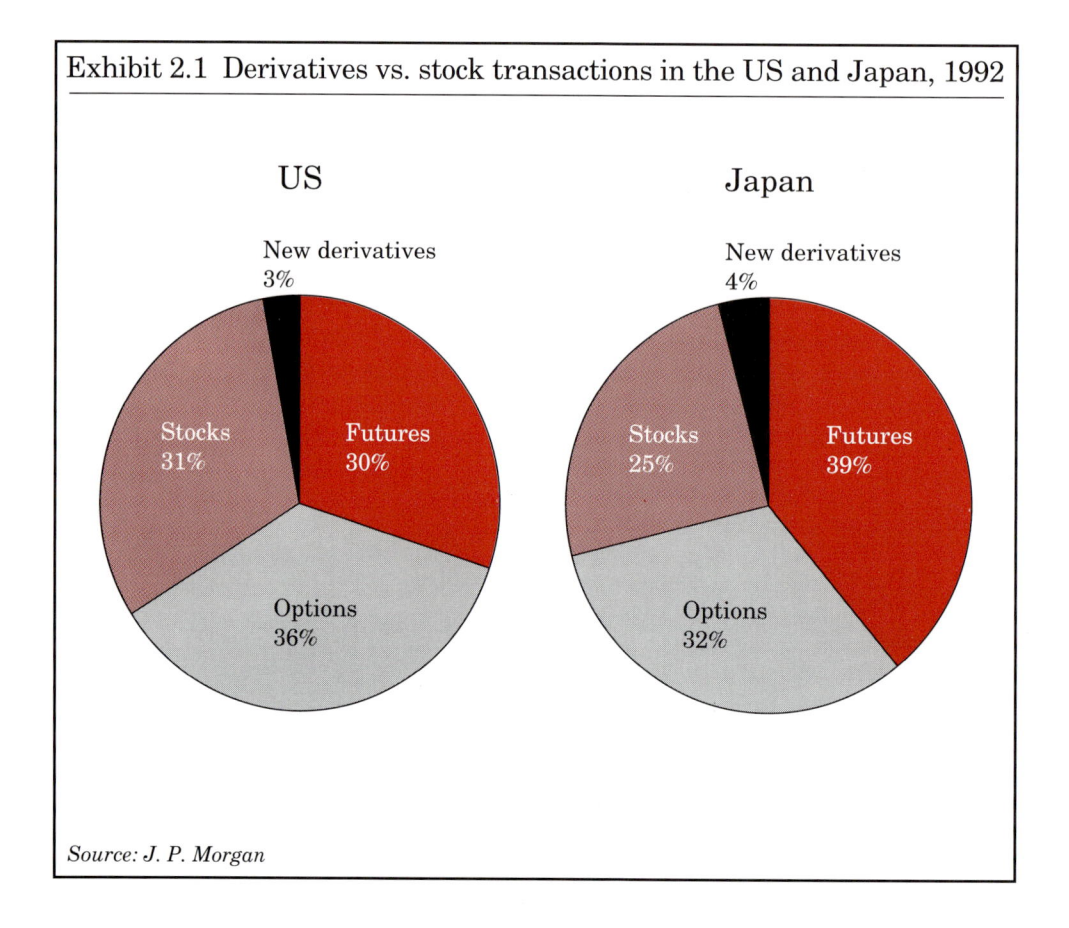

Exhibit 2.1 Derivatives vs. stock transactions in the US and Japan, 1992

US
- New derivatives 3%
- Stocks 31%
- Futures 30%
- Options 36%

Japan
- New derivatives 4%
- Stocks 25%
- Futures 39%
- Options 32%

Source: J. P. Morgan

on this strategy appeared in 1991–92. In each case, overstated claims regarding the adverse influence such arbitrage had on the share markets was found in the press. Ignored were the natural and proper functions performed by this and other forms of arbitrage in linking related markets and in reducing overall price volatility for the larger equity market-place.

By implication the interface between stock index futures and stock index options also must be characterised by arbitrage. This arbitrage is primarily conducted by professional participants and is largely unseen by the public. Such arbitrage once again keeps markets orderly. In addition, within a single derivative class there is arbitrage among class members. For example, S&P 500 futures are arbitraged against NYSE futures and OEX options are arbitraged against SPX options, tying together related markets so they act more coherently.

The smallest market share in 1992 was held by OTC derivatives such as index swaps, options and index-linked bonds. The primary reason for this situation was certainly not a lack of interest by institutional investors. Indeed this segment of the equity market was the fastest growing. In countries outside the US and Japan the market share of OTC derivatives is estimated to be considerably higher. In 1992, however, this market was quite new and relatively unknown. Expectations are for OTC applications to grow globally and exceptionally fast in the next five years.

Stock portfolios
In some senses, stock portfolios, whether partially or fully constructed to mimic underlying indices, can be considered equity derivatives. They too are derived from equity just as are index options, index futures and OTC products. They are often intimately involved in the execution of derivative-related strategies. Finally, stock portfolios today are traded globally, often as easily as listed options and futures, and frequently as substitutes for derivatives. All these factors encourage the view among derivative users that stock portfolios in some senses are derivatives too.

The use of stock portfolios in a derivatives context arises in several different situations. Investor limitations on the use of OTC and listed derivatives, whether partial or complete, self-imposed or regulatory, often lead to the use of such portfolios in place of potentially preferred derivatives. At other times, implementation of certain investment strategies is completed most cost-effectively by the use of some combination of stock portfolios and derivatives. Also, shifting from stock-based to other derivative strategies usually creates entry and exit transactions solved most efficiently by means of portfolio trades.

To understand fully the potential uses for stock portfolios in derivative strategies we need to explore briefly the evolution of portfolio trading technology and to explain certain current investor applications. Discussions of portfolio trading technology often appear under the title of "program" trading. Accordingly, to complete the profile of stock portfolios a short history of program trading follows.

A brief history of program trading
As US investors placed increasing amounts of money into index funds in the mid to late-1970s, a need arose on the part of index fund managers to put these monies efficiently into the market. The best way to effect this injection of new funds was to buy entire indexed stock portfolios as if they were one single stock issue. The creative response of the broker/dealer community at that time was to offer the ability to trade portfolios provided the user supplied a computer programmed list of securities to buy or sell. A computer program was necessary to quickly and accurately calculate the

number of shares of each stock in the index to purchase, given an initial dollar investment. This quick and convenient style of trading stocks became known among users as "program trading".

Early in 1982, index futures were listed for trading in the US for the first time. Alert money managers realised quickly that a synthetic index fund could be constructed using these new investment instruments by combining them with a cash portfolio. Careful but simple calculation of the fair value of the futures contract provided the price below which a manager would be willing to buy futures and construct such a fund. Because index futures contracts spend virtually all their lifetime mispriced relative to this fair value, it became easy to place orders with brokers to purchase cheap futures and outperform standard index funds. An index fund manager with investments entirely in stocks could take advantage of this mispricing only if stocks were sold and the futures purchased simultaneously. Such transactions were made possible by uniting program trading with futures trading. Similarly, a manager with cash to invest in an index fund could compare the relative returns of the stock and synthetic funds and choose the better of the two. Further, once in an index fund, switches between stock and synthetic could be effected each time a mispricing in the futures permitted. Each switch resulted in an incremental gain to the performance of the total index fund.

Separate from the investment needs of index fund managers were the needs of cash managers seeking superior short-term returns. Many of these cash managers also realised that such returns could be obtained by simultaneously purchasing a stock index basket and shorting a dollar equivalent amount of index futures contracts. Whenever the futures were trading expensive to fair value a return over similarly dated Treasury bills could be obtained with minimal risk. Until the middle years of the early-1980s returns over that of bills were commonly in excess of 100 basis points, occasionally reaching 900 to 1000 basis points. Without the prior development of stock portfolio trading technology, this activity would never have been possible.

At this point in the evolution of program trading three definitions of the term were possible. To avoid confusion, in the balance of this section we choose to differentiate

Exhibit 2.2   The evolution of portfolio trading

Decade	Trading application	New users
1950s	Round lots (100 shares)	Individuals
1960s	Block trades (10,000+ shares)	Institutions
1970s	"Program" trades on indexed portfolios	Index managers
1980s	Portfolio trades on active portfolios; multicountry portfolios; indexed portfolios	Active managers Global managers Index enhancers Cash managers
1990s	Portfolios trades to hedge customised equity derivatives	Global OTC providers

the three as follows: (i) portfolio trading will refer to the simple trading of stock portfolios (an activity which provides the historical roots for the next two definitions); (ii) index switching refers to the trading of stock portfolios in conjunction with index futures for the purpose of enhancing the returns of an index fund; and (iii) index arbitrage refers to the taking of simultaneously offsetting positions in a stock portfolio and index futures. Common and essential to each is the ability to trade a diversified portfolio of stocks in a brief period of time.

So valuable was portfolio trading technology that in the 1970s it rapidly became a standard means for US passive managers to assist investors with new index fund purchases and redemptions. In the 1980s portfolio trading evolved to include applications for US actively managed portfolios as well as for passively managed non-US portfolios. Also, as we have seen, portfolio trading united with index futures helped create new investment strategies for enhancing both index funds and cash returns. Emerging too in this decade was the ability to trade for actively managed multicountry portfolios, often lowering international stock trading costs. During the 1990s portfolio trading technology has allowed the new OTC equity derivatives market to grow by giving providers of these products alternatives to hedges in markets where listed index derivatives are absent or are ineffective.

With continuing experimentation, portfolio trading has found new applications over time. Managers today seeking to rebalance portfolios, enhance index funds or cash, shift asset allocations to or from equities, implement listed derivative strategies, put new funds to work or raise cash will find portfolio trading to be a generally effective tool. Professional investors seeking to arbitrage price inefficiencies or to hedge trading positions will also need to understand and utilise this technology.

Investor uses of equity derivatives

Equity derivatives are versatile instruments which can be used both speculatively to reinforce a view and defensively to hedge an existing portfolio. This section looks at the various reasons why investors should choose to use a derivative rather than take an underlying position.

Management of risk and return
In general a simple distinction can be made between hedging in which the investor is concerned to limit downside and which can only be achieved reliably by buying options, and revenue enhancement which effectively can only be done by selling options.

Hedging risks in an existing portfolio
The simplest form of hedging involves the investor buying put options at or near the money, these puts providing compensation if the stock or index falls below the strike, though of course the upfront premium lowers the level of protection. The following description of costless collars incorporates the simple put option and is illustrative of a popular defensive strategy.

Collars Equity costless collars are hedges consisting of a put plus a call arranged in such a way that the initial cash outlay to the buyer is zero and hence "costless". These collars are most frequently used to hedge broadly diversified investment portfolios which have a good correlation with a recognised equity index. To hedge a portfolio, an out-of-the-money index put is purchased and paid for exactly by the premium received from the sale of an out-of-the-money index call. The put and call must be on the same index and are usually the same maturity. Typically the put strike price is chosen first, which then by calculation determines the strike price of the call.

The index put provides a protective floor on the downside market price movements, while the short call creates a cap on the upside market price movement. Should the index on which the collar is based end at maturity below the floor (put strike price) or rise above the cap (call strike price), a payment will be due to (or by) the collar buyer respectively. Depending on how closely the underlying portfolio tracks the index on which the collar is constructed, these payments will represent a better or poorer hedge.

Finally, certain variations of collars can be constructed to allow continuing participation in upside market movements with no cap. Such variations will not be costless, but will involve a small premium payment.

Implementation   In addition to the cap, floor and zero premium characteristics described above, costless collars have other aspects important to consider during implementation. These features include portfolio correlation, credit exposure and liquidity.

To provide an effective portfolio hedge, the underlying equities should in the aggregate have a reasonable correlation with the index chosen for the collar construction. Otherwise the buyer may be assuming an undesirable basis risk.

Credit exposure is also a consideration. Collars are typically constructed and offered on a customised basis (OTC) by a bank or broker-dealer. In this case buyer and seller have credit exposure to one another. Therefore clients contemplating purchase of a costless collar should carefully examine their counterparty's credit to ensure it meets their highest standards. In the case where the collar is constructed using listed options, the buyer's credit exposure is confined to the clearing house associated with the options.

Finally, collar buyers are generally best served by holding their hedges to maturity rather than by unwinding them early. This approach allows the buyer to avoid payment of the bid/offer spread.

Collars may be implemented in the listed markets whenever the appropriate index has associated calls and puts. Such collars, however, are often limited in size, expiration dates and choices for floors and caps. The more flexible OTC market is used whenever strike prices, maturities, transaction sizes and indices are not readily available or unsuitable. It should be noted that the short call leg in a listed market transaction generally will involve escrow or margin requirements. Such escrow or margin requirements will not apply in the case of OTC options.

Example   An insurance company wishes to protect its equity portfolio over the next 12 months against a drop of more than 8 per cent from the prevailing S&P 500 Index level of 409. Observing a high correlation between its portfolio and the S&P 500 Index, it decides to purchase a one-year costless collar having a floor of 8 per cent below the market. A triple-A rated bank calculates an acceptable cap of 9.2 per cent above the market and the collar is implemented on the OTC market. The insurance company and bank are each satisfied with one another's credit. No initial cash changes hands as the collar takes effect.

Collar providers hedge their risks by offsetting transactions in listed derivatives, stock portfolios or some combination thereof. Index futures contracts, when available, often provide the lowest cost hedge. The ready availability of index futures in most large capital markets means that buyers can purchase collars on most of their international equity exposure at any time. Following completion of their own offsetting hedges, collar providers are generally market neutral. Their profits therefore

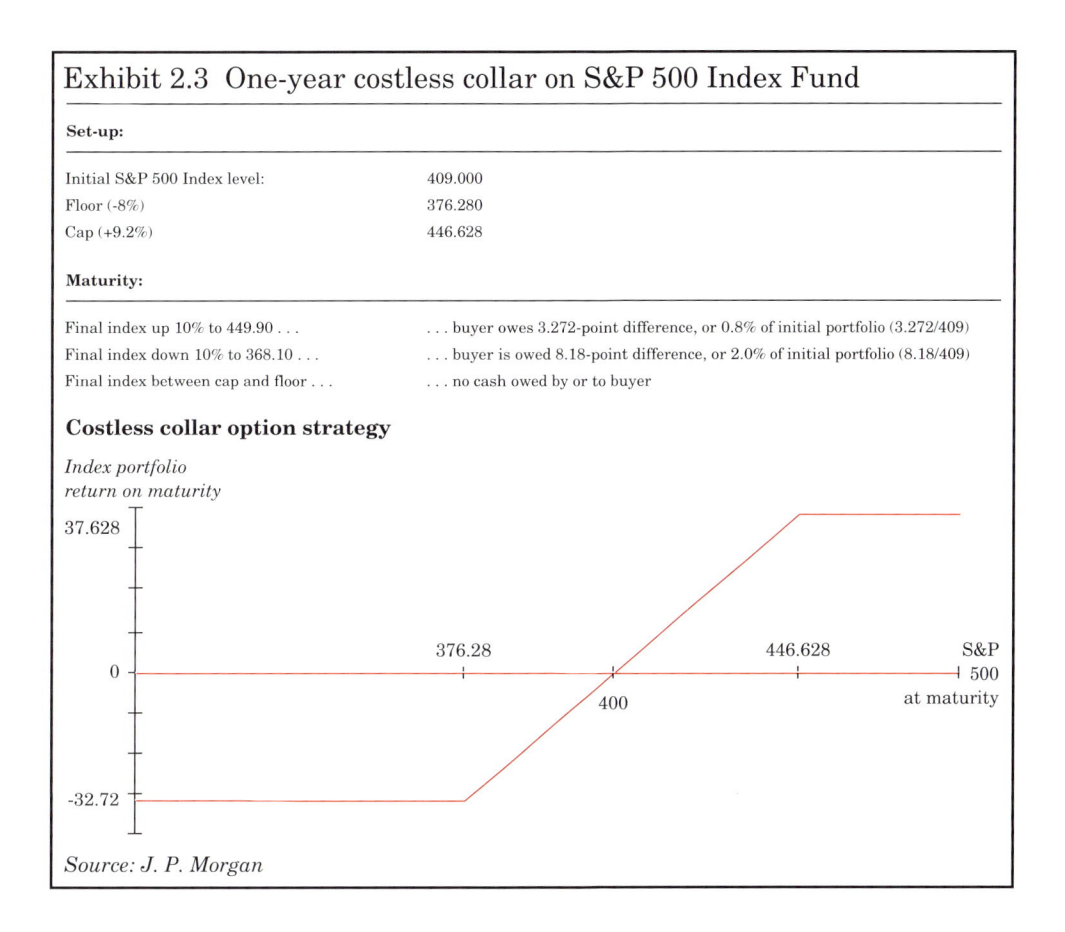

Exhibit 2.3 One-year costless collar on S&P 500 Index Fund

Set-up:

Initial S&P 500 Index level:	409.000
Floor (-8%)	376.280
Cap (+9.2%)	446.628

Maturity:

Final index up 10% to 449.90 . . .	. . . buyer owes 3.272-point difference, or 0.8% of initial portfolio (3.272/409)
Final index down 10% to 368.10 . . .	. . . buyer is owed 8.18-point difference, or 2.0% of initial portfolio (8.18/409)
Final index between cap and floor . . .	. . . no cash owed by or to buyer

Costless collar option strategy

Index portfolio return on maturity

Source: J. P. Morgan

come from spread pricing, management of hedged positions or from commissions on listed executions, and not from assuming investment positions opposite to that of their customers.

Collars need not be "costless", but can be designed to provide a premium upon initial purchase, or to create an initial cash outlay when first implemented. Also the caps on collars need not be total but rather can be designed to allow for a continuing percentage participation in upside price movements. As an example, consider an investor wishing to protect a portfolio against a 10 per cent portfolio loss, while at the same time wanting to participate in upside market moves. Such a pattern of risk and return can be created, but at the cost of a small premium. First, a put is purchased to provide the 10 per cent floor. Next, a call is sold on 50 per cent of the underlying portfolio value. This creates a participation of 50 per cent in any upside market moves above the strike price of the call.

Finally, collars can be applied to individual stocks as well as stock indices. A portfolio manager with a concern about the future course of a particular stock may elect to collar its current price pending a meaningful change of direction. Often listed calls and puts are not available for this purpose making the design and implementation more suitable for an OTC provider.

Improving portfolio return

Writing covered calls An investor selling short a single stock call option must deliver to the buyer the number of shares controlled by the call should it be exercised. If at the time of sale the investor has (does not have) the required number of shares,

Exhibit 2.4 At-the-money covered call

Profit/loss at maturity

Stock position

Upper breakeven

Covered call position

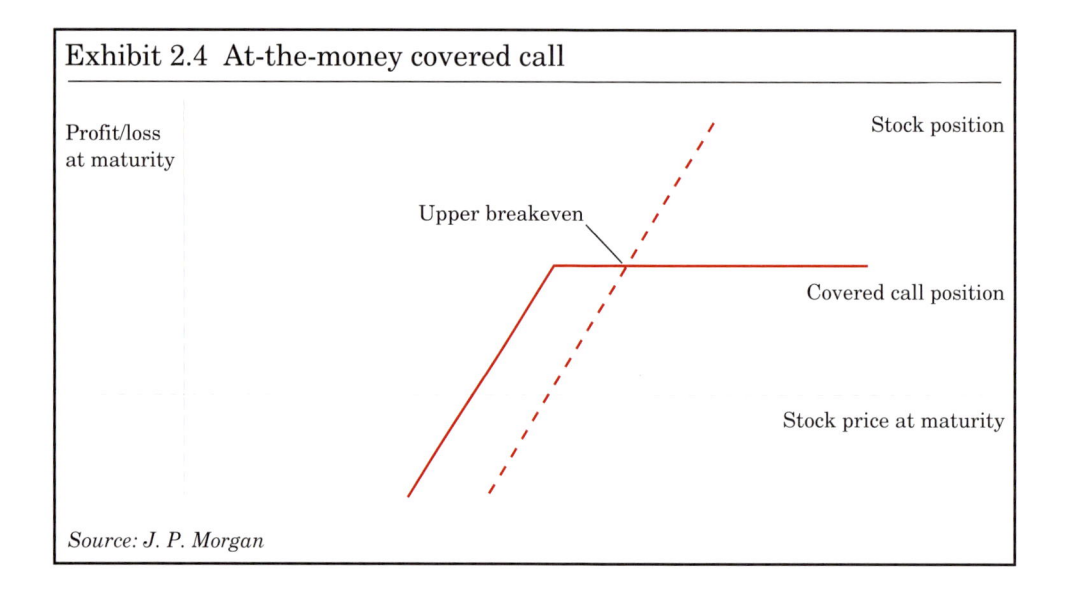

Stock price at maturity

Source: J. P. Morgan

the call is said to be covered (uncovered). In the case of a cash settled index call, the cover can be provided by a portfolio of securities with an asset value sufficient to satisfy margin requirements prescribed by the exchange on which the option trades. In the case that the cash settled option is OTC the required collateral is negotiated with the buyer.

A covered call position on a single stock has a risk-return profile very different from the underlying stock. Returns are limited above the call strike price, and buffered but not limited below the strike price (see Exhibit 2.4).

An investor holding such a position receives a premium from the sale of the call which reduces the risk of stock ownership. Beyond a certain price rise, however, the investor will be subject to opportunity losses compared with a holder of stock alone. This point is called the upper breakeven point and is equivalent to the strike price of the option plus premium received. Covered call writing as a strategy will thus outperform simple stock ownership provided the stock at call expiration is below the upper breakeven. Also, it is easy to see that this strategy carries less volatility of return and less downside risk than direct ownership of stock.

Premium received from the sale of a call will enhance the returns from stock ownership at all points below the upper breakeven. The historical average premium received ranges between approximately 6 per cent and 15 per cent depending upon the underlying market volatility, option demand and option maturity. To achieve this, a diversified portfolio of stocks is purchased and options sold selectively on issues from which premiums received are expected to be retained.

Corporate treasurers seeking enhanced yield on short-term cash also can look to covered call writing programmes to produce favourable results in such market periods. In addition, in the US the dividends received from common stock holdings normally qualify for the dividend received deduction of 70 per cent, further enhancing the yield of this strategy for corporate cash management. In this case, a portfolio of dividend yielding stocks is chosen and calls are written to protect the equity holding while dividends are captured. For the dividends to qualify for preferred tax status, stock must be owned for a minimum number of days and call options sold must meet certain qualifying characteristics set down by the Internal Revenue Service.

Certain managers of index funds offer enhancement strategies based upon underweighting overvalued stocks and overweighting undervalued stocks. Instead of selling an overvalued stock, a call option can be sold to buffer projected downside price movements. The deeper in-the-money the call option is, the more downside protection is available for the covered writer. Alternatively, index calls can be sold to raise premium whenever the market conditions are appropriate. Pursued properly, this strategy too results in an enhancement of portfolio returns.

Risk reduction feature   By varying the degree to which a call is in-the-money, a portfolio manager can adjust flexibly the stock exposure assumed. In this sense, covered calls have adjustable risk features. In-the-money calls will neutralise more existing stock exposure than will at-the-money or out-of-the-money calls of the same maturity. By the same token an in-the-money call immediately removes all the upside in an existing stock position. For an out-of-the-money covered call the stock can rise to the strike price before the return is capped. A trade-off therefore exists between the degree of downside exposure to be neutralised and the upside potential to be retained. The skill of a portfolio manager lies in correctly striking the balance between the two.

In a falling market the protection afforded by the call premium received can be exhausted if no defensive action is taken. However, covered call managers will actively roll out-of-the-money calls with little premium left, to calls with lower strike prices in order to capture additional premium. This strategy can prove to be very effective in protecting portfolios. In markets with an upward price trend, managers can remain less than fully covered to avoid excessive opportunity losses above the upper breakeven points. Here too, call contracts can be rolled to higher strike prices as the market advances. The objective in such a market is to be fully covered when the

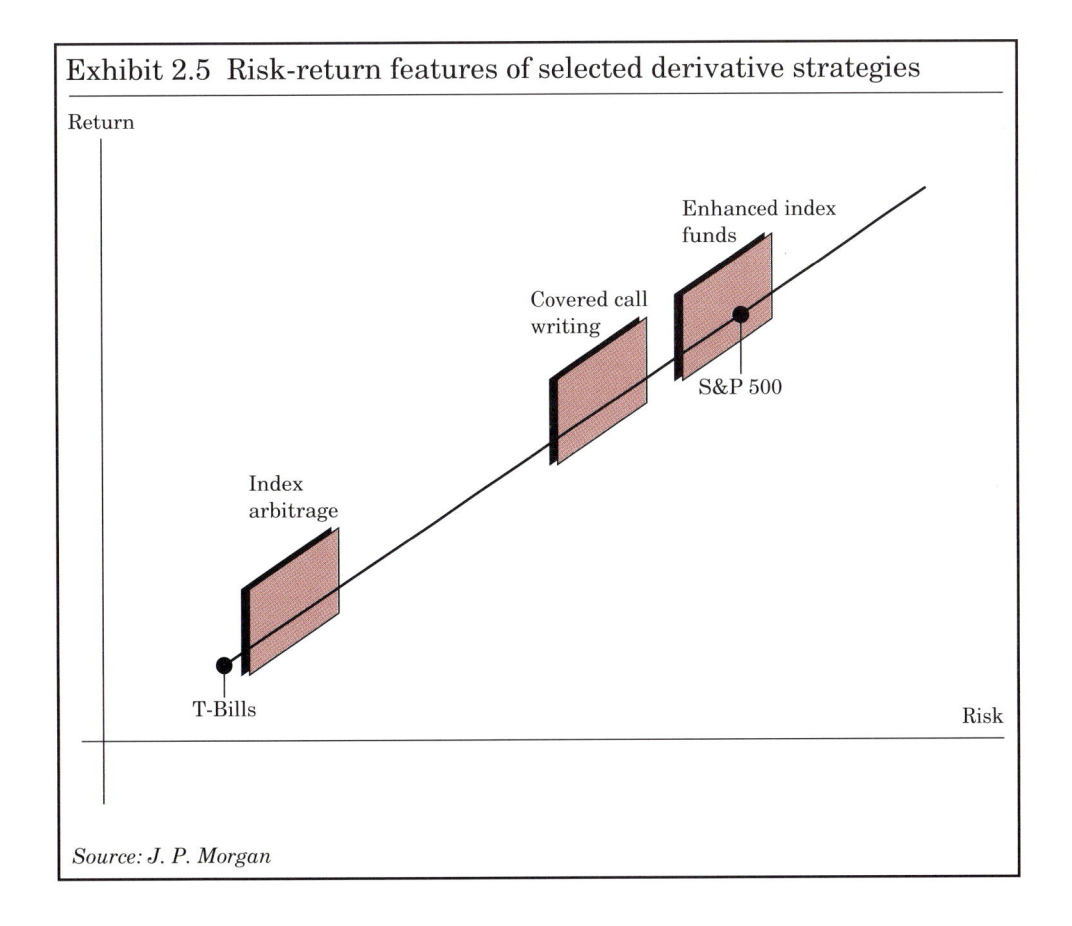

Exhibit 2.5 Risk-return features of selected derivative strategies

Source: J. P. Morgan

stock reaches its point of maximum appreciation. Hence, covered call managers need to have valuation views on the stocks in their portfolios. The major risk to a covered call writer is the same as that for a stock only manager – namely, a steeply falling market. In this case it is difficult to generate enough option premium to compensate for price losses.

On a risk adjusted basis, covered call writing is often a very attractive strategy. When compared with a benchmark index such as the S&P 500, risks are lower and returns can at times be higher.

Benefits and concerns   Return enhancements can be negated by opportunity losses as stocks rise above their covered call upper breakeven points. In this case portfolio returns are capped, but not negative. Some observers are quick to criticise this strategy in rising markets as underperforming the S&P 500 as a benchmark. This ignores not only the overall result over a full market cycle, but also the performance of such a strategy adjusted for the risk reduction if offers. Generally, historical results have qualitatively resembled those sketched in Exhibit 2.5. Here we see that a range of returns is possible relative to the S&P 500.

The options used in covered call writing programmes usually are the most liquid ones available. Managers need this liquidity to book sizeable positions. They therefore choose carefully in such programmes to avoid being locked into losses from illiquid options when markets move. Nevertheless, because returns depend upon holding many covered calls to maturity, abrupt termination of such a programme can be costly and should be avoided. An orderly unwind is far better for the investor if time permits. Accordingly, the liquidity of such an investment should not be expected to be exeptionally high.

Rebalancing the portfolio

Probably the area with the greatest growth potential for the equity derivative market is the use of swaps, puts and calls as asset allocation elements. Most typically this will be in the form of an overlay strategy but increasingly derivatives will actually replace the underlying investment rather than just complement it.

Overlay strategies   Asset allocation decisions are generally made on a strategic rather than tactical basis and are therefore not easily modified to take account of short-term price movements. In some institutions there is a conflict between the traders who have strong views on the short-term market and the asset allocation committee. Again there can be conflict between the committee and particular portfolio managers during the process of the quarterly reallocations if the decision to lighten the weighting of a particular market involves selling a position laboriously and expensively acquired. It is particularly difficult to justify reducing exposure for the upcoming quarter if the portfolio managers suspect that in three or six months they will want to reinstate the position. Seen in this light there is an inertia in the decision-making process. In order to avoid incurring the bid and offer spread as well as two sets of commission, a committee may opt to leave the status quo. However, on pure economic fundamentals the investment portfolio probably should have been adjusted.

Using derivatives to make such adjustments, while leaving the underlying portfolio untouched, can therefore resolve many of the problems of the periodic asset allocation decision. Portfolio managers can maintain a stock portfolio while complying with the committee's decision; the traders can trade at low cost on their market views by using derivatives; and perhaps most importantly the committee's hands are untied by the ability to make important adjustments promptly to the overall asset mix.

These overlay strategies can take many forms, for example:

1. Equity swaps provide a useful way of reducing one market exposure and increasing another, netting out the Libor flows in between. Thus an investor who decides strategically to reallocate assets by reducing exposure to the US from a 30 per cent weighting to 25 per cent and increasing French exposure by 3 per cent and UK exposure by 2 per cent could execute an equity swap where the S&P 500 return is paid and the CAC-40 and FT-SE 100 returns are received. The notional amount would be the 5 per cent reduction sought with fixed exchange rates between dollars, francs and sterling and the maturity could be one year. One year is the most liquid maturity at present for most equity swaps. For periods shorter than this the futures market is often cheaper and for periods longer the market bid/offer swap spreads increase.

2. A stock investor who is medium-term bullish but short-term bearish buys a three-month put option to protect the investment. If internal rules stipulate the portfolio must be sold when its market value drops below a specified level, then the put purchase may prevent the sale. As the market drops, the put value rises, preventing portfolio sale and eventual repurchase with all attendant commission and trading costs.

Shifting management expertise Equity investors are increasingly looking at index options and equity swaps to replicate their portfolios rather than just to complement them. Thus when a decision is made to increase the weighting of a particular overseas market, a portfolio manager convinced of the value of buying downside protection may choose either to buy the stock together with an index put or, instead, simply to buy an index call and invest the cash balance elsewhere. The equity performance should in theory ("put/call parity") be exactly the same if the cash remaining from buying the call is invested in a note which has the same coupon as his expected dividend. However, the main reason for taking this approach is to gain the advantages, mentioned above, of saving the equity market commission, eliminating dividend risk, and, above all, simplifying administration. UK institutions have started to buy FT-SE calls in combination with UK gilts to accomplish this very objective. Gilts carry higher coupons than the stock market's dividends so that there will be an initial cash shortfall in the combination by comparison with simply buying a put option. However, the collection of these gilts' coupons is a much simpler process, being twice a year on entirely predictable dates.

Such an investor also has the added flexibility of being able to enhance the return by selecting gilt portfolio managers skilled at return enhancement. An investor who feels comfortable with the gilt market, and has successfully used his in-depth knowledge to outperform a passive approach, but who feels that for prudential reasons he should diversify into equities will be able to keep 100 per cent of his investment in gilts and use his edge here to add to his passive equity exposure. Thus any competitive advantage in a different market can be transferred as enhanced performance in the equity market.

Taking market views Portfolio managers wishing to acquire positions in selected stocks sometimes use individual listed stock options to implement their buying strategies. Usually the portfolio manager has a general idea about price levels where purchases seem attractive, a time over which purchases are anticipated, and the number of shares to be purchased. To implement this strategy, puts with strike prices at or below the current market level are sold and if exercised result in the purchase of shares at the targeted strike price values. By selling puts with a maturity within the desired time frame for stock acquisition, and also covering the number of shares eligible for purchase, a target buying programme is initiated.

To illustrate this strategy, suppose a manager wishes to acquire 50,000 shares of a stock over the next two months at prices less than or equal to the current market price. Half the shares are purchased at the currently attractive market price of $50 and the balance is targeted for purchase at lower prices with a put selling programme. Should the price rise, direct purchases will be made to a limit price of $58, a target breakeven price calculated by the manager. Listed puts with a strike price of $45 are available with a one-month maturity. The manager sells puts at this strike price representing 20,000 shares. The balance of 5000 shares is to be purchased as the manager sees fit. There will be three scenarios possible at expiration of the puts:

1. The stock price closes at or above the strike price of $45. The puts sold expire worthless and the premium initially received from the sale, less the commissions paid, is retained as net premium income. This income received can be viewed as lowering the cost of eventual stock purchase at whatever price the acquisition takes place.
2. The stock price closes at a price below $45. In this case the puts are exercised creating a functional purchase of stock at a price of $45 per share. As the initial sale premium received is always retained, the effective purchase price can be viewed as $45 less this premium. This price is sometimes referred to as the lower breakeven price. Suppose the net premium received is $3. Then the stock could fall to $42 at put expiration and still not create an opportunity loss from selling the put.
3. The stock price can potentially close significantly below the strike price of $45, in which case the effective purchase price of $45 less net premium received may still be above the then current market price and accordingly represent an opportunity loss. Should the stock gradually drop in price below the lower breakeven price the manager can take defensive action by repurchasing the puts sold. Stock can then be purchased directly at a lower level or puts can be sold with a yet lower strike price.

Targeted selling programmes, much like targeted buying programmes, are implemented with options. In this case, however, call options are sold having strike prices corresponding to levels where the portfolio manager would be willing to sell shares. The premium received is always retained if options are held to expiration. Again, the number of shares covered by the call options and the option maturities are calculated to correspond to the portfolio manager's view of the stock's potential.

Cost and execution advantages

Clearly the usefulness of derivatives in asset allocation mix changes depends on several factors. In order to compete with making adjustments to the portfolios in securities markets, portfolio managers must be able to buy or sell options quickly and cheaply, whether OTC or listed.

Cost benefits of equity alternatives

The argument that using derivatives as an overlay is cheaper than shifting the underlying portfolio depends chiefly on economies of scale. An options house which has two-way flows in OTC options or equity swaps will be able to run a smaller net delta than would be required for just one option position. The smaller overall position will lead to reducing financing costs and lower commission. By way of illustration let us take one example of an equity swap.

Equity swaps A rational investor will only use an overlay equity swap to, for example, swap out of the S&P 500 into a synthetic index fund if the synthetic equity fund shows better economics. The investor needs to compare costs (commissions on liquidation of shares; dividends not received; spread below Libor which he receives for investing cash; commissions paid to repurchase the portfolio; and stock lending income foregone) with the enhanced swap quote and the interest which can be earned on the cash released from sale of the stock. A dealer offering this equity swap as its first, and possibly only, derivative position should charge the investor exactly the same costs and when including a credit charge the economics of the swap will immediately look worse for the investor. This is true even if the options house hedges itself using S&P futures, since arbitrage ensures that the futures basis always has cost of carry and commissions included. However, an options warehouse which has many other positions will be able to save many of these costs. The best possible case would be that the dealer manages to synchronise two opposing positions and thus save all the stock commissions, though this is clearly unlikely. Alternatively it can sometimes be arranged that the two parties trade the underlying stock required for the dealer's hedge between themselves, and more frequently that an equity payer can lend stock to the dealer who needs to short stock on the market. These private arrangements can also save commissions and other costs. Even without this help it is assumed by the options house that its net long equity position will be reduced at some stage, thus eliminating the stock borrowing charge and the spread below Libor for investing cash. These anticipated savings are passed on to the investor in the form of the spread below Libor agreed at the outset of the swap.

As well as using derivatives as part of an overlay on an existing portfolio, they are increasingly used in asset allocation in the place of the underlying shares. Equity swaps where the investor receives the equity dividends and price appreciation, or loses the depreciation, can represent a cheaper form of investment than buying the underlying shares, depending on the spread above or below Libor. For example an investor whose cost of funds is deemed to be Libor flat and who expects to suffer commissions of 10 basis points on buying and selling would achieve a better return over 1 year by entering an equity swap where his spread vs. Libor is only 5 basis points, as determined in the swap market. This is particularly true for those investors who for various reasons do not, or cannot lend their stocks to enhance the return.

Equity swaps should also appeal particularly to those funds who like to recognise capital gains on the portfolio, possibly in order to allocate the profit to the fund investors on an annual basis. This would otherwise require turning the portfolio in order to cash in the gains, whereas these gains can be paid conveniently at the maturity of a one year swap. The swap can then be restarted on the same terms with the original investment, the only risk being that the spread to Libor might have worsened a year from now. A mark-to-market swap would achieve the same effect, but the Libor spread for longer swaps is often unattractive relative to the risk of rolling the position.

There is one additional feature of equity swaps which can prove to be an overwhelmingly persuasive argument for some investors. Through the equity swap mechanism, foreign investors can recover some tax, which is usually only due to domestic taxpayers. This is part of the explanation for the sub-Libor margins in the DAX and CAC swap markets, the other major component being the returns of lending (or costs for borrowing) stock.

For example, in a one-year DAX swap an investor could receive the return of the DAX which includes reinvested dividends in cash after one year, and in the meantime pay Deutschmark Libor less 70 basis points on a principal amount which is the initial amount invested. The most neutral market for index swaps is the S&P with very small stock borrowing or lending influence and no tax effects, so that we may conclude that some of the extra 70 basis points given to the investor in a DAX swap are tax-related. In fact there are two taxes withheld from German dividends: one is a 25 per cent withholding tax which is levied on the net dividend paid and is in most cases recoverable by foreign investors; the other is a form of advanced corporation tax (*Körperertragsteur*) withheld at 36 per cent from the gross dividend and reclaimable only by German institutions and individuals against their own taxes. This 36 per cent is clearly different for each of the 30 stocks, depending on the dividend, but it is generally regarded that the average tax on the DAX as a whole amounts to between 1.2 and 1.5 per cent per annum. Clearly not all of this is passed on to the swap market but there is now sufficient depth in the market to feel confident that until the tax rules change DAX swaps will be sub-Libor. The risk that the tax law may change is indicated by the tighter spreads to Libor in medium-term maturities (ie, only 20 basis points in three years and maybe Libor plus a margin in five years or beyond). Stability to these spreads is given by the number of participants who seek to make money by arbitrage. There are now many fixed or floating investors who have realised that by buying stocks at Libor flat and swapping out the equity risk through an equity swap they can still make a margin despite the 70 basis point deficit between the floating legs by claiming the tax relating to the stocks. In fact the arbitrage is more often done via DAX futures than through equity swaps, but even so the value of the tax credit is partially given by the regular cheapness of DAX futures to cash.

In summary, an equity swap provided by a dealer which sees good two-way flows of business and has a large in-house reservoir of stocks will provide generally better economics than an investor liquidating a portfolio. In fact the above analysis of how to "manufacture" a swap will be overtaken increasingly by the dynamics of a growing swap market. The spread below Libor will vary mainly according to the supply and demand of payers and receivers, and this will mean that sometimes they will represent good value for an investor and sometimes not. Swap spreads are no more predictable than in the interest rate swap market, since even in the manufactured position shown above there are variables which can change at any time, the most sensitive being the dividend yield and stock lending income.

The same analysis can be performed for ordinary OTC put and call options. In theory a large investor could create an in-house option hedge by dynamically trading the delta in the same way as an options trader. However, the pay-off profile of such a process will not be exactly that of an option. The only way to guarantee 100 per cent pay-out on a put below a certain strike is to buy an option from another party. Furthermore if you factor in the management time and expertise required as well as the systems and technologies support, it is most unlikely that a home-made product will be cheaper than an option provided by an active dealing participant.

When it comes to straightforward put and call options there is one further element which makes a third party presence vital, namely volatility risk. This is the one options element which is unhedgeable except by finding offsetting positions, and if an investor left this unhedged then the eventual return from even the most accurate, dynamic hedging process may prove to be more or less than anticipated.

Therefore, provided that derivatives meet the investors' requirements in efficiency of execution and cost-effectiveness, they represent the most flexible and simplest way to shift overall exposures without disturbing established portfolios.

Finally, the fact that most swap and option structures are off balance sheet is an advantage for insurance companies and other corporates, to which they should attribute a monetary value. In other words when making the cost comparison above of buying a basket of shares or doing an equity swap, a corporate should allocate a certain annual cost (say 50 basis points) to the use of its balance sheet. Derivative profits improve the return of assets, whereas stocks funded by debt balloon the balance sheet. This analysis depends on the size of the balance sheet and the company's sensitivity to its financial ratios.

Synthetic index funds One of the most important uses for equity derivatives by investors is in the construction of synthetic index funds. The two primary motivations in pursuing these substitutes for stock equivalent investments are return enhancement and cost savings.

The newest methods for enhancement of index fund returns have emerged in conjunction with the growth of three related markets: global futures, global portfolio trading and OTC derivatives. The general form of these funds is:

"Cash" underlay + derivative overlay = enhanced index fund

This equation, while revealing a simplicity of construction, also shows there are two possible sources for enhancement: the "cash" underlay or the derivative overlay.

Underlays today can include a huge variety of cash and cash-like instruments. Examples other than Treasury bills include:

- corporate and government bonds;
- actively managed bond portfolios;
- synthetic fixed income assets;
- simultaneously held long and short stock portfolios; and
- stock index arbitrage positions.

Examples of derivative overlays include:

- stock index futures
- stock index option pairs; and
- stock index swaps.

The sources of risk and sources of enhancement will differ in each case and accordingly will require careful analysis before investing. Generally, however, every synthetic fund in the matrix will have some combination of credit, interest rate, basis and event risk. Therefore, making an investment in an enhanced index fund requires some understanding of these risks and how they can be managed successfully.

A simple example will illustrate these points:

Underlay:	Single A-rated, fixed rate, three-year, US corporate bond which swaps to US dollar Libor plus 20 basis points.
Overlay:	Three-year S&P 500 Total rate of return index swap with triple-A rated counterparty priced at US dollar Libor plus 5 basis points.
Result:	S&P 500 synthetic index fund plus 15 basis points per year for three years.
Primary risk:	Normal corporate bond credit risk (A); swap has minimal counterparty risk (AAA).

A second example provides an interesting variation and illustrates yet other features of synthetic funds. A pension fund owns five-year fixed rate, illiquid Canadian provincial bonds, but wants to shift exposure to the German equity market for a period of one year. The fund does not wish to sell the Canadian bonds if possible so as to avoid paying the bid/offer spread.

Underlay:	Canadian AA-rated, fixed coupon, five-year provincial bonds.
Overlay:	German DAX index swap paying total rate of return plus 70 basis points per year vs. Canadian fixed coupon. Swap provider is AAA-rated.
Result:	Provincial bond assets are fully exposed to the German stock market for one year. Returns equal the total rate of return of the DAX index plus 70 basis points per year.
Primary risk:	Normal provincial bond credit risk (AA). Swap has minimal counterparty risk (AAA). Currency risk on equity appreciation (not principal).

Here we see the versatility of the OTC derivatives market. A preferred holding by a customer remains in place while being fully converted into an enhanced synthetic index fund in the country of choice with full currency exposure.

Equity-linked notes An index call on the S&P 500 is characterised by limited downside loss and full participation in any upside market gains, less of course, the initial purchase premium. Purchase of a call represents a bullish statement on the US market as the investor can gain only in a rising market. Similarly, purchase of an index put represents a bearish position because gains are realised only in a declining (bear) market. These investment positions and related ones such as call and put spreads, can be joined with fixed income CDs, notes and bonds to form a family of index-linked securities known loosely as bull and bear bonds or equity-linked notes (ELNs).

There are generally three parties to ELN transactions: the investor, the issuer and the bank/market-maker. The investor, dealing with the market-maker, specifies investment requirements, including credit of the issuer, size of offering, term, coupon and index. The bank arranges for an issuer to meet the credit size, term and coupon needs, and itself provides the OTC call. The issuer, which stands between bank and investor, then issues the bond, containing the index-linked option. To hedge the option pay-

Exhibit 2.6 Sample term sheet for an S&P 500 bull bond

Term	Details
Issuer	AA-rated US Corporation
Principal	$50 million
Maturity	Two years
Coupon	Zero
Issue price	Par
Redemption	Principal amount plus S&P 500 payment
S&P 500 payment	Higher of zero or the following result: Principal $\times$ 85% $\times$ (SMP/SPI – 1) SMP = S&P 500 Index at maturity SPI = S&P 500 Index at issuance

ment, it obtains the OTC call from the bank in a separate transaction, thereby making itself market neutral. By acting as an intermediary for this transaction, the issuer is able to lower its total cost of financing by two to five basis points. A term sheet for a simple two-year bull bond is shown in Exhibit 2.6. Here we see that this bond is issued at par, and redeemed at par plus an equity-linked payment representing the pay-off, if any, on the call option.

Notice that in no case does the investor redeem below par. This capital preservation feature is especially attractive to tax-exempt investors. Notice too that the investor participates at less than a full 100 per cent rate in market gains. The factor is referred to as the participation rate.

It is easy to calculate the participation rate once the issuer's financing cost is known and the bank's OTC option is priced. This calculation proceeds as follows. First, the present value of a zero coupon bond is evaluated using the issuer's targeted cost of funding. We imagine for the sake of discussion that this number is 83 per cent. If the cost of the OTC option is 20 per cent then only a partial call can be purchased with the balance of funds available from the investor. The ratio of the balance of funds available to the option premium is by definition the participation rate.

$$\text{Participation rate} = (100 - 83 \text{ per cent})/20 \text{ per cent} = 85 \text{ per cent}$$

An investor can constrain the option provider to a bull bond design containing a 100 per cent participation rate, in which case other bond features will have to be adjusted. For example, there are three ways in which a 100 per cent participation rate might be achieved:

1. raise the call strike price;
2. lower the issuer credit;
3. capping potential upside gains.

If the call strike is raised the purchase cost of the call is lowered until the price just reaches the 17 per cent value required for a 100 per cent participation rate. It is easy to see that the investor begins participation only after the new strike price is reached. All market gains up to this new strike price result in no additional equity-linked payment.

If the credit quality of the issuer is lowered sufficiently the present value of the zero coupon bond falls below the critical 80 per cent threshold necessary for full upside participation. It is seldom the case that investors have a large degree of flexibility to adjust their credit requirements. Nevertheless some flexibility is maintained and may play a role in meeting participation rate requirements.

If the investor is willing to cap upside returns, full participation can be achieved between the current market level on the index cap level through the sale of an out-of-the-money call option. The market-maker calculates the upper level strike price required to generate the 3 per cent missing premium necessary to achieve full participation. The investor now retains 100 per cent of any upside between the present market level and the upper strike price.

Many variations on the ELN structure are possible. Choices are available to investors depending upon country exposure, currency exposure and risk-return exposures. Equity indices exist in most major and many minor equity markets making possible the construction of ELNs around the world. Such bonds would be useful for obtaining hedged entry into selected markets. A Nikkei 225 bull bond would have limited downside risk and upside appreciation, much the same as a Nikkei 225 Index fund hedged with a put purchase.

Currency exposure can be altered to suit the investor's preference. A German DAX put currency-hedged back to the Canadian dollar could be paired with a zero coupon Canadian bond to create a Canadian dollar bear bond. Whenever the investor's home currency is preferred, the option embedded can be currency-hedged to create a bond fully denominated and payable in that home currency.

Option-like risk-return combinations can be also created and embedded in a bond. A bull call spread involves purchase of a call with a lower strike price and sale of a call with a higher strike price but having the same maturity. This call spread can be joined with a zero coupon bond to create an instrument with a cap, a floor and an upside participation between the two strike prices.

Coupon levels can be changed as well. It is not necessary to design bonds having zero coupons. One variation is to set the coupon equal to the dividend yield on the underlying index. Most dividend yields are less than the corresponding matched-to-maturity bond coupon rates leaving an excess with which to purchase embedded options.

Investors unable to use OTC or listed derivatives due to regulatory or self-imposed constraints find it attractive to make implicit use of them through the purchase of securities with the derivative features embedded. There is also the matter of administrative simplicity: if a bond is constructed by two separate purchases of the zero coupon portion and the option, separate documentation and negotiations must take place for each portion. Some investors are willing to undertake this task themselves, usually by making deposits rather than buying a bond. Many, however, prefer to purchase one single instrument which combines the features they desire. Simplicity too has a cost saving potential in the reduced time allocated to manage the investment exposure.

Exhibit 2.7   Features of index futures and OTC swaps

Feature	*Futures*	*OTC swaps*
Credit	Clearing house	Counterparty
Margin	Initial + variation	None
Maturity	1–12 months	6 months–5 years
Listing	Exchanges	None
Commissions	Negotiated	None
Users	Retail + institutional	Institutional
Underlying	Selected indices	Most equity indices, customised indices, single stocks and stock baskets
Availability	Major capital markets	Major global markets
Liquidity	Low to high	Low to moderate
Settlement	Normally 1–2 days	Negotiated
Special features	None	Negotiated

Comparison of derivative features

The following section compares the practical aspects of using various derivative instruments and outlines the factors which should influence an investor's choice.

Listed futures vs. OTC swaps Because equity index futures and equity index swaps exhibit generally similar investment characteristics, it is natural to want to compare their features and uses in institutional portfolios. Each instrument can be used to create synthetic index funds, to hedge stock portfolios and to implement certain asset allocation strategies. Each instrument too carries with it some aspect of credit, maturity, margin, size and liquidity. A brief summary of selected features appears in Exhibit 2.7.

Credit: Buyers and sellers of futures must look to the clearing house associated with the exchange on which the contract is traded for credit satisfaction. The particular arrangements made between the clearing house and its members will determine the nature of this credit assessment. Clearing houses do not normally carry credit ratings by independent rating agencies. Swap counterparties each have potential exposure to one another's credit and so the choice of counterparty assumes a high degree of importance. A triple-A rated provider with a commitment to the swap and OTC markets will be preferable to a lesser credit with a similar profile.

Margin: Futures generally require initial margin by the investor. This margin acts as a good faith deposit to insure performance on the contract should it move against the investor. Variation margin on futures corresponds to a daily flow of funds between the investor and the clearing house which settles the contracts between buyers and sellers. No such margins, initial or variation, are generally required for OTC swap contracts. Instead, swaps may be marked-to-market periodically and cash differences exchanged between the two counterparties to the swap. A final exchange takes place at the maturity as the swap terminates.

Maturity: Futures contracts carry maturities as long as a year and sometimes more. As a practical matter, however, liquidity is constrained to the shortest-term maturities. Therefore investment strategies longer in term than three months or so will require that futures positions be rolled over as expiration is approached. In such rolls, the existing position is extinguished and replaced simultaneously with a new position in the next nearest maturity contract. Three rolls per year would then complete a one-year investment position. With swaps, no such activity is required. Maturities range from six months to five years or more and often require no action on the part of the investor prior to maturity.

Listing: Futures contracts are standardised with respect to their maturity, face value, price movement, margin requirements and trading hours. All these design features are meant to facilitate the trading of contracts on listed exchanges with the greatest convenience. Without the growth of these futures markets, expansion of the equity OTC derivatives would have been inhibited. Swap contracts, on the other hand, are not standardised. It is in fact rare to see many equity swaps which are alike with respect to terms of size, currency or maturity. None are listed. Herein lies not only a major difference between these two types of contracts but a key to understanding how best to use then to achieve investment objectives.

Commissions: Commissions on futures are negotiated between executing brokers and customers. They can range from approximately three to ten basis points per year based on the face value of the contract. Swaps have no commissions charged. All costs are priced into the contract at initiation.

Availability: Index futures contracts are available in most major and many minor capital markets globally. Swaps can be constructed to cover not only the local indices on which futures are based, but also customised indices, single stocks and stock baskets.

Liquidity: In most major markets, liquidity of futures is moderate in the shortest maturity contracts and much less in longer-term contracts. If the bid/ask spread is used as a measure of liquidity this can be very high for certain contracts such as for the S&P 500 futures. Swaps have liquidity anywhere between low and high depending on the market, but even so should probably be entered with the intention of holding to maturity.

Settlement: Settlement terms for futures are standard and set by the exchange on which the contract is listed. The actual settlement normally takes place within two days of maturity. Swaps are settled on the basis of terms negotiated between the counterparties and are set at initiation.

Special features: Listed futures carry only standardised features. Swaps have no such requirements and accordingly reflect greater variability. Chapter Six deals with "exotic" structures that can be adapted for equity swaps.

It is probable that in time swap contracts will grow to encompass a wider range of investment activity than futures contracts. Much will depend upon investor demand for the flexibility and global reach which swaps can provide. In some narrow areas of activity, such as in index fund construction, swaps will provide a useful alternative to futures from time to time. An investor seeking a three-year investment may prefer the certainty of return offered in a swap to the return uncertainty and higher liquidity of a futures-based implementation. Each derivative in this case offers its own features to a potential investor.

Listed options vs. OTC options   A comparison of listed and OTC options can be made which largely parallels that between listed futures and OTC swaps. Many of

Exhibit 2.8   Features of listed vs. OTC options

Feature	*Listed option*	*OTC option*
Credit	Clearing house	Counterparty
Margin	Primarily for sales	Not generally
Maturity	1–9 months	6 months–5 years
Listing	Exchanges	None
Commissions	Negotiated	None
Users	Retail + institutional	Institutional
Underlying	Single stocks and selected indices	Single stocks, most indices, customised indices and stock baskets
Availability	Major capital markets	Major global markets
Liquidity	Low to moderate	Moderate
Settlement	Normally 1–2 days	Negotiated
Special features	None	Negotiable

the observations here are similar if not identical to those above. Exhibit 2.8 will help this comparison and, again, notable features are discussed in the following paragraphs.

Credit: Buyers and sellers of listed options must look to the clearing house associated with the exchange on which the options are traded for credit satisfaction. Once again, as in the case of futures, the credit of the clearing house will depend upon the capital arrangements made by the clearing house with its members. Buyers of OTC options have potential exposure to the sellers and so the credit rating of the latter becomes an important issue.

Margin: Listed options purchased by an investor and paid for in full involve no margin. Such options sold short will involve margin if no assets are available to cover potential losses. Similarly, OTC options bought and paid for in full will involve no margin. OTC options sold short by an investor may require collateralisation to cover a portion or all of the potential obligations on the OTC contract.

Maturity: Listed option contracts can carry maturities as long as three to five years. As a practical matter, however, liquidity is constrained as in futures markets to the shorter-term contracts. In many cases liquidity is available only in the nearest term contract. OTC options have maturities ranging from six months to five years or more and liquidity is moderate.

Listing: Listed option contracts are standardised in maturity, face value, price movement, margin requirements trading hours and strike prices. This standardisation facilitates the trading of contracts for users. Counterparties are removed by interposing the clearing house as the party to all transactions. OTC options are specific in their terms, being variable in maturity, underlying amount, strike price and currency exposure to suit customer needs.

Commissions: Commissions on listed options are negotiated between brokers and investors. OTC options have no commissions, only net prices.

Availability: Listed options are available in most major and many minor capital markets around the world. OTC options are available on virtually all global markets covering customised indices, standard indices, single stocks and stock baskets.

Liquidity: In shorter maturities listed options are more liquid than for longer maturities. OTC options have only moderate liquidity depending on the credit of the seller, and should be entered into with an intention of holding positions until maturity.

Settlement: Listed options have standardised settlement terms often being only one or two days. OTC option settlement terms are negotiable.

Special features: Listed options have standardised and well-publicised features. OTC options have no such requirements and therefore greater variability is found.

Arbitrage

Stock index arbitrage is the taking of simultaneous offsetting positions in two related stock index financial instruments. Examples of this type of arbitrage appear in Exhibit 2.9, the simplest and purest of which involves purchase of a basket representing the stock index and the sale of stock index futures in equal asset size.

In a typical transaction a synthetic money market position can be created by combining an S&P 500 stock basket and S&P 500 futures. This combination produces an annualised return approximating:

$$\text{Arbitrage return} = \frac{(\text{futures price} - \text{index}) \times 365}{\text{index} \times \text{holding period in days}} + \text{dividend yield}$$

The actual realised return differs from this approximate formula due to several factors, including margin requirements, tracking error, dividend variations and commission costs.

Exhibit 2.9   Examples of stock index arbitrage

Long	Short
Basket of Nikkei 225 stocks	Nikkei 225 futures
CAC-40 calls	CAC-40 puts and CAC-40 futures
FT-SE 100 swap	FT-SE 100 future

Margin requirements   Purchase or sale of a stock index future requires deposit of a good faith sum to assure performance on this contract. This sum, called the initial margin, also assists in ensuring the financial integrity of the market-place for all participants. It is often the case that Treasury bills are used to satisfy this requirement. The amount of this deposit per contract is specified by the exchange on which the contract trades and is a sum which generally amounts to about 3–5 per cent of the contract face value.

A second margin requirement also must be satisfied by participants in the futures markets. This requirement arises as the futures rise and fall in value daily in line with settlement price changes realised at the end of each business day. Differences in the value of the contract must be settled daily, usually by the opening of business on the following day. To settle these differences funds must be wired into or out of a cash account associated with the customer's futures positions. Settlement of this difference, called the variation margin, also enhances the financial integrity of the futures markets by causing all parties to settle differences daily. Because this variation margin is uncertain in magnitude and direction, a cash pool must be maintained to satisfy obligations. Thus it is easy to see that an investor with $100 million to invest in this strategy cannot fully deploy all funds directly in the arbitrage. The actual rate of return realised on investment funds will be a blended rate related to the sums deployed in the initial margin, variation margin pool and the stock index arbitrage. As the object of entering the arbitrage is generally to achieve returns superior to Treasury bills, it is easy to see that the blended rate will fall short of that estimated by the return equation above.

Tracking error   Stock baskets to mimic the S&P 500 Index are often designed for purchase with a round lot constraint. This constraint requires that any issue in the index be purchased in multiples of 100 shares. For investment sums below about $25 million the round lot constraint implies that many issues will not be purchased. The basket which mimics the index then contains less than a full 500 issues. This means that the two values, of basket and index, will not precisely track each other at all times. Hence the basket is said to have a tracking error. Tracking error induces yet another uncertainty in the realised return arising from stock index arbitrage. Wherever good price statistics are readily available on stock issues this tracking error can be measured historically and its effects evaluated. Further, with portfolio construction techniques, baskets can be designed which assist in minimising or containing the tracking error. Finally, for sums above about $25 million, no large tracking errors need be assumed as stock purchases in round lots or odd lots will allow full representation in the basket of all 500 issues.

Dividend variations Historical analysis of dividend payments from stocks in the index is valuable in assessing the effect on the realised arbitrage return. As most stocks in the S&P 500 infrequently experience dividend cuts, the dividend variation is small. The arbitrage return accordingly can be expected to be stable in most business circumstances.

Commissions Commissions must be paid on futures contracts and on stock purchases and sales as the arbitrage is set up and unwound. Futures commissions will cause a reduction in the numerator of the return equation while the stock commissions will cause a decrease in both the numerator and denominator. In each case the return approximated in the above equation is reduced.

Prior to entering an arbitrage position, the investor should estimate the spread of futures over the index net of all costs and uncertainties required to achieve a targeted return. Once this spread is determined, an order is placed to execute both the futures sale and stock purchase when the market permits. Because futures spend most of their lifetime mispriced, obtaining the desired spread is primarily a matter of time and market conditions.

Conclusion

In this chapter the main focus has been on the basic building blocks of the equity derivative market, and particularly on comparisons of both listed and OTC derivatives with the underlying equity.

The main theme has been that the imaginative use of derivatives can solve many problems faced by equity investors, and that even the simplest forms of derivative have a flexibility and versatility which can be employed in a vast number of situations. However, it should particularly be noted that it is the OTC market which offers the most ingenuity in problem solving and where product development is running faster than anywhere else in finance.

3

The issuer's perspective

Timothy Lindberg[1]
Goldman Sachs

The use of equity derivatives by corporate issuers is perhaps five to ten years behind their use of fixed income derivatives. However, with increased liquidity and improved pricing efficiency, the equity derivatives market has the potential to transform the equity market for issuers in the same way as the swap market transformed the debt markets in the 1980s. The varieties and types of equity-related issues will continue to increase and the choice of such assets available to investors will continue to diversify. Markets will become more efficiently priced and corporates will have greater flexibility in managing their cost of capital.

The potential of this market is unlikely to grow to the extent of that for fixed income derivatives given the relative size of the underlying markets. However, the impact of a developing equity derivatives market is already changing the way corporates and investors view their alternatives. It is now possible for corporates is issue equity-related securities (eg, convertibles, debt with warrants) and to hedge so as to suffer little or no dilution. It is also now common for investors to gain exposure to a company's equity price (or an equity index value) by purchasing a security issued by an unrelated third party.

The issue of equity derivative securities is "driven" either by the issuer or by the investor. Whoever drives the issue will determine its structure – the market will determine the pricing and the driver will pay the transaction costs.

Comparisons with the fixed income derivatives market

Market efficiency and access
Fixed income derivatives (swaps, swaptions, etc) opened up the international debt markets to many borrowers. Investors and issuers were no longer limited to a restricted selection of issues and issuing opportunities. Issuers could tap any market where they had a comparative advantage in issuing, and "transform" the obligation with

---

[1] The material in this chapter is based upon information which the author believes to be reliable, but he does not represent that it is accurate or complete, and it should not be relied upon as such. Where opinions are expressed, they are the personal opinions of the author and do not necessarily represent those of any other person or organisation.

derivatives into the liability of their choice. Markets and credits were arbitraged and the international capital markets became more efficient.

For example, there is the famous case of the single-A rated US corporate that could borrow in the Swiss capital market at the same rate as a triple-A rated corporate. Since the swap rate from Swiss francs to US dollars is basically the same regardless of credit rating, the single-A rated corporate could issue in Swiss francs and swap its liability into US dollars for a net cost below which it could otherwise have borrowed dollars. Similarly, the Swiss capital market lost its position as the sole source of capital for a US-based corporate with a need to fund its Swiss operation. In fact, a US corporate could find it more cost advantageous to issue dollars in its domestic market and swap into Swiss francs rather than raise Swiss francs in Switzerland.

The chasms between different regional debt markets have thus been bridged with the use of fixed income derivatives. Once bridged, any corporate, government, or agency can issue in the market where its reception is best, and swap the resulting liabilities into the desired currency and terms (eg, a fixed or floating interest rate). In the past, if investors in a particular market were keen to invest in the local market, they would buy up paper and force down yields until issuers who wanted to issue debt in the currency and maturity offered by the local market found the levels attractive enough to issue and create new supply. Now, an issuer, regardless of its need for debt in the currency of a particular market, will use swaps to take advantage of lower yields wherever it finds them to issue debt and swap into its desired terms. The different markets have been arbitraged and relative value is more transparent.

Investors, on the other hand, can also arbitrage with fixed income derivatives by locating "cheap" assets in any market and swapping into their desired terms. In effect, the swap market keeps assets from trading at too high a yield, and issuers from borrowing at too low a yield.

Debt markets are now more efficient, but by no means perfectly efficient. Differing capital markets still have their own unique features of desired maturities, legal and regulatory constraints, technical and other factors. However, the playing field has never been more level.

Diversity of issue structures

A whole new generation of securities has evolved with the use of derivatives. Since a swap allows an issuer to transform fixed into floating debt or a Swiss franc issue into a US dollar liability, the security purchased by investors may bear no relation to the economic liability held by the issuer.

If the debt capital market demanded securities that allowed investors to profit from a steeper yield curve, issuers would sell "inverse floaters" that pay twice the term fixed rate of interest less six-month Libor. The issuer then could swap into Libor-based debt. "Min/max floaters", dual-currency bonds, Euro-Australian dollar bonds and a host of other structures were created to meet investor demand, all made possible because derivatives could hedge issuers into the debt terms they found acceptable.

The derivative-driven changes that have already taken place in the fixed income capital markets are similar to the changes currently taking place in the equity markets.

Equity derivative securities

The universe of potential investments presents an almost limitless variety of equity-related structured securities from which to choose. In order to simplify this broad universe, we have differentiated between types of securities that are issuer or investor driven. Every security in existence is a match between what the investor and the issuer desires. However, some securities are created due to the specific need of an investor (investor driven) or the particular preference of an issuer (issuer driven).

Until the mid-1980s the variety of equity-related structured securities was very limited. A new type of security or a change in structure was only possible if a critical mass of investor interest called for it. Otherwise corporates issued either straight debt or straight equity, with some equity derivative securities issued as a "sweetener" (or as a necessity), usually for lesser rated entities.

The advent of an efficient equity derivative market has started to have a dramatic effect on the equity capital market. Issuer driven transactions now have a firmer basis in theoretical pricing, and investor driven securities have exploded in types and varieties.

Issuer driven securities

An equity derivative financing may be more advantageous for a corporate than an issue of either straight debt or straight equity. Traditionally, most structures involve a debt financing with some potential for the investor to convert part or all of the debt into equity. The rationale for issuing such structures usually involves a desire to issue cheap debt, or to sell shares at a premium to current values.

The exact structure depends primarily on the issuer's desired probability of conversion. If the issuer wants cheap debt, it (in effect) sells a call option with a low probability of conversion. The premium from the call option is reflected in a lower coupon or accrued yield to call or maturity. An example of such a structure would include a zero coupon convertible. If the issuer's intent is to sell shares at a premium to its spot price, it will issue under a structure with a high probability of conversion. For example, a low premium conventional convertible. If the issuer wishes to raise debt cheaply and sell shares at a premium, then it can issue debt with warrants. There are also tax and capital classification considerations depending on issuer jurisdiction, but we will focus more on pure economics in this chapter.

In either case the corporate has effectively sold a call on its equity in return for a premium that is reflected in a lower coupon or yield. With hindsight, the issuer may have waited for a more opportune time to sell its options and therefore could have an opportunity cost upon issuance. Because of this, issuers usually tend to sell equity derivative securities when they feel their share price is at an attractive level.

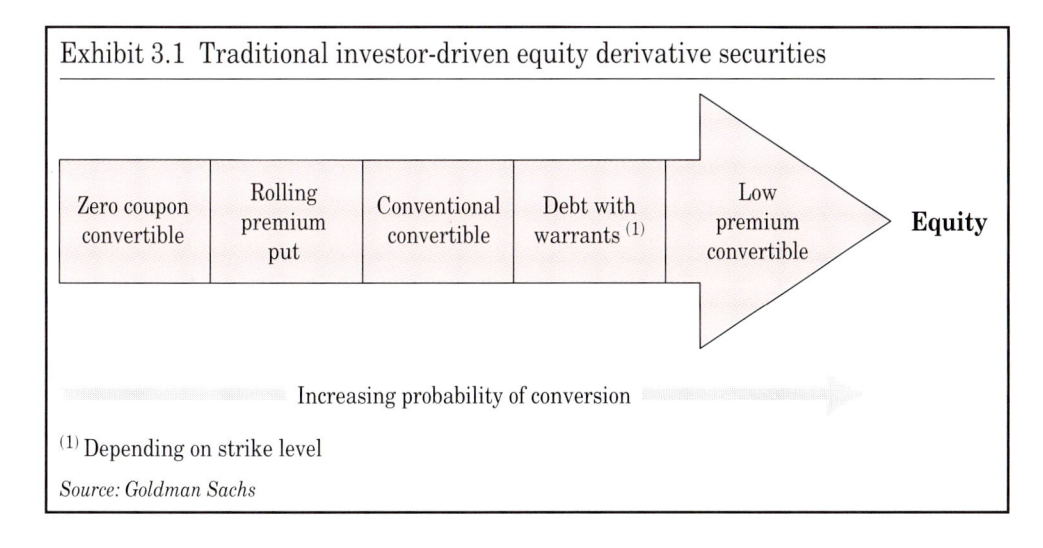

Exhibit 3.1 Traditional investor-driven equity derivative securities

| Zero coupon convertible | Rolling premium put | Conventional convertible | Debt with warrants [1] | Low premium convertible | Equity |

Increasing probability of conversion

[1] Depending on strike level

Source: Goldman Sachs

Convertibles
There are two main traditional forms of issuer driven structures – convertibles and debt with warrant issues. Convertibles are debt obligations which allow the investor to "convert" the debt into a fixed number of shares. Should the investor exercise the right of conversion, the debt is extinguished and shares are delivered. If the investor never exercises the right to convert then either:

– the bond will be redeemed for cash at par at maturity; or
– the bond may be called at a premium; or
– conversion may be forced, depending on the exact terms of the issue.

Since the debt is extinguished upon exercise, convertibles have an effective debt option in their structure. The issues usually have fixed rate coupons which give the debt part of convertibles a certain value relative to market interest rates. Should market interest rates increase, the debt value of the convertible decreases. When conversion occurs, this is equivalent to both exercising a call on the equity and exercising a put on the bond. Most investors only focus on the equity option as it is by far the more valuable of the two options. The two option nature of traditional convertibles is most relevant when valuing them, creating them synthetically or arbitraging them.

Each convertible issue is different and terms vary widely. The main difference, however, is in the probability of conversion which runs from the high conversion probability of a low premium conventional convertible to zero coupon convertibles where there is a rising effective conversion premium and a relatively higher probability of cash redemption.

Debt with equity warrants
Debt with equity warrant issues differ from convertibles in several aspects. Warrants are quite separate from the "host" bond and may be "stripped" and sold (or exercised) independently. The maturity of the host bond is thus unaffected by what happens to the warrant, which makes it possible for the issuer to swap out of the bond liabilities. If the warrants are exercised, then shares are sold at the strike price but the debt lives on until maturity. The cost of the debt portion is known, quantifiable and cash flow can be planned.

In contrast, the convertible is outstanding only as long as it is not converted and therefore the cost of the debt is not directly quantifiable and financial planning can be more difficult. On the other hand, convertibles have more flexibility with higher call premiums and the ability to force conversion. There are other differences in terms of possible maturities, tax and accounting differences and technical factors that differ by market and the jurisdiction of the issuer.

PERCs
A third, more recent type of security enables corporates to limit dilution when issuing equity. If a corporate wants to issue equity, but feels its shares are undervalued, then it can issue what are commonly referred to as preferred equity redemption certificates (or 'PERCs'). Investors receive special shares which pay dividends well above normal levels, but have a limited potential to appreciate. Upon maturity these special shares may be redeemed for the same number of ordinary shares provided the share price is below a predetermined level. However, if its share price rises above a predetermined level (say 30 per cent in three years) then these securities would be redeemed for a smaller number of ordinary shares, and the issuer suffers less dilution.

In effect the corporate issues equity and buys a call option (out-of-the-money) on its own shares from the investor. In this case the issuer drives a transaction whereby instead of selling a call option and charging for it in the form of a lower coupon (as in standard convertibles) it purchases an option and pays for it in the form of a higher dividend or coupon.

The equity derivative market's effect on issuer driven structures
Ten years ago issuers' derivative structures were priced at what the market could bear. Depending on size, market appetite, and the prospects for the issuer, the underwriters would establish a new issue level. The secondary market would establish a clearing price as a function of supply and demand, taking into account the change in the underlying share price. New issues could be conservatively priced, and secondary trading levels could move to a very high premium or drop to where there was no value attributed to the effective option. Liquidity on smaller issues could be poor given the lack of any value buyers.

The markets are now adjusting to the discipline of the equity derivatives market. First, secondary prices have found more and more support among arbitrage houses who will buy convertibles and, with the help of a developed stock loan market, short shares or sell options and create "floors" on the prices of secondary issues. This is more technically difficult, but the same in theory, as asset swaps supporting a corporate debt security's spread to government issues. In the bond market this works as follows – suppose:

– a bond trades at 150 basis points over a reference government's debt; and
– the swap spread is Libor vs. 80 basis points over the government yield; and
– asset buyers would invest at 50 basis points over Libor.

In this case the asset swap market will tighten the corporate's issue toward 130 basis points over Libor by purchasing the debt on a fixed rate basis and selling it on to other asset buyers on a spread over Libor basis. By the same method, a developed equity derivatives market is searching for secondary warrants or convertibles that are trading too low in implied volatility and will purchase such securities and effectively strip out the cheap implied call to capture a spread between implied and anticipated volatility. The swap yield level in the fixed income derivatives market equates in function to the volatility level in the equity derivatives market.

Not only has the equity derivatives market increased the efficiency of the secondary pricing of equity derivative securities, it has also more recently affected the new issue pricing of issuer driven securities. New issues are now often priced keeping in mind where a synthetic security giving the same pay-out characteristics could be constructed. Not long ago only premium and gearing were important in warrant pricing – now the implied volatility is watched closely. The pricing available in the over-the-counter equity options market now has a bearing on primary issue pricing.

Corporates may also use the equity derivatives markets effectively to guarantee conversion of convertibles at maturity by purchasing puts. (The purchase of a put converts the short call position which resulted from the čonvertible issue into a forward sale of shares – see the section on put-call parity in Chapter Seven.) Similar uses of derivatives include the execution of share repurchase programmes by selling puts, and hedging and covering positions to manage dilution and outstanding shares. Regulations vary by jurisdiction and corporates may face certain restrictions on dealing in options on their shares.

Investor driven securities

In response to specific perceived investor demands, market professionals have originated a variety of securities where they themselves act as issuer or, in rather fewer cases, procure an issuer who "fronts" the security but which will normally be swapped out of the equity derivative exposure into straightforward fixed or floating rate debt liabilities. In general, either through being the issuer or through acting as swap counterparty, it is the originating market professional which is the effective issuer of the equity derivative position held by the investor. The issuer's viewpoint in respect of investor driven securities issues is therefore that of a market professional who "synthesises" the position by dynamically hedging the position owned by the investor.

In fact the greatest impact of equity derivatives has been on the market for investor driven securities. Investors in many markets now have a more highly defined idea of how they want to invest their funds. In the past the investor could only choose from available (commodity product) assets in the market. If an underlying risk, preferred maturity or other terms were not available in the market, the investor had no option but to take the next best alternative.

In the late-1980s it became possible to purchase securities which provided a desired equity-linked payout, but where the issuer was hedged against any risk and simply ended up with fixed or floating rate debt. The early inefficiency of the equity derivatives markets only allowed a few types of structure, and early structures were often expensively priced. However, with the maturing of the market and the relative pricing efficiency that can be obtained, synthetic equity securities have multiplied in both number and type.

The types of securities driven by investors fall into three general categories:

– synthetic warrants ("covered" warrants);
– equity-index-linked notes; and
– stock-linked notes.

There are many variations, but in this chapter we will focus on the markets for these three.

Synthetic warrants

There is a significant market in Europe for geared instruments on stocks, bonds and foreign exchange rates. Many types of institution look for geared securities to minimise cash usage and obtain a leveraged investment: however, the market for these securities is more often underpinned by retail demand.

Starting in the mid-1980s, investment houses noticed that there was a lack of instruments to allow smaller investors to profit from movements in equities, bond yields and foreign exchange. In particular, investors in the Swiss market wanted more Swiss franc denominated primary securities to invest in the Japanese equity market. Investment houses therefore issued public warrants in their own names allowing investors to have a securitised call option on a particular Japanese share.

The success of the Japanese equity market, especially after the 1987 Crash, propelled the "covered" warrant market. Investment houses simply purchased US dollar denominated warrants and used them as a hedge, or "cover", for an issue (in the name of the investment house) of Swiss franc denominated warrants (often on the exact same terms). These covered warrants on Japanese stocks soon evolved into dynamically hedged warrants on other equities and indices. Issuers of these warrants simply hedged by purchasing the required delta in physical shares or futures. The hedge was rebalanced dynamically as the share price rose or fell. The market in these synthetically created warrants grew to offer investors a wide variety of securities to invest in and trade. As long as the underlying physical shares are liquid enough to set up and rebalance the hedge, it is theoretically possible to construct a synthetic warrant on any share, basket, or other underlying instrument.

Synthetic warrants are now one of the most flexible, competitive, investor driven segments of the capital markets. Although synthetic warrants have been issued in North America and Asia (mainly Hong Kong), the vast majority have been issued in the Euromarkets. It is the ultimate investor driven security in the sense that the issuer is most often the underwriting bank. If a bank feels that there would be investor interest in a geared security giving the market an ability to profit from appreciation in a particular share or market, the bank can construct, hedge, issue and sell a synthetic warrant within one day. The issues are frequently listed on an appropriate regional stock exchange but the trading takes place OTC on an information screen-based system such as Reuters.

Many banks and investment firms now issue synthetic warrants to create a broad range of products to offer their clients for secondary trading purposes. For example, Bank XYZ may issue call and put warrants on the S&P 500 Index struck at US$380, $400 and $420 for a one-year maturity. Investors would have a choice of six warrants to trade (puts and calls on three strikes). Six months later Bank XYZ may reissue one-year put and call warrants at three new strike levels. Eventually Bank XYZ creates a full compliment of securitised options for clients to trade the S&P 500 Index. In effect, Bank XYZ has created its own "exchange" where, instead of the exchange's credit risk, investors have Bank XYZ credit risk, and instead of an open outcry or computer-based, market-making system, investors look to Bank XYZ to provide liquidity. Exchange-traded options are often limited in their variety of strike prices, maturities and liquidity. The synthetic warrant market now largely complements the main exchange-traded options markets in Europe.

The synthetic warrant market now often exceeds the secondary trading volume and (depending on the issuing firm) the liquidity of direct company issued warrants. In many instances in the past, however, investors had been disappointed with overpriced issues that traded poorly. Investors in synthetic warrants have the disadvantage of relying on only one market-maker for most of the issues. Therefore, it is often most important to know who is the underlying issuer, underwriter, and market-maker on a synthetic warrant.

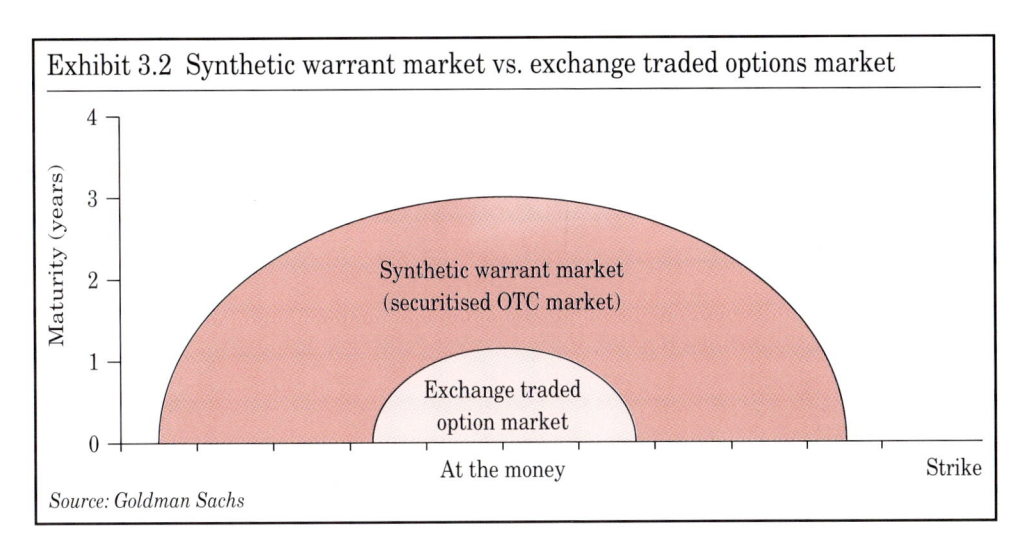

Exhibit 3.2 Synthetic warrant market vs. exchange traded options market

Source: Goldman Sachs

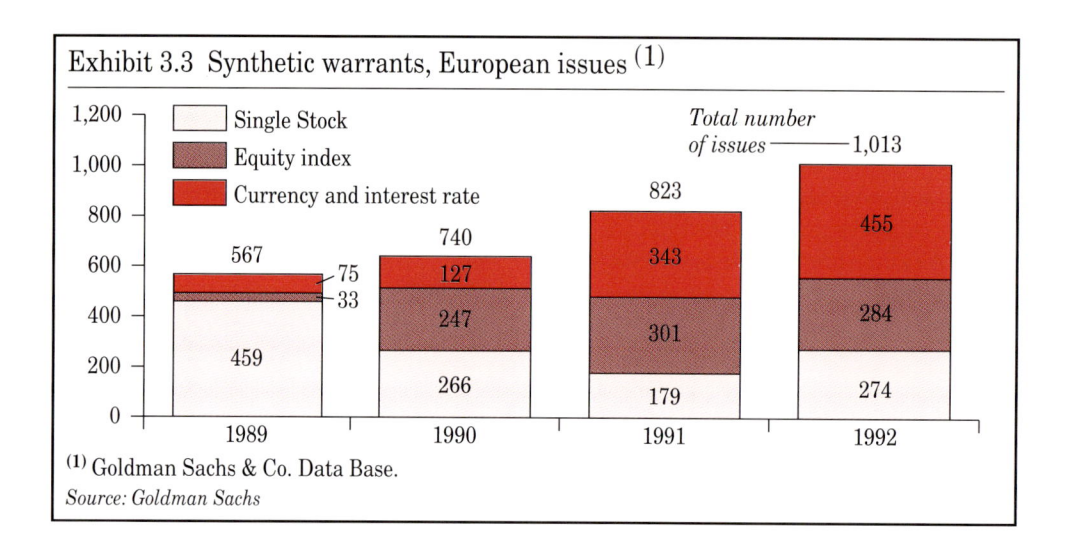

Exhibit 3.3 Synthetic warrants, European issues [1]

Year	Single Stock	Equity index	Currency and interest rate	Total number of issues
1989	459	33	75	567
1990	266	247	127	740
1991	179	301	343	823
1992	274	284	455	1,013

[1] Goldman Sachs & Co. Data Base.
Source: Goldman Sachs

The amount, diversity and trading volume of synthetic warrants outstanding in Europe now amounts to a significant market. Approximately 1,000 new warrants are issued per year. It is generally acknowledged that 100 per cent of the new warrant issues are not sold in the initial launch period. In fact, it is most likely that a low percentage of the face number of warrants are initially distributed. However, it is reasonable to assume that the amount of funds invested annually in new issue synthetic warrants well exceeds US$1.0 billion with a multiple of that amount traded in the secondary market.

The types of warrants issued vary widely from single call warrants to complex structures with caps, lookback strikes and other variations. In the late-1980s, the bulk of the market was based on single stocks (usually Japanese) with 1990 seeing an explosion in equity index warrants at the expense of single stock warrants due to the Gulf War. Now the market is reasonably equally divided between single stock, equity index, and currency or interest rate warrant issuers. However, given the flexibility and investor driven nature of the synthetic warrant market, it is reasonable to assume that the types and structures of future issues will change as rapidly as investor sentiment changes.

Equity-index-linked notes

Many institutional investors are increasing their equity allocation outside of their domestic markets. At the same time, these investors tend to prefer to index their foreign equity exposure. They do not have the time to actively follow and pick stocks in far away markets and indexing allows them to gain exposure with minimal resources and expense.

This has led to the concept of market-indexed notes on equity ("Mines") and similar constructions which:

1 Allow investors to gain equity index exposure with no tracking risk.
2 Guarantee investors a minimum redemption value of their investment.
3 Allow investors other potential flexibility such as:

  – no foreign exchange rate exposure;
  – gearing their investment to obtain greater than 100 per cent exposure; and
  – obtaining their desired investment maturity.

This market began in the late-1980s with simple notes which generally paid no interest but where principal was indexed to a particular stock index (eg, the S&P 500, Nikkei 225, FT-SE 100 etc). Structures were put together by a bank or securities firm which would arrange for a corporate, bank, governmental agency or other borrower to issue the new security desired by the investor. The issuer would then be hedged with a series of options and swaps into floating rate funding. In effect, the investor has purchased a zero coupon note and an option where the option premium plus the present value of the notes are equal to par. The incentive for the issuer is cheaper funding that would not otherwise be available. The investor obtains a security which provides for its required pay-out characteristics. However, the investor would effectively pay all the costs and expenses of the issuer and the arranging bank.

At present, the market continues in a similar way except that the costs and expenses of creating such a structured security have come down. It is now possible to construct such securities in much smaller sizes, and there is much greater flexibility available to investors in terms of more complex option pay-out characteristics. It is possible to gain exposure to many more equity indices in this way (eg, indices on Hong Kong, Spain and Mexico). Many structures contain terms which allow investors to lock-in any gains above a certain level (eg, ladder options). Possible structures are only limited by the range of the OTC options available to be embedded in the notes. Depending on jurisdiction there may be various tax, regulatory or accounting reasons to structure synthetic equity. Expenses are reduced because most issuers in this market simply issue via medium-term note (MTN) programmes that allow for a wide variety of maturities and structures at minimum issuing expenses. MTNs also allow for smaller issues (US$5–10 million equivalent) and therefore suit a wider range of investors.

Stock-linked notes
The latest development in investor driven equity derivatives are notes linked to single stock prices. This market began as a direct outgrowth of the traditional convertible bond market and from fixed income investors seeking ways to increase potential yield.

The traditional issuer driven convertible bond market has several drawbacks, including:

1 Issuer timing: Issuers tend to want to come to market when their stock price is at an attractive price to the issuer. Timing for primary deals may not be to all the investors' liking.
2 Issuer selection: There has been a general lack of convertibles on high quality, blue chip corporate names in most markets. Investors who prefer to invest using convertibles have a very limited selection of issuers to choose from.

Many investors would like to see new convertibles on shares they prefer, issued when they prefer them. This shortage of supply has left room for investment houses to create convertibles synthetically in the same way as market-indexed notes, except using options on single stocks, rather than on indices.

Since the notes are constructed to meet particular investor demand, they can take many forms. Exhibit 3.4 outlines the spectrum of notes that have been created and the equivalent option structure involved. These structures have included everything from low coupon notes with principal indexed to a share price (ie, giving investors upside equity participation with protected principal) to high coupon notes with redemption in either cash or shares of a company (ie, allowing investors to effectively write a put on the shares and take the premium income in the form of a higher coupon). The notes usually have embedded long options (ie, long volatility) or embedded short options (ie, short volatility) with varying equity content (ie, deep in-the-money to far out-of-the-money effective strike prices).

Most of the stock-linked notes created do not allow for early exercise as in a traditional convertible. Notes with early conversion are more expensive to construct and do not guarantee the underlying issuer funding with a determinate maturity. Therefore they tend to be created with short maturities (eg, two to four years) based on MTN programmes issued by other corporates, banks and government agencies.

Different markets have seen different structures for single stock synthetic notes. These differing structures reflected the different investor bases driving the issues. For example, several high quality French corporates have taken advantage of demand for notes linked to their share price to obtain lower cost straight funding. The shortage of blue chip French corporate equity-linked paper together with positive investor sentiment and certain technical constraints on issuers of standard convertibles led to several new synthetic issues in 1991. The French corporates usually issued four-year zero coupon paper with an embedded call spread on their own share price. They then hedged their redemption risk by purchasing calls on their shares from the equity derivatives market, thereby guaranteeing themselves pure debt financing. Conservative portfolio managers then had a protected vehicle to take their bullish views on high quality share prices. Fixed income portfolio managers had a vehicle which allowed them to obtain some exposure to the equity market and potentially increase their yields without risking principal. French corporates effectively raised debt from (primarily) the equity capital market through the use of equity derivatives.

On the other hand, investors searching for high yield income in Germany have purchased the "cash or share" notes on quality corporate names. In return for higher interest rates, investors purchased securities that were redeemed in either cash or shares at the option of the issuer. The ratio of shares per standard note denomination determined the effective purchase price of the shares.

Since the redemption alternative is at the issuer's option, the investor has effectively sold a put on the underlying shares at the above defined purchase price. Investors were looking for yield and believed the spot share price would most probably be above the effective purchase price at maturity. Synthetic and company-issued PERCs are basically the same type of security where investors receive a high yield,

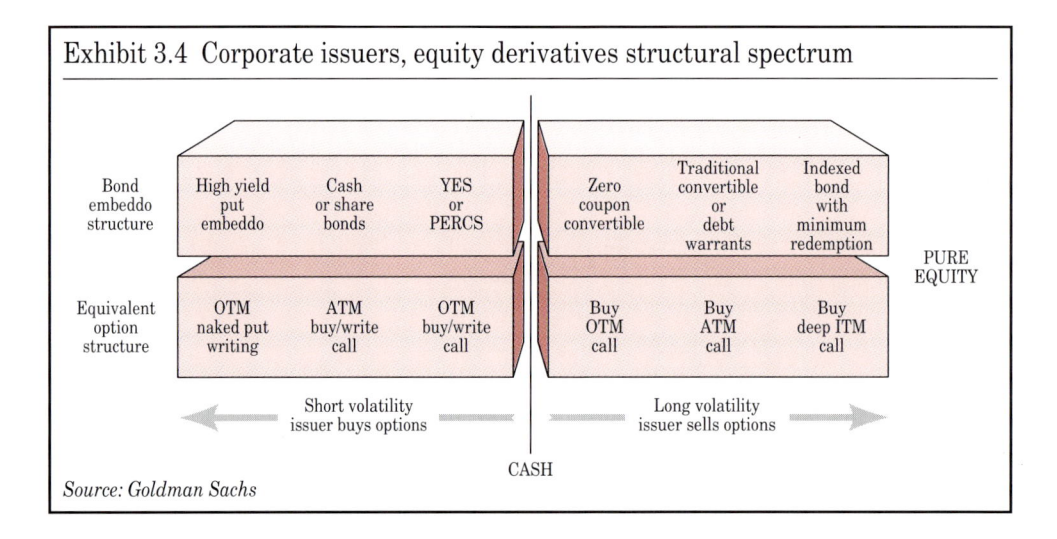

Exhibit 3.4 Corporate issuers, equity derivatives structural spectrum

Bond embeddo structure	High yield put embeddo	Cash or share bonds	YES or PERCS	Zero coupon convertible	Traditional convertible or debt warrants	Indexed bond with minimum redemption
Equivalent option structure	OTM naked put writing	ATM buy/write call	OTM buy/write call	Buy OTM call	Buy ATM call	Buy deep ITM call

← Short volatility issuer buys options | CASH | Long volatility issuer sells options →

PURE EQUITY

Source: Goldman Sachs

retain all the downside price risk and have limited upside price potential. The only difference is in equity content. The cash or share notes are equivalent to buying debt and writing an at-the-money put (or equally, buying shares and writing at-the-money calls) whereas the synthetic PERCs have a higher strike price (ie, buying shares and writing out-of-the-money calls).

Summary

An established, efficient equity derivatives market has allowed corporate issuers much greater flexibility in meeting the demands of the investment community as well as the ability to manage their equity exposure and potential dilution.

Only time will tell how this market will develop and how corporates will make further use of equity derivatives in their capital raising and exposure management. However, it seems reasonable to assume that the market, once created, will continue to deepen and more corporates and investors will discover ever more uses for equity derivatives in their capital raising and investment decisions.

4

Equity-index-linked derivatives

Salomon Brothers

Overview of the market

As the world's financial markets continue to become more integrated, asset managers have recognised the advantages of gaining exposure to foreign equity markets. A manager can no longer ignore the financial opportunities that exist abroad or the benefits that are associated with increased portfolio diversification. Since 1987, a series of new instruments, known as equity-index-linked (EIL) derivatives, has been developed in response to this demand for international equity exposure. An EIL derivative is a financial instrument (security or contract), the return on which is linked to the performance of an equity index. An investor can simulate the outright purchase of an entire equity index with one of these instruments. EIL derivatives are ideal for investors who wish to invest in a foreign equity market while avoiding the actual foreign market transactions, index managers seeking to outperform their benchmarks, investors who must protect the value of their asset portfolios, and investors who desire to alter their market exposures without selling existing assets.

The EIL derivatives market in swaps, notes, options and warrants provides an attractive alternative to direct investment for achieving equity market exposure. First, replicating an index (or multiple indices) with a limited number of direct equity share investments subjects the investor to the risk of tracking error and adverse selection. An EIL derivative tracks an index accurately and avoids these risks. Secondly, maintaining such diverse equity portfolios can be costly in terms of custodial fees, rebalancing costs and stamp taxes. These costs are avoided with EIL derivatives because the investor does not actually purchase shares. Thirdly, it can be difficult to hedge against adverse movements of some indices using exchange-traded futures and options; these instruments may be illiquid for some international indices, and certain investors may be prohibited from using them by law or internal policy. EIL derivatives offer an alternative hedge vehicle to futures and options. Finally, investment in foreign equities exposes the investor to foreign currency risk. While traditional foreign currency instruments can reduce this exposure, currency hedging of the foreign investment can be incorporated directly into EIL derivatives, thus avoiding separate currency hedging transactions.

Some of the indices on which EIL derivatives are available are set out in Exhibit

Exhibit 4.1 Some popular indices for EIL derivatives[1]

Country	Equity index	Description
Australia	All-Ords	All-Ordinaries Index. Capitalisation-weighted index of more than 250 companies, mostly industrial.
Canada	TSE-35	Toronto Stock Exchange 35 Index. Capitalisation-weighted index of 35 stocks.
France	CAC-40	Capitalisation-weighted index based on 40 of the 100 most highly capitalised companies listed on the forward segment of the Official List. Calculated by the Société des Bourses Français.
Germany	DAX	Deutsche Aktien Index. Capitalisation-weighted, total rate-of-return index of 30 blue chip stocks.
Great Britain	FTSE 100	*Financial Times* Stock Exchange 100 share index. Based on the 100 largest companies by market capitalisation.
Hong Kong	Hang Seng	Capitalisation-weighted index of 33 stocks, including 4 financial, 9 property, 6 utility, and 14 commerce and industry.
Japan	TOPIX	Tokyo Price Index. Capitalisation-weighted index of all shares listed on the first section of the Tokyo Stock Exchange.
	Nikkei 225	Price-weighted index of 225 Japanese blue chip stocks that are traded on the first section of the Tokyo Stock Exchange.
The Netherlands	EOE	European Options Exchange Dutch Stock Index. Based on prices quoted on the Amsterdam Stock Exchange for 25 leading Dutch stocks.
Spain	FIEX	Capitalisation-weighted index of the 35 most liquid companies quoted on the four Spanish stock exchanges (Barcelona, Bilbao, Madrid, and Valencia).
Sweden	OMX	Capitalisation-weighted index of 30 stocks quoted on the A1 list of the Stockholm Stock Exchange. The composition of this index changes quarterly according to trading volume.
Switzerland	SMI	Swiss Market Index. Capitalisation-weighted index currently consisting of 22 Swiss companies.
United States	S&P 500	Standard & Poor's Index of 500 widely held common stocks, including 400 industrial, 40 public utility, 40 financial, and 20 transportation issues.

[1] Options on these indices are not in all instances available to US individuals.

4.1. In addition to the individual indices listed, an investor may participate in the performance of a sub-sector of an index or in a combination of several indices.

The instruments

This section discusses in brief the structure and applications of three types of EIL derivatives: EIL swaps, EIL notes, and EIL options and warrants. In-depth descriptions of the instruments, their specifications and their cash flow calculations are included later in the chapter.

EIL swaps

An EIL swap is a contractual agreement to exchange payments with a counterparty. The investor receives a stream of payments that mimic the return of a direct investment in an equity index and makes a stream of payments based on a short-term interest rate index. Typically, both the index return payment and the floating rate payment occur monthly or quarterly. The payments are calculated based on a notional principal amount. No principal is actually exchanged; the notional sum is only used for determining the cash flows of the swap. The index return payment is typically the total rate of return of the equity index plus or minus a fixed spread, while the floating rate payment is typically Libor (London inter-bank offered rate) flat. The payment streams may be denominated either in the same currency or in different currencies, and the index return payment may be hedged into a currency other than the natural currency of the index. These swap agreements are similar to traditional interest rate and currency swaps and may have maturities as long as ten years.

An EIL swap is often used as an overlay to a portfolio of fixed income assets to create a synthetic equity investment. The asset manager invests funds in floating rate assets with yields based on the same short-term index as the floating rate swap payment. The money market index of the swap will then offset the index of the floating payment. The investor's performance relative to the equity index is the spread

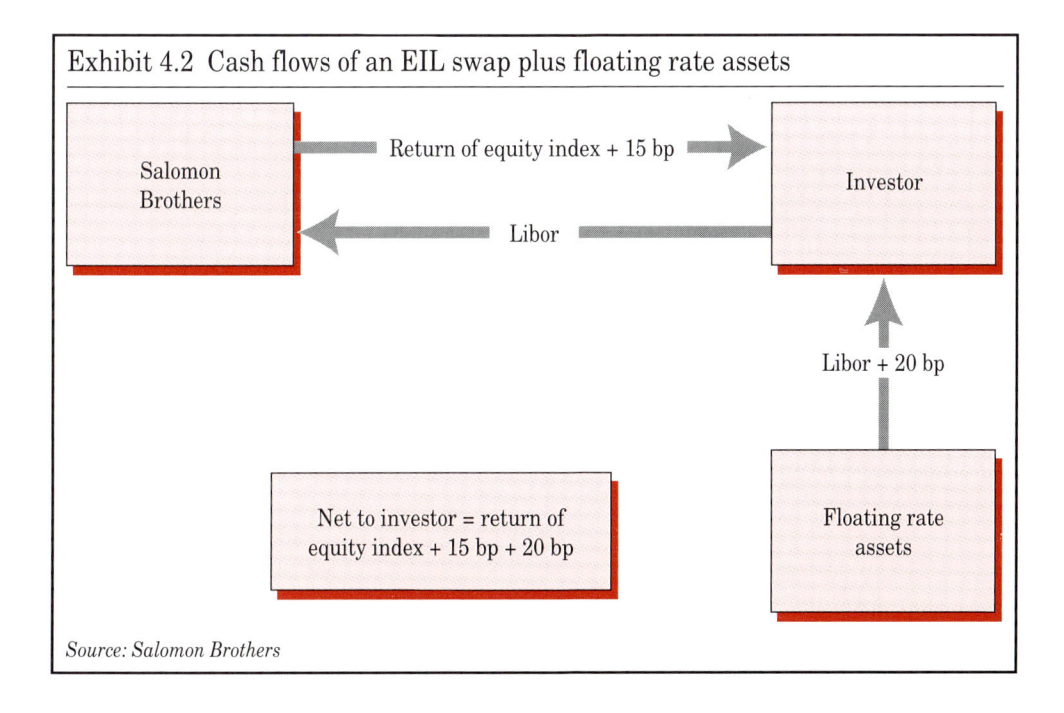

Exhibit 4.2 Cash flows of an EIL swap plus floating rate assets

Salomon Brothers → Return of equity index + 15 bp → Investor

Salomon Brothers ← Libor ← Investor

Floating rate assets → Libor + 20 bp → Investor

Net to investor = return of equity index + 15 bp + 20 bp

Source: Salomon Brothers

received over or under the index on the swap, plus any spread received over or under the floating rate index on the assets. For example, as shown in Exhibit 4.2, if the swap is priced at the equity index return plus 15 basis points versus Libor and floating rate investments earn Libor plus 20 basis points, then the synthetic equity investment earns the index return plus 35 basis points.

In a case such as that just discussed, in which the swap spread and floating rate asset spread are both positive, an EIL swap plus a portfolio of floating rate assets may routinely outperform the target equity index. An active manager may invest part of his portfolio in this synthetic equity investment while keeping the remaining assets in an actively managed equity portfolio. By using EIL swaps as the core position and managing around it with direct investments, the overall return of an equity fund may be enhanced.

EIL notes
An EIL note is a fixed income security issued by a corporation, bank or sovereign, and consequently requires a cash investment of principal. The principal repayment of the note at maturity is linked to the performance of an equity index. The formula for principal repayment can reflect a long or short position in an equity index and can also provide an exposure to the equity market which is similar to an option or combination of options. The options can be puts or calls on the index and can be long or short positions. There is tremendous flexibility in designing an EIL note to reflect the market views and desired equity exposures of an investor.

The note usually carries fixed periodic coupon payments, although zero coupon structures can be created. The level of the coupon payment can be above or below the normal coupon on the issuer's debt and will depend on the nature of the equity exposure incorporated into the principal repayment as well as the currency, maturity and quality of the issuer of the bond.

EIL options and warrants
Options and warrants are vehicles that create one-sided (asymmetric) exposure to the equity markets. Call options provide profits when the equity market index rises above the strike level of the option. It is similar to a long position in the equity market in that profits are realised when the market advances; however, call options avoid losses when the market declines. Conversely, put options produce profits when the equity index falls below the strike level. It is similar to a short position in the market in that profits are produced when the market index declines in value; however, put options avoid losses when the market increases in value. In order to obtain such one-sided exposures that eliminate losses, the investor pays a premium up-front to purchase the option. The maturities of EIL options usually range from one week to five years.

EIL options and warrants are often used as hedging vehicles. An investor, for example, can protect an existing indexed equity portfolio against a decline in the market by purchasing a put option on the index or sub-index that is being replicated. The option will set a minimum value of the portfolio equal to the strike of the option (less the option premium plus perhaps dividends). At times, an asset manager may find that the cost of purchasing a put option to hedge the value of the portfolio may be less than the transaction and execution costs associated with liquidating investments as the market falls and then repurchasing an entire equity portfolio after the market has moved. By purchasing the option, an asset manager will not miss an opportunity if the market rises unexpectedly. Alternatively, options can be used to protect previously realised gains.

With options, synthetic equity investments with downside protection can be created. Instead of investing in a foreign equity market and purchasing put options on the foreign equity index to protect against a falling market, the investor can purchase call options on that market and invest the remaining cash (which would have otherwise been used to purchase actual foreign market shares) in fixed income assets. (A similar structure can be achieved with an EIL note.)

By buying or selling calls or puts on an equity index with individually tailored strikes and expiration dates, an investor can easily and quickly implement his views on the market.

Advantages of EIL derivatives

Ease of investing in foreign markets   The use of EIL derivatives simplifies many operational aspects of investing in foreign markets. For example, the investor can avoid the delivery and receipt of foreign currency amounts and the attendant spot currency transactions that are required for investments in foreign shares. The investor can save time and effort, because EIL derivatives avoid any rebalancing of portfolios, which may be required with the purchase of shares; tracking error is eliminated as well. The derivative can be structured to include reinvestment of dividend income in the index, thus eliminating income reinvestment decisions for the investor.

Improved returns   Participation in the performance of an equity index through the use of EIL securities can produce higher net returns, compared with those of a direct equity investment. An investor will incur costs when replicating an index with a portfolio of equities. These costs vary from stamp taxes to costs associated with having to rebalance the portfolio to remain matched with the characteristics of the underlying index. Exhibit 4.3 summarises the costs associated with direct equity ownership.

Exhibit 4.3   Estimated percentage costs associated with direct equity ownership[1]

Equity index	Round-trip costs[2]		Annual costs	
	Stamp taxes and commissions	Dealer spread[3]	Portfolio rebalancing[4]	Custody[5]
All-Ords	1.60	1.60	0.32	0.15
CAC-40	0.90	1.40	0.23	0.15
DAX	0.50	1.40	0.19	0.15
FTSE-100	0.90	1.20	0.21	0.15
TOPIX	0.80	0.90	0.17	0.15
EOE	0.75	1.50	0.23	0.15
SMI	0.80	1.50	0.23	0.15
S&P 500	0.25	0.70	0.10	0.05

[1] These are estimated costs to a US investor. Actual costs may vary significantly.
[2] Round-trip costs are transaction costs that occur when the shares of the equity portfolio are purchased and later sold.
[3] Assumes that investor pays one-half of the market spread on entry plus one-half on exit.
[4] Rebalancing costs assuming 10% portfolio turnover because of round-trip costs.
[5] Estimate of annual safekeeping, dividend collection, reporting, and other miscellaneous expenses.

Transfer of asset management expertise   EIL swaps allow a manager to transfer his expertise in managing one class of assets to another market. For example, a money manager with a relative advantage in managing short-term, fixed income investments can improve his chance of outperforming an equity index by creating a synthetic equity investment via an EIL swap funded with a portfolio of floating rate assets. Similarly, a manager with expertise in managing a portfolio of domestic equities can transfer this skill to other equity or fixed income markets by using a swap in which the investor pays the return on a domestic equity index and receives the return from a second market, as an overlay to a portfolio of domestic equities.

Investment vehicle for asset allocators   Many investors in today's markets attempt to achieve the highest possible return through the selection of which particular markets to invest in and not through individual equity share selection. The investment strategy of these investors is not focused primarily on outperforming a particular index through the "correct" choice of companies in which to invest; rather, they select shares in order to hold a portfolio that replicates the return of an index. For these asset allocators, EIL derivatives that allow the purchase of an entire index with a single transaction are an ideal investment vehicle.

Return pattern flexibility   EIL derivatives offer the investor the ability to customise his exposure to an equity market. Virtually any return pattern can be achieved – long or short, symmetric or asymmetric, and more complex patterns. Option positions, with or without an underlying portfolio of equities, are the most traditional way to customise exposures. However, the same performance characteristics can be obtained in a single EIL note transaction. Passive and risk-averse managers are likely to select return patterns that reflect the purchase of options and the elimination of downside risk. More active managers may expand the use of options beyond providing protection against a down market, instead taking positions that profit from market moves in accordance with their views. For example, by selling call options when an investor feels that the market will not rise in value, an investor will attempt to create excess returns by taking in the option premium.

Currency-hedged returns   The return from an investment in a foreign equity market is a function of changes in both the equity market and in the exchange rate between the domestic currency of the investor and the currency in which the investment is denominated. An unfavourable move in this exchange rate may reduce or eliminate any gain on the underlying investment resulting from a favourable move in the equity market, or compound a loss if the market has fallen. An asset manager may want exposure to changes in a foreign equity market without incurring any currency risk. EIL derivatives provide the investor with the flexibility to choose whether or not the return from the exposure to a foreign equity index includes the sensitivity to exchange rates. To obtain exposure to a foreign equity market through direct equity ownership without incurring any currency risk, an investor must use traditional foreign exchange instruments to hedge the domestic value of the equity portfolio. When using foreign exchange instruments, the amount of foreign currency to be hedged must be determined at the time of purchasing the hedge. Because it is unlikely that the investor will be able to predict accurately the foreign currency value of the equity portfolio at hedge maturity, the investor will have hedged a foreign currency amount that does not match the index portfolio. The currency hedge of an EIL derivative, however, can be constructed to be a quantity-adjusting hedge that matches the index value at maturity. When using these instruments, the investor will not have to worry about rebalancing a hedge position as the foreign currency value of the equity portfolio changes.

Market exposure with limited capital   EIL options and warrants allow a manager to gain exposure to an equity market in return for the cash investment of the option premium. By purchasing a call option, an investor has created a leveraged position in an equity index with limited downside. For the cost of the option premium, the investor will obtain upside exposure to an equity market to the extent of the full underlying amount. This presents a way to gain exposure to markets with a very small commitment of capital and resources.

Issues in the selection of an EIL derivative
An investor can participate with relative ease in the performance of an equity market via the use of one of the EIL derivatives, which offer investors much flexibility and several alternatives for obtaining equivalent exposures. When selecting the vehicle with which to obtain this exposure – be it a swap, note or option – and the structure of the derivative, an individual investor should consider the following issues.

What are the investor's objectives?   When selecting an EIL product, an investor must consider which alternative will best fulfil the fund's objectives. All three types of derivatives discussed in this chapter can be used to create synthetic investments in equity markets. Investors whose goal is to outperform an equity index may find desirable the use of a swap in conjunction with a portfolio of assets that the investor has a relative advantage in managing. Options are most suitable for investors who wish to hedge an existing equity exposure, because they require small cash investment. Active investment managers who want to short the market or otherwise implement market views will find both EIL notes and options the most flexible vehicles.

Do investment constraints exist?   Some asset managers are prohibited from selling or purchasing options; however, entering into a swap or purchasing an EIL note may be permissible. Other investors may be unable to enter into swaps.

Which equity index is desired?   The investor will have to choose the equity market or markets – and the corresponding equity indices – in which to invest. The return of a sub-set of an index is also possible.

What form of equity exposure is desired?   EIL derivatives allow customised return patterns to be created. The choice of the direction, limits and size of market exposure will depend on the objectives of the investor, his market views, and the ability and desire to undertake or eliminate risk. The derivative can even be customised to provide the better of the returns from two indices.

Does the investor wish exposure to exchange rates?   Some investors may desire the currency exposure of foreign market indices, while others – whose benchmark may be a currency-hedged one – may prefer an EIL investment that hedges foreign currency risk.

Is the investor an active or passive asset manager?   EIL swaps and notes are usually one or more years in maturity and lend themselves to passive equity market exposure. However, short-term options allow a manager to more quickly alter the fund's equity market exposure in accordance with the investor's short-term view.

Which classes of assets does the investor have expertise in managing?   If the investor has expertise in managing a particular type of asset, an EIL swap allows the investor to utilise this advantage by transferring those skills to another market.

What credit risks are acceptable?   The credit risk associated with each alternative is unique to the product type. An asset manager must decide what type and level of risk is acceptable when making a selection.

Summary

EIL derivatives provide a simple and cost-efficient means to participate in the performance of an equity index. EIL swaps, notes and options can be structured to customise market exposures for an investor and, thus, are flexible alternatives to direct equity ownership for any investor. An asset manager may use these instruments to invest in a new market, adjust the size and direction of equity market exposures in accordance with market views, hedge an existing portfolio, or enhance the overall return of an equity fund.

EIL swaps

Description and terms

An EIL swap is a contract between two counterparties, such as Salomon Brothers and an investor, to exchange two streams of payments. Over the life of the swap, Salomon Brothers agrees to pay the investor the rate of return of an equity index, while the investor agrees to pay Salomon a floating rate based on a short-term interest rate index (see Exhibit 4.4). These payments are based on a notional principal amount; no principal is actually exchanged. It is only assumed for calculating the payment amounts. The currency in which these cash flows are denominated must be specified and need not be the same currency for both sides of the swap. The payments will be exchanged according to the reset frequency and terminate on the swap maturity date. The terms of a generic EIL swap are set out in Exhibit 4.5.

Index return payment

Salomon Brothers will pay the investor the return of an equity index plus or minus a spread (or fixed number of basis points). Typically, the return has been the index plus a spread, but the spread will depend on market conditions and the particular structure of the transaction. Some of the equity indices on which this return payment could be based are listed in Exhibit 4.1. The investor receives the total return of the index,

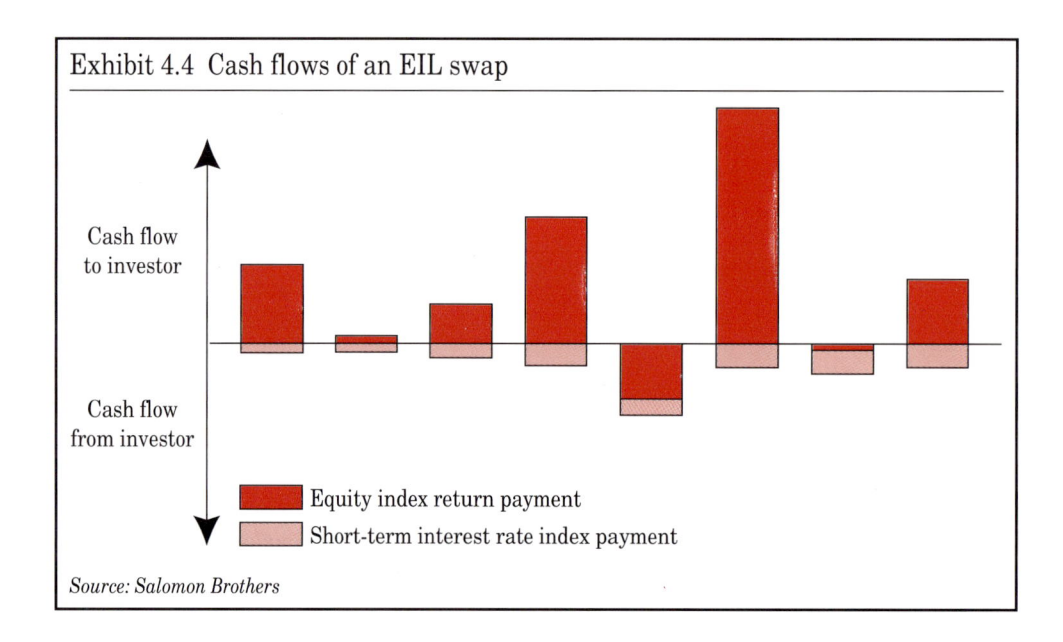

Exhibit 4.4 Cash flows of an EIL swap

Source: Salomon Brothers

Exhibit 4.5 Terms of a generic EIL swap

Term	Definition
Maturity	One to ten years
Settlement date	Day on which floating interest starts to accrue
Reset frequency	Periodicity with which indices are reset, which is typically the term of the floating rate index
Payment frequency	Periodicity of the exchange of payments, depending on the reset frequency: one-, three-, or six-month intervals starting from settlement date
Payment date	Date on which payments are exchanged; two business days following reset
Index return payment	
Equity index	Equity index on which return payments are based
Spread	Number of basis points to be added to or subtracted from the return payment
Currency	Currency in which payments are denominated
Currency hedge	Foreign exchange rate risk is hedged or unhedged
Floating rate payment	
Floating index	Money market index on which floating payments are based
Day count	Market convention (for example, Actual/360 for US dollar Libor)
Currency	Currency in which payments are denominated

which is defined as the percentage change in the index plus dividends. If the return over the period is negative, then the investor will make the return payment to Salomon Brothers in addition to the floating rate payment.

In a typical swap, the index return is calculated in the currency of the selected index. If the swap is denominated in a currency other than that of the index, then the return associated with the change in exchange rates between the index and swap currencies will be factored into the return payment calculation. The investor may hedge this foreign currency exposure by requesting a currency-hedging return payment. In so doing, the payment to the investor will be based on the movements in the index alone. The spread (over or under the index) will depend on whether the contract provides for a hedged or unhedged payment.

Floating rate payment
The investor may select one of several available money market indices on which the floating rate payment is based, although it is typical to use Libor of the currency in which the swap is denominated. For example, the floating rate payment of a Japanese yen-denominated swap would be based on yen Libor. This rate is set at the beginning of a payment period for the cash flow that occurs at the end of the period. The day count used in calculating the payment depends on the market convention for quoting the short-term index.

Notional principal amount

An EIL swap typically has a variable notional principal amount. In the variable case, the notional principal amount – which is used to calculate both the index return and floating rate payments – increases or decreases by the return payment made or received by Salomon Brothers. A swap with variable notional principal simulates the cash flows of a direct equity investment.

A swap may also have a fixed notional principal, in which case the principal amount is set on the swap settlement date and remains unchanged throughout the life of a swap. A fixed notional swap simulates selling part of the equity investment whenever the market rises and purchasing more of the equity investment whenever the market falls. This keeps the amount invested in the index constant and is similar to a dollar cost-averaging strategy.

Credit considerations

When entering into an EIL swap with a counterparty, the investor is exposed to the counterparty's credit between payments. An EIL swap is simply a swap of the return payments on two investments (for example, the Libor interest payment and the index return). Because the swap does not involve an exchange of principal, an investor is not exposed to the counterparty's credit for his principal equity investment. Because the swap is marked to market according to the payment frequency, the size of the exposure is limited to the movement of the equity index (in excess of the Libor payment) over a single payment period, which is typically one month or a quarter. If the investor funds the swap with a portfolio of floating rate assets, then the investor is exposed to the credit risk of the issuer of those assets. Clearly, this risk can be reduced by diversifying among several floating rate issuers.

To demonstrate the mechanics of EIL swap transactions, we outline the cash flows of four distinct EIL swap structures. For the purposes of comparison, all of these swaps are linked to the German DAX Index, reset quarterly and have a two-year maturity. The first example can be considered the base case. The cash flows of this swap are denominated in Deutschmarks, the domestic currency of the DAX Index. The

Exhibit 4.6   Historic index levels

Pricing date	Three-month US$ Libor[1]	Three-month DM Libor[1]	DAX Index	DM/US$ exchange rate
29/07/88	8.313%	5.125%	1,181.70	1.8785
31/10/88	8.500%	4.813%	1,300.70	1.7870
31/01/89	9.250%	6.000%	1,312.70	1.8795
28/04/89	9.875%	6.375%	1,370.90	1.8802
31/07/89	8.438%	6.813%	1,554.10	1.8647
31/10/89	8.563%	8.188%	1,472.70	1.8380
31/01/90	8.250%	8.125%	1,822.70	1.6820
30/04/90	8.563%	8.250%	1,813.20	1.6705
31/07/90	NA	NA	1,919.12	1.5895

[1] US dollar and Deutschmark Libor rates are quoted on a certificate of deposit (CD) basis. Rate for 360 actual days.

notional principal amount is variable, and the floating rate is Deutschmark Libor. The second example is similar to the first with the exception that the two sides of the swap have different currency exposures. The DAX equity return is in Deutschmarks; however, the floating rate payments are in US dollars and based on US dollar Libor. As before, the notional principal amount is variable. In the third example, all cash flows are denominated in US dollars, and the DAX equity return is hedged to US dollars. The fourth, and final, example is similar to the first, but the notional principal amount is fixed.

Assuming an initial pricing date of 29 July 1988, the swaps will settle on 2 August 1988, two business days after pricing. A two-day lag also occurs between the swap reset dates and the days on which the cash flows actually change hands. Each of these examples is calculated from the historical levels set out in Exhibit 4.6.

Example 1: Cash flows denominated in Deutschmarks; variable notional principal

Situation
A German investor with a portfolio of Deutschmark floating rate assets desires to shift some of his investments to the German equity market. The investor simply wants exposure to the equity market, rather than a selection of individual stocks. In addition, he does not want to sell his floating rate assets, because some are illiquid; if the investor wants to reverse his market exposure, selling and then repurchasing the floating rate assets could be costly. For these reasons, an EIL swap is an attractive way to change the allocation of the investor's assets

The swap
On 29 July 1988, a Deutschmark investor enters into a two-year EIL swap with Salomon Brothers for settlement on 2 August. Salomon agrees to pay this investor the price return of the DAX Index plus 25 basis points per annum, while the investor pays Deutschmark Libor on a variable notional principal amount, which is set initially at DM100,000,000. All cash flows are denominated in Deutschmarks, the domestic currency of the DAX Index. At the initiation of the swap, three-month Deutschmark Libor is equal to 5.125 per cent, and the DAX Index is at 1,181.70. The first set of payments is exchanged on 2 November, 1988, three months from the swap settlement date. The floating rate payment by the investor is calculated according to the following formula:

$$\text{Payment} = \text{floating rate} \times \text{principal amount} \times \frac{\text{days in period}}{360}$$

The actual number of days over the 2 August–2 November period is equal to 92. Substituting this value – as well as the notional principal and Deutschmark Libor rate, which were set on the initial pricing date – into the above formula, results in a floating payment by the investor of the following:

$$5.125\% \times \frac{92}{360} \times \text{DM}100{,}000{,}000 = \text{DM}1{,}309{,}722$$

The return payment by Salomon is equal to the percentage change in the DAX Index plus the 25 basis point spread. The new level of the DAX Index, which is used for calculating the return payment, is the level of the index on 31 October 1988, two days prior to the first payment date. The first component of this payment is calculated as follows:

$$\text{Payment} = \text{principal amount} \times \left(\frac{\text{index}_2 - \text{index}_1}{\text{index}_1}\right)$$

where index_1 is equal to the index level at the beginning of the period, and index_2 is equal to the index level at the end. The DAX Index on this reset date is 1,300.70, resulting in a cash flow of:

$$\text{DM}100{,}000{,}000 \times \left(\frac{1{,}300.70 - 1{,}181.70}{1{,}181.70}\right) = \text{DM}10{,}070{,}238$$

The spread payment is calculated using the same methodology as the floating payment, only substituting the basis point spread for the floating rate:

$$\text{DM}100{,}000{,}000 \times 0.25\% \times \frac{92}{360} = \text{DM}63{,}889$$

The net payment to the investor is, therefore, equal to the index return, plus the spread, minus the floating payment:

$$\text{DM}10{,}070{,}238 + \text{DM}63{,}889 - \text{DM}1{,}309{,}722 = \text{DM}8{,}824{,}404$$

The indices for the next period's swap flows are also reset on 31 October 1988. For the second payment period ending on 31 January 1989, the DAX Index is set to 1,300.70, three-month Deutschmark Libor is set to 4.813 per cent, and the principal amount is adjusted by the index return. The new notional principal amount is now equal to the original principal of DM100,000,000 plus the return of DM10,070,238, or DM110,070,238. This notional principal amount is to be used when calculating the next set of swap payments. On 31 January 1989, the DAX Index is 1,312.70, and the actual number of days over the 2 November–2 February period is 92. Substituting these values into the appropriate equations produces the following flows:

$$\text{Floating payment} = \text{DM}110{,}070{,}238 \times 4.813\% \times \frac{92}{360} = \text{DM}1{,}353{,}852$$

$$\text{Index return} = \text{DM}110{,}070{,}238 \times \left(\frac{1{,}312.70 - 1{,}300.70}{1{,}300.70}\right) = \text{DM}1{,}015{,}486$$

$$\text{Spread} = \text{DM}110{,}070{,}238 \times 0.25\% \times \frac{92}{360} = \text{DM}70{,}323$$

for a net payment by the investor of DM268,043.

After the swap flows are determined, the indices are once again reset to new levels. The DAX Index is set to 1,312.70, three-month Deutschmark Libor is set to 6.000 per cent, and the notional principal amount is set to DM111,085,724 for calculating the next swap payments on 28 April 1989. The remaining flows for this EIL swap are presented in Exhibit 4.7.

How does a variable notional principal swap simulate a direct equity investment? Examine the index return payments in Exhibit 4.7. If the Deutschmark investor had invested DM100,000,000 on 29 July 1988, in the DAX Index, then at the

Exhibit 4.7 Two-year DAX Index-linked swap vs. Deutschmark Libor – variable notional principal

Cash flow date	Notional principal (DM)	Floating payment (DM)	Return payment		Net payment to investor (DM)
			Index (DM)	Spread (DM)	
02/11/88	100,000,000	(1,309,722)	10,070,238	63,889	8,824,404
02/02/89	110,070,238	(1,353,852)	1,015,486	70,323	(268,043)
02/05/89	111,085,724	(1,647,772)	4,925,108	68,657	3,345,993
02/08/89	116,010,832	(1,890,010)	15,503,089	74,118	13,687,197
02/11/89	131,513,921	(2,289,789)	(6,888,381)	84,023	(9,094,147)
02/02/90	124,625,539	(2,607,776)	29,618,346	79,622	27,090,193
02/05/90	154,243,886	(3,098,267)	(803,927)	95,331	(3,806,862)
02/08/90	153,439,959	(3,235,026)	8,963,358	98,031	5,826,363

end of two years this investment would have grown to the following:

$$DM100,000,000 \times \frac{1,919.12}{1,181.70} = DM162,403,317$$

Subtracting the original investment from this amount results in a net return of DM62,403,317. This amount is equal to the sum of the index component of the return payments in Exhibit 4.7.

Consider the interpretation of an EIL swap funded with floating rate assets as a direct investment in the equity index. With a variable notional principal amount, the investor purchases DM100,000,000 of the equity index and does not withdraw or add to the investment over the term of the swap. In addition, all dividends are reinvested in the index. The following illustrates the equivalence of the cash flows:

1. *At the beginning of the swap.* The investor purchases DM100,000,000 of assets paying interest of Deutschmark Libor minus 25 basis points, and the swap calls for no cash flows. Equivalently, the investor purchases DM100,000,000 of shares in the DAX Index.

2. *On the first payment date.* The investor's floating rate payment on the swap minus the 25 basis point swap spread exactly offsets the interest earned on the floating rate assets. There is a positive cash flow of the index return on DM100,000,000 (namely, DM10,070,238). The investor uses this payment to purchase an additional DM10,070,238 of floating rate assets; therefore, there is no net cash flow to the investor. The notional principal increases to DM110,070,238 for the next period. Equivalently, with the direct purchase of the index, the investor has no cash flows but now has an investment worth an additional DM10,070,238.

3. *On subsequent payment dates.* The comparison is similar. The interest received on the floating rate assets exactly offsets the floating rate payment minus the swap spread. If the index return payment is positive, then additional floating rate assets are purchased (and, if negative, sold) so that the value of the floating rate investments equals the market value of the index. Neither the synthetic nor the direct investment have any net cash flow.

4. *Last payment date.* As on other payment dates, the interest received on the floating rate assets exactly offsets the floating rate payment and swap spread. The

floating rate assets mature (or are sold) for DM153,439,959, and the last index return payment (DM8,963,358) is received for a total value of DM162,403,317. Equivalently, the investor sells his equity investment, which now has a market value of DM162,403,317.

Example 2: Deutschmark equity; US dollar Libor; variable notional principal

Situation
A US dollar investor would like to be exposed to the DAX Index as well as the Deutschmark currency. While the swap of Example 1 would provide this exposure, the US dollar investor has expertise in managing US dollar floating rate assets and prefers such an investment to a Deutschmark floating rate note. Therefore, the investor enters into a two-year EIL swap with Salomon Brothers in which the investor receives the Deutschmark return of the DAX Index plus 20 basis points per annum and pays US dollar Libor on a variable notional principal amount. The index return payment is denominated in Deutschmarks, and the floating rate and spread payments are denominated in US dollars.

The swap
This EIL swap is equivalent conceptually to the swap of Example 1 plus a Deutschmark Libor to US dollar Libor cross-currency swap. In the cross-currency swap, the investor receives Deutschmark Libor minus 25 basis points and pays US dollar Libor minus 20 basis points. The Deutschmark Libor received in the currency swap cancels with the Deutschmark Libor payments of the EIL swap, netting to a DAX Index versus US dollar Libor swap. This additional swap accounts for the reduction in the EIL swap spread of five basis points over the EIL swap spread in Example 1.

The cross-currency aspect of this swap makes the cash flows somewhat more complicated and is similar to the differences between currency and interest rate swaps. First, consider the Deutschmark-to-Deutschmark EIL swap of Example 1. On each payment date, the investor paid the floating rate interest (adjusted by the spread), and the swap was then marked to market. The market value of the swap was the Deutschmark notional amount of the DAX Index "investment" at the beginning of the period plus the return over the period minus the Deutschmark notional amount of the floating rate side. Because the two Deutschmark notional amounts were the same, the market value of the swap was simply the index return, and this marked-to-market payment was made to the investor. After the mark, the notional amounts for both sides of the swap were reset to be equal at the new level of the index.

In the cross-currency EIL swap of this example, the process of identifying the cash flows is similar. On each payment date, the investor paid the US dollar floating rate interest (adjusted by the spread), and the swap was marked to market. Again, the market value equals the Deutschmark notional amount of the DAX Index "investment" at the beginning of the period plus the return over the period minus the US dollar notional amount of the floating rate side. However, here, because of changes in exchange rates, the two notional amounts – which were equal at the exchange rates at the beginning of the period – are not likely to be equal at the end of the period. Therefore, the market value of the swap is the index return (in Deutschmarks) plus the change in the US dollar value of the Deutschmark principal over the period, and this marked-to-market payment is made to the investor. After the mark, the notional amount for the Deutschmark side of the swap is reset according to the new level of the index, and the US dollar notional amount is reset to equal the new Deutschmark amount at the new exchange rate.

At the initiation of the swap, three-month US dollar Libor is equal to 8.313 per cent, the DAX Index is at 1,181.70 and the DM/US$ exchange rate is equal to 1.8785 DM/US$. The notional principal amount is set initially at DM100,000,000 for calculating the index return payment, and the US dollar notional amount (for computing the spread and floating rate payments) is determined by converting this initial Deutschmark principal to US dollar at the DM/US$ exchange rate, or US$53,233,963. On each subsequent reset date, the Deutschmark notional principal amount will increase or decrease by the return of the DAX Index as seen in Example 1. The US dollar principal, however, is reset to equal the Deutschmark notional principal amount converted to US dollars at the prevailing DM/US$ exchange rate. The US dollar principal amount fluctuates with changes in the equity index, as well as with changes in the DM/US$ exchange rate.

On 31 October 1988, the first set of swap payments is determined. Three of the cash flows can be calculated according to the equations provided in Example 1 by substituting the appropriate Deutschmark and US dollar values into the expressions:

$$\text{Index return} = \text{DM}100{,}000{,}000 \times \left(\frac{1{,}300.70 - 1{,}181.70}{1{,}181.70}\right) = \text{DM}10{,}070{,}238$$

$$\text{Floating payment} = \text{US\$}53{,}233{,}963 \times 8.313\% \times \frac{92}{360} = 1{,}130{,}920$$

$$\text{Spread} = \text{US\$}53{,}233{,}963 \times 0.20\% \times \frac{92}{360} = \text{US\$}27{,}208$$

During the period, the Deutschmark has strengthened against the US dollar from an exchange rate of 1.8785 DM/US$ at the beginning to 1.7870 DM/US$ at the end. The investor was long Deutschmarks and short US dollars in amounts of equal value at the beginning of the period. Now, the investor's long Deutschmark position is worth more than the investor's short US dollar position. When the swap is marked to market at the end of the period, this exchange rate gain is passed on to the investor by the following payment.

Change in US dollar value of Deutschmark equity investment equals:

$$\frac{\text{DM}100{,}000{,}000}{1.7870 \text{ DM/US\$}} - \frac{\text{DM}100{,}000{,}000}{1.8785 \text{ DM/US\$}} = \text{US\$}2{,}725{,}746$$

On this reset date, the indices for the next period's swap flows are set to new levels. The DAX Index is set to 1,300.70, and three-month US dollar Libor is set to 8.500 per cent. The US dollar and Deutschmark principal amounts are adjusted. The Deutschmark notional principal amount is now equal to the original principal of DM100,000,000 plus the index return of DM10,070,238, or DM110,070,238. The US dollar notional principal amount is equal to the new Deutschmark principal amount of DM110,070,238 converted to US dollars at 1.7870 DM/US$, or US$61,594,985. These notional principal amounts are to be used when calculating the next set of swap payments on 31 January 1989. With a DAX Index equal to 1,312.70 and the DM/US$

exchange rate at 1.8795 DM/US$, the following cash flows are exchanged at that time:

$$\text{Index return} = \text{DM}110{,}070{,}238 \times \left(\frac{1{,}312.70 - 1{,}300.70}{1{,}300.70}\right) = \text{DM}1{,}015{,}486$$

$$\text{Floating payment} = \text{US}\$61{,}594{,}985 \times 8.500\% \times \frac{92}{360} = \text{US}\$1{,}337{,}980$$

$$\text{Spread} = \text{US}\$61{,}594{,}985 \times 0.20\% \times \frac{92}{360} = \text{US}\$31{,}482$$

Change in the US dollar value of the Deutschmark equity investment equals:

$$\frac{\text{DM}110{,}070{,}238}{1.8795 \text{ DM/US}\$} - \frac{\text{DM}110{,}070{,}238}{1.7870 \text{ DM/US}\$} = \text{US}\$(3{,}031{,}411)$$

The indices are once again reset to new levels. The DAX Index is set to 1,312.70, three-month US Libor is set to 9.250 per cent, the Deutschmark notional principal amount is set to DM111,085,724, and the US dollar notional principal amount is set to US$59,103,870 for calculating the next swap payments on 28 April 1989. The remaining flows for this index-linked swap are contained in Exhibit 4.8.

How does a variable notional principal swap simulate a direct equity investment? Consider the interpretation of a DAX Index-linked swap funded with US dollar floating rate assets as a direct investment in the equity index. As in Example 1, dividends are reinvested in the equity index; otherwise, no change in the investment occurs for the term of the swap.

1. *At the beginning of the swap.* The investor purchases US$53,233,963 of assets paying interest at US dollar Libor minus 20 basis points, and the swap calls for no cash flows. Equivalently, the investor purchases DM100,000,000 (US$53,233,963) of shares in the DAX Index.
2. *On the first payment date.* The investor's floating rate payment on the swap minus the 20 basis point swap spread exactly offsets the interest earned on the floating rate assets. There is a positive cash flow of the index return on

Exhibit 4.8 Two-year DAX Index-linked swap vs. US dollar Libor – variable notional principal

Cash flow Date	Deutschmark		US dollar			
	Principal outstanding (DM)	Index return payment (DM)	Principal outstanding ($)	Floating payment ($)	Spread payment ($)	Principal adjustment[1] ($)
02/11/88	100,000,000	10,070,238	53,233,963	(1,130,920)	27,208	2,725,746
02/02/89	110,070,238	1,015,486	61,594,985	(1,337,980)	31,482	(3,031,411)
02/05/89	111,085,724	4,925,108	59,103,870	(1,351,591)	29,224	(22,004)
02/08/89	116,010,832	15,503,089	61,701,325	(1,557,102)	31,536	512,882
02/11/89	131,513,921	(6,888,381)	70,528,193	(1,520,854)	36,048	1,024,539
02/02/90	124,625,539	29,618,346	67,804,973	(1,483,791)	34,656	6,288,689
02/05/90	154,243,886	(803,927)	91,702,667	(1,870,352)	45,342	631,296
02/08/90	153,439,959	8,963,358	91,852,714	(2,010,033)	46,947	4,680,761

[1] Change in US dollar value of Deutschmark equity investment.

DM100,000,000 (namely, DM10,070,238 or US$5,635,276) plus a positive cash flow of US$2,725,746, which represents the change in the US dollar value of the Deutschmark investment. The investor uses these payments to purchase an additional US$8,361,022 of floating rate assets; therefore, there is no net cash flow to the investor. The notional principal increases to DM110,070,238 (equal to US$61,594,985) for the next period. Equivalently, with the direct purchase of the index, the investor has no cash flows but now has an investment worth an additional DM10,070,238.

3 *On subsequent payment dates.* The comparison is similar. The interest received on the US dollar floating rate assets exactly offsets the US dollar floating rate payment and US dollar swap spread. If the DAX Index return payment plus the change in US dollar value of the Deutschmark investment is positive, then additional US dollar floating rate assets are purchased (and, if negative, sold), so that the value of the US dollar floating rate investments equals the Deutschmark market value of the index at the payment date. Neither the synthetic nor the direct investment have any net cash flow.

4 *Last payment date.* As on other payment dates, the interest received on the US dollar floating rate assets exactly offsets the US dollar floating rate payment and US dollar swap spread. The US dollar floating rate assets mature (or are sold) for US$91,852,714 (equal to DM145,999,890), and the last index return payment (DM8,963,358) plus a payment of US$4,680,761 (equal to DM7,440,070) – representing the change in US dollar value of the Deutschmark investment – is received for a total value of DM162,403,317. Equivalently, the investor sells his equity investment, which now has a market value of DM162,403,317.

Example 3: Deutschmark equity; currency hedged to US dollars; variable notional principal

Situation
The US dollar investor in Example 2 would like to participate in the performance of the DAX Index without being exposed to the volatility of the DM/US$ exchange rate. This investor, therefore, enters into a two-year DAX Index-linked swap that is currency hedged to US dollars. Salomon Brothers agrees to pay the investor the Deutschmark return of the DAX Index plus 120 basis points per annum, hedged to US dollars, while the investor pays US dollar Libor. The swap has a variable notional principal amount initially set at US$100,000,000. At the initiation of the swap, three-month US dollar Libor is equal to 8.313 per cent, and the DAX Index is at 1181.70.

The swap
The 100 basis point difference in spread between this currency-hedged swap and the unhedged swap in Example 2 reflects the difference between forward and spot exchange rates. The forward exchange rate is the rate that can be fixed for exchanging a set amount of one currency for another on a future date and is a function of the spot exchange rate on the settlement date and the interest rate differential between the two currencies in the respective debt markets. Because interest rates for maturities less than or equal to two years were lower in Germany than in the United States in August 1988, a Deutschmark would have been exchanged for more US dollars when converted at the forward exchange rate than at the spot exchange rate.

However, when entering into a currency-hedged swap, Salomon Brothers agrees to pay the future returns of the DAX Index converted to US dollars at the spot exchange rate prevailing at the beginning of the swap, rather than at an appropriate forward rate. Because these forward contracts are quantity adjusting and off-market, an adjustment must be made to the swap spread to compensate the investor. Because, in this example, conversion at the spot rate is worth less in dollar terms than conversion at the forward rate, the spread on the EIL swap is increased (here, by 100 basis points). If Deutschmark interest rates were higher than US dollar rates, then this spread would have been decreased.

On 31 October 1988, the first set of swap payments is determined. Because the impact of changes in exchange rates can be ignored, the cash flows of this swap are calculated according to the formulae provided in Example 1:

$$\text{Floating payment} = \text{US\$}100{,}000{,}000 \times 8.313\% \times \frac{92}{360} = \text{US\$}2{,}124{,}433$$

$$\text{Index return} = \text{US\$}100{,}000{,}000 \times \left(\frac{1{,}300.70 - 1{,}181.70}{1{,}181.70}\right) = \text{US\$}10{,}070{,}238$$

$$\text{Spread} = \text{US\$}100{,}000{,}000 \times 1.20\% \times \frac{92}{360} = \text{US\$}306{,}667$$

The net payment to the investor is equal to the index return plus the spread minus the floating payment:

$$\text{US\$}10{,}070{,}238 + \text{US\$}306{,}667 - \text{US\$}2{,}124{,}433 = \text{US\$}8{,}252{,}471$$

Once the payments are determined, the indices for the next set of swap flows are specified. The DAX Index is set to 1,300.70, three-month US dollar Libor is set to 8.500 per cent, and the notional principal amount is set to US$110,070,238, to be used in calculating the swap payments on 31 January 1989. The remaining payments for this index-linked swap are set out in Exhibit 4.9.

How does a currency-hedged swap simulate a currency-hedged direct equity investment? Consider the interpretation of a currency-hedged DAX Index-linked swap funded with US dollar floating rate assets as a combination of a direct investment in

Exhibit 4.9 Two-year currency-hedged DAX Index-linked swap vs. US dollar Libor – variable notional principal

Cash flow date	Notional principal ($)	Floating payment ($)	Return payment Index ($)	Return payment Spread ($)	Net payment to investor ($)
02/11/88	100,000,000	(2,124,433)	10,070,238	306,667	8,252,471
02/02/89	110,070,238	(2,390,970)	1,015,486	337,549	(1,037,935)
02/05/89	111,085,724	(2,540,315)	4,925,108	329,554	2,714,348
02/08/89	116,010,832	(2,927,662)	15,503,089	355,767	12,931,193
02/11/89	131,513,921	(2,835,937)	(6,888,381)	403,309	(9,321,009)
02/02/90	124,625,539	(2,727,208)	29,618,346	382,185	27,273,323
02/05/90	154,243,886	(3,145,933)	(803,927)	457,590	(3,492,269)
02/08/90	153,439,959	(3,357,761)	8,963,358	470,549	6,076,146

the equity index and a currency hedging contract that guarantees that the investor will be able to convert Deutschmarks to US dollars in two years at the initial exchange rate. Again, dividends are reinvested; otherwise, there is no change in the investment over the term of the swap.

1. *At the beginning of the swap.* The investor purchases US$100,000,000 of assets paying interest at US dollar Libor minus 120 basis points, and the swap calls for no cash flows. Equivalently, the investor purchases DM187,850,000 (equal to US$100,000,000) of shares in the DAX Index.

2. *On the first payment date.* The investor's floating rate payment on the swap minus the 120 basis point swap spread exactly offsets the interest earned on the floating rate assets. There is a positive cash flow of the index return on US$100,000,000. The investor uses this payment to purchase an additional US$10,070,238 of floating rate assets; therefore, there is no net cash flow to the investor. The notional principal increases to US$110,070,238 for the next period. Equivalently, with the direct purchase of the index, the investor has no cash flows but now has an investment worth DM206,766,942, which, if converted at the initial exchange rate, equals US$110,070,238.

3. *On subsequent payment dates.* The comparison is similar. The interest received on the US dollar floating rate assets exactly offsets the US dollar floating rate payment and US dollar swap spread. If the index return payment is positive, then additional US dollar floating rate assets are purchased (and, if negative, sold), so that the value of the US dollar floating rate investments equals the market value of the index converted to US dollars at the initial exchange rate. Neither the synthetic nor the direct investment have any net cash flow.

4. *Last payment date.* As on other payment dates, the interest received on the US dollar floating rate assets exactly offsets the US dollar floating rate payment and US dollar swap spread. The US dollar floating rate assets mature (or are sold) for US$153,439,959, and the last index return payment (US$8,963,358) is received for a total value of US$162,403,317. Equivalently, the investor sells his equity investment, which now has a market value of DM305,074,632, and the forward currency contract allows the investor to convert the Deutschmarks to US dollars at the initial exchange rate for a value of US$162,403,317.

Example 4: Cash flows denominated in Deutschmarks; fixed notional principal

Situation
This example is similar to the first example. A German investor desires to change part of his floating rate Deutschmark assets to Deutschmark equity exposure without selling the underlying assets. However, the swap in Example 1, which has a variable notional principal, may require him to buy additional floating rate Deutschmark assets over the term of the swap. At the current time, the investor thinks that it may be difficult to find good quality, cheap Deutschmark floating rate assets if he needs to. Therefore, the investor desires a swap that will keep the notional amount fixed at DM100,000,000 throughout the life of the swap. This swap simulates a constant asset allocation strategy.

The swap

A Deutschmark investor enters into the same two-year DAX Index-linked swap as in Example 1, except that the notional principal amount is fixed rather than variable. Salomon Brothers agrees to pay the return of the DAX Index plus 25 basis points per annum in return for Deutschmark Libor on a fixed notional principal amount of DM100,000,000. As in Example 1, all cash flows are denominated in Deutschmarks. The first set of swap payments, which are determined on 31 October 1988, are calculated as in Example 1:

$$\begin{aligned} \text{Floating payment} &= \text{DM}(1{,}309{,}722) \\ \text{Index return} &= 10{,}070{,}238 \\ \text{Spread} &= \underline{63{,}889} \\ \text{Net payment to investor} &= \text{DM}8{,}824{,}404 \end{aligned}$$

On this reset date though, the DAX Index is set to 1,300.70 and three-month Deutschmark Libor is set to 4.813 per cent. The notional principal amount remains at DM100,000,000 and is to be used when calculating the next set of swap payments. On 31 January 1989, the DAX Index is 1,312.70, and the actual number of days over the 2 November–2 February period is 92. Substituting these values into the appropriate equations produces the following flows:

$$\text{Floating payment} = \text{DM}100{,}000{,}000 \times 4.813\% \times \frac{92}{360} = \text{DM}1{,}229{,}989$$

$$\text{Index return} = \text{DM}100{,}000{,}000 \times \left(\frac{1{,}312.70 - 1{,}300.70}{1{,}300.70}\right) = \text{DM}922{,}580$$

$$\text{Spread} = \text{DM}100{,}000{,}000 \times 0.25\% \times \frac{92}{360} = \text{DM}63{,}889$$

for a net payment to the investor of DM(243,520).

After the swap flows are determined, the indices are once again reset to new levels. However, the notional principal amount is never reset and always remains at DM100,000,000. The remaining flows for the index-linked swap are set out in Exhibit 4.10.

Exhibit 4.10 Two-year currency-hedged DAX Index-linked swap vs. US dollar Libor – variable notional principal

Cash flow date	Notional principal (DM)	Floating payment (DM)	Return payment Index (DM)	Return payment Spread (DM)	Net payment to investor (DM)
02/11/88	100,000,000	(1,309,722)	10,070,238	63,889	8,824,404
02/02/89	100,000,000	(1,229,989)	922,580	63,889	(243,520)
02/05/89	100,000,000	(1,483,333)	4,433,610	61,806	3,012,082
02/08/89	100,000,000	(1,629,167)	13,363,484	63,889	11,798,206
02/11/89	100,000,000	(1,741,100)	(5,237,758)	63,889	(6,914,969)
02/02/90	100,000,000	(2,092,489)	23,765,872	63,889	21,737,272
02/05/90	100,000,000	(2,008,681)	(521,205)	61,806	(2,468,080)
02/08/90	100,000,000	(2,108,333)	5,841,606	63,889	3,797,162

How does an EIL swap with fixed notional principal simulate a direct equity purchase? Consider the interpretation of an EIL swap funded with floating rate assets as a direct investment in the equity index. With fixed notional principal, the comparison is with an asset allocation strategy in which the equity market exposure is kept constant – in this case, at DM100,000,000.

1. *At the beginning of the swap.* The investor purchases DM100,000,000 of assets paying interest at Deutschmark Libor minus 25 basis points, and the swap calls for no cash flows. Equivalently, the investor purchases DM100,000,000 of shares in the DAX Index.
2. *On the first payment date.* The investor's floating rate payment on the swap minus the 25 basis point swap spread exactly offsets the interest earned on the floating rate assets. There is a positive cash flow of the index return on DM100,000,000 (namely, DM10,070,238). Equivalently, with the direct purchase of the index, the investor has no cash flows, but now has an investment worth an additional DM10,070,238. Because the investor wants to keep his investment in the DAX Index at DM100,000,000, part of the equity is sold, providing the investor with DM10,070,238 in cash.
3. *On subsequent payment dates.* The comparison is similar. The interest received on the floating rate assets exactly offsets the floating rate payment minus the swap spread. The investor receives cash from the index return payment, if positive, and makes a payment, if negative. Equivalently, if the index return is positive, then the investor sells part of his equity position (and, if negative, purchases additional equity), so that the value of the equity investment remains at DM100,000,000. Both the synthetic and the direct investment have the same net cash flow.
4. *Last payment date:* As on other payment dates, the interest received on the floating rate assets exactly offsets the floating rate payment and swap spread. The floating rate assets mature (or are sold) for DM100,000,000, and the last index-return payment (DM5,841,606) is received for a total value of DM105,841,606. Equivalently, the investor sells his equity investment, which now has a market value of DM105,841,606.

EIL notes

Description and terms

An EIL note is a fixed income security issued by a corporation, bank or sovereign on which principal redemption at maturity is linked to the performance of an equity index. Unlike a swap, which is simply an exchange of cash flows, this debt instrument is a loan from the investor to the issuer. Typically, these are new issues; therefore, they are priced at par. In return for lending to the issuer, the investor will receive a fixed coupon over the life of the note and a principal payment at maturity, representing repayment of the loan. The principal payment will vary according to the performance of a specified equity index and a pre-determined repayment formula. The terms of EIL notes are set out in Exhibit 4.11.

Principal
The principal repayment at maturity is linked to the performance of an equity index and can be structured to meet the needs of a particular investor. For example, the asset manager may choose between an unprotected or protected principal payment.

An unprotected EIL note is similar to a direct investment in equities; the investor participates in all market moves – both favourable and unfavourable – and, therefore, may risk losing some of the initial investment. In a protected EIL note, the investor participates in favourable market moves only and is guaranteed full repayment of the initial investment; this structure is similar to a direct investment in equities with long put option overlays. (As discussed at the start of this chapter, EIL notes can have more complex equity return patterns.) The principal repayment at maturity reflects the performance of a specified amount invested in the index. This underlying investment amount is specified as a fixed percentage (the participation rate) of the principal amount of the note.

The investor may choose whether the equity index is a price or total rate-of-return index. In addition, this return may be currency hedged to eliminate any foreign exchange rate risk if the currency in which the note is denominated is different from the domestic currency of the equity index.

In a typical EIL note, the principal repayment formula reflects a one-sided exposure to the market. The investor participates in market upside moves above a floor level. The principal payment at maturity is equal to the original principal amount plus the following "index payment" if the index level at maturity is greater than the floor index level specified:

$$\text{Index payment} = \text{principal amount} \times \text{participation rate} \times \frac{(\text{index}_m - \text{index}_o)}{\text{index}_o}$$

Index_m is equal to the index level at maturity, and index_o is equal to the floor index level, which is specified at issue. An investor may set index_o equal to the market level at issue or another desired level. In a protected EIL note, the equation above does not apply if the index level at maturity is less than the floor level, in which case the principal amount at maturity is equal to the original principal.

Conversely, an EIL note may be structured to achieve a return pattern such that the investor benefits if the equity index falls over the life of the note. In this case, the

Exhibit 4.11 Terms of an EIL note

Term	Definition
Issuer	Corporation, bank or sovereign
Quality rating	Credit quality of note issuer
Maturity	One to ten years
Principal amount	Minimum amount US$10 million
Coupon	Fixed coupon rate to be paid periodically
Coupon frequency	Periodicity of coupon payments
Equity index	Equity index to which principal of note is linked
Currency	Currency in which payments are denominated
Currency hedge	Foreign exchange rate risk is hedged or unhedged
Protection type	Principal is protected or unprotected
Return type	Total return or price return
Participation rate	Percentage exposure to equity market

principal payment at maturity is equal to the original principal amount plus the following payment, if the index level at maturity is less than the index level specified:

$$\text{Index payment} = \text{principal amount} \times \text{participation rate} \times \left(\frac{\text{index}_o - \text{index}_m}{\text{index}_o}\right)$$

Index_m is equal to the index level at maturity, and index_o is equal to the index level specified at issue. The principal payment at maturity is equal to the original principal if the index level is above that specified at issue.

Issuer

Because an EIL note is a debt security, the asset manager must decide the credit quality of the issuer and the industry sector in which to invest. For example, a manager may select an industrial corporation that is rated double-A or better by any rating agency or a single-A financial institution.

Coupon

The coupon of an EIL note can be below or above the market yield of a similar borrowing by the same issuer with a normal fixed principal repayment. Whether the coupon is above or below market levels depends primarily on the structure of the equity exposure. One attractive structure to some investors is to set the fixed coupon of an EIL note to mirror the dividend yield of the equity market to which it is indexed.

Pricing issues

The structure of the note, as well as market factors, enters into the pricing of an EIL note. These include the following: interest rates, the credit of an issuer, equity market volatility, maturity, and exchange rates. These factors combine to determine the coupon levels and participation rates that can be achieved at any time in the market. Generally, the investor specifies either the coupon level or participation rate, and the other will be determined accordingly.

For example, when the coupon in a protected EIL is below market, the difference between the market yield and the lower coupon offsets the cost to the issuer of linking the principal repayment to a protected equity index. A lower coupon rate, therefore, results in a higher participation in the performance of the index; zero coupon notes have the highest possible participation rate.

In a protected EIL note, the participation rate will vary not only according to the coupon level but also to the floor level selected. The lower the floor level is, the higher the coupon will be. The lower the index volatility and the longer the maturity, the higher is the participation rate. The participation rate also depends on the issuer of the security and its corresponding credit quality. In general, for a given coupon, a lower credit-quality issuer will result in a higher participation in the index. This is to compensate the investor for taking a greater credit risk.

In a note linked to a foreign equity index, the investor may wish to protect gains in the performance of the index from unfavourable movements of the currency. Compared with the similar note that is not currency hedged, the coupon on the hedged note will increase (decrease) if the foreign currency is at a premium (discount) to the domestic currency.

Credit considerations

The investor is exposed only to the credit of the issuer of the note. The credit exposure is identical to that of any fixed-income obligation of the same issuer.

An example of an EIL note

Situation

A US dollar investor would like long-term exposure to the Japanese TOPIX Index without any risk of losing the original investment or incurring losses from the depreciation of the yen versus the US dollar.

The note

The investor may purchase a five-year protected TOPIX Index-linked note. The issuer of this security is an industrial corporation that is rated double-A. The note pays a coupon of 0.75 per cent semi-annually, which is more than 10 basis points above the current dividend yield of the TOPIX Index. Because the coupon simulates the payment of dividends over the horizon, the investor elects to receive the price return of the index hedged to US dollars at maturity. The principal amount is equal to US$100,000,000 and is protected against any adverse movements in the index. The index level is set at 1,659.46, the TOPIX Index on issue date. Given current market conditions and an issue price of par, the resulting participation rate is equal to 102 per cent, with a minimum of par received at maturity. Every six months, the investor will receive a coupon equal to the following:

$$\frac{US\$100,000,000 \times 0.75\%}{2} = US\$375,000$$

The principal repayment at maturity will depend on the movement of the TOPIX Index over the five-year period. If, at the maturity of the note, the index is less than or equal to the level specified at issue (1,659.46) then the investor will receive US$100,000,000. The investor is guaranteed a minimum return of 0.75 per cent semi-annually. However, if the index has achieved a positive return and is at a level that

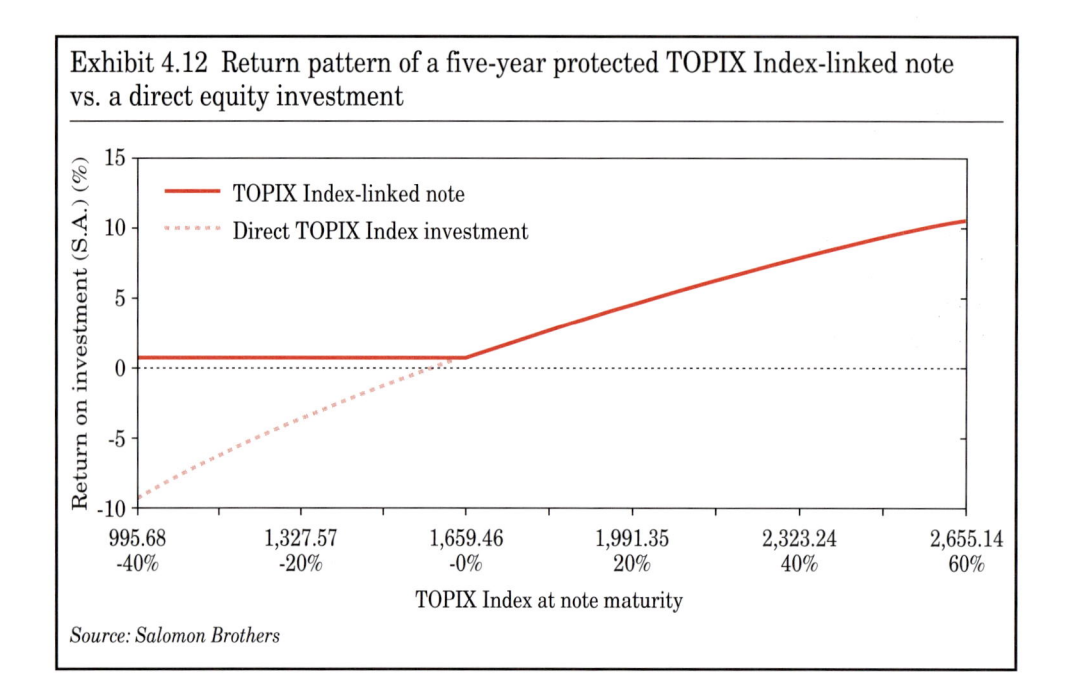

Exhibit 4.12 Return pattern of a five-year protected TOPIX Index-linked note vs. a direct equity investment

Source: Salomon Brothers

exceeds 1,659.46, then the principal payment will equal the original principal plus the following:

$$102\% \times US\$100{,}000{,}000 \times \left(\frac{\text{index}_m - 1{,}659.46}{1{,}659.46}\right)$$

where index_m is equal to the index level at maturity.

For example, if the TOPIX Index has realised a 50 per cent increase – reaching a level of 2,489.19 at note maturity – then the investor will receive US$100,000,000 plus the following:

$$102\% \times US\$100{,}000{,}000 \times \left(\frac{2{,}489.19 - 1{,}659.46}{1{,}659.46}\right) = US\$51{,}000{,}000$$

for a total payment of US$151,000,000. The net return to the investor over the five years is equal to 9.04 per cent semi-annually. Exhibit 4.12 plots the return of this TOPIX Index-linked note against a direct investment in the TOPIX Index, given the change in the underlying equity index. It is assumed that the direct equity investment is purchased when the TOPIX Index is at 1,659.46, is held for five years, realises a dividend yield of 0.64 per cent annually, and is then liquidated. All portfolio maintenance costs are ignored.

If the index payment were not currency hedged, then the formula for the index payment given above would be adjusted for the change in the ¥/US$ exchange rate. More specifically, the index payment would be multiplied by

$$\frac{\text{Curr}_o}{\text{Curr}_m}$$

where Curr_m is the ¥/US$ exchange rate at maturity, and Curr_o is the ¥/US$ exchange rate at issuance.

Over-the-counter EIL options and warrants

Description and terms

An EIL option is the right, but not the obligation, to sell or purchase an equity index at a specified index level (or option strike) for a specified period of time. A call option is the right to buy the index, and a put option is the right to sell the index. The amount that can be bought or sold is the underlying investment amount. The purchase price of the option is the option premium and is typically quoted as a percentage of the underlying investment.

Generally, an EIL option is cash settled on exercise. The option purchaser will receive from the option seller not the basket of equities that comprise the index, but a cash payment equal to the intrinsic value of the option. The intrinsic value of a call option is equal to the increase in the index above the strike (expressed as a percentage of the strike) or zero, whichever is greater, times the underlying investment amount. For a put option, the intrinsic value is equal to the decline in the index below the strike (expressed as a percentage of the strike) or zero, whichever is greater, times the underlying investment amount. Exhibit 4.13 displays this asymmetric pay-off pattern of options, where the option buyer participates only in favourable moves while limiting any downside exposure. These figures do not include the option premium.

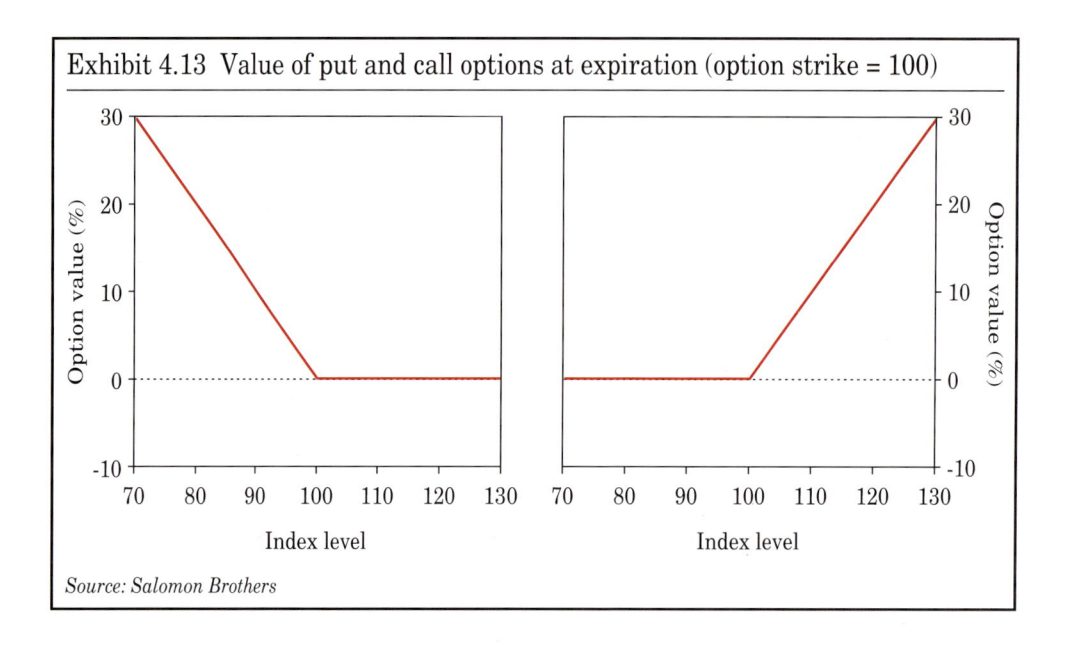

Exhibit 4.13 Value of put and call options at expiration (option strike = 100)

Source: Salomon Brothers

In EIL options, the value of the underlying index is generally taken to be the price return on the index, although options can be written on the total return of the index as well. The payment at option exercise, if the intrinsic value of the option is greater than zero, is calculated according to the following equations. For a call option:

$$\text{Payment} = \text{underlying amount} \times \left(\frac{\text{index}_x - \text{index}_s}{\text{index}_s}\right)$$

and for a put option:

$$\text{Payment} = \text{underlying amount} \times \left(\frac{\text{index}_s - \text{index}_x}{\text{index}_s}\right)$$

where index_x is equal to the index level at option exercise and index_s is equal to the option strike.

Exhibit 4.14 gives the terms of generic EIL options. Typically, the underlying

Exhibit 4.14 Terms of generic EIL options and warrants

Term	Definition
Option type	Put or call option; American or European
Maturity	One week to five years
Equity index	Equity index that can be bought or sold (typically does not include dividend income)
Option premium	Purchase price of option as percentage of underlying amount
Underlying amount	Amount of equity index that can be bought or sold
Option strike	Level of index where option may be exercised
Currency	The natural currency of the index

investment amount of an EIL option is denominated in the domestic currency of the index, and the strike level is specified as a level of the index. However, other types of options are possible. Two such are discussed below.

Currency-hedged EIL options

In a generic option, an investor whose domestic currency differs from that of the equity index is exposed to exchange rates at option exercise. He will receive the return in the currency of the index and must convert it to his currency at the then current spot rate. The value of the payment to the investor will increase or decrease with changes in exchange rates. The option buyer may select to hedge this exchange rate risk by purchasing an option that is perfectly currency hedged. In this case, the return of the option will depend solely on the performance of the equity index, and the underlying amount is denominated in the hedge currency. In effect, the foreign equity return received at expiration is converted to the domestic currency at the spot exchange rate when the option was purchased. Because forward exchange rates are not typically equal to spot exchange rates, the cost of the hedge embedded in this type of option (related to the difference between the forward and spot exchange rates) will adjust the price of the option.

Compound EIL options

A compound option provides a different type of cross-currency protection. Such an option is similar to the typical EIL option with one difference. In the typical option, the strike level is a level of the index. In the compound option, the strike price is a fixed amount of another currency. For example, a compound call option on the DAX Index will provide a pay-off at expiration if the then current value of the DAX Index (on an underlying Deutschmark investment amount) is greater than some fixed US dollar amount (the US dollar strike). The purchase of such an option combined with a US dollar fixed income investment is equivalent to an unhedged investment in the DAX Index, which is protected so that the US dollar value of the investment does not fall below a minimum level (the strike). Again, the premium for such an option, compared with the premium for a generic option, will be adjusted by an amount that is related to the forward/spot exchange rate differential.

Credit considerations

The option purchaser is exposed to the credit of the option writer. However, the option writer has no exposure to the option purchaser. This is because after the initial premium is paid, the cash flow, if any, is only from the writer to the purchaser. The size of the exposure to the purchaser is only the value or pay-off of the option. For example, if the option is struck at the level of the index at purchase, the size of the exposure is only the change in value of the index and not the full amount of the index. In this way, options are similar to swaps and different from notes. However, if the market moves in the option purchaser's favour, the credit risk of a long-term option can be significantly greater than that of a swap. Payments on a typical swap are marked to market quarterly, while a typical option has no mark to market, and exposure continues until option maturity.

If the option or warrant is combined with a short-term fixed income investment, then the investor is exposed to the credit of the option writer (exposure is approximately equal to the change in value of the index), as well as the credit of the issuer of the short-term security (exposure is approximately equal to the value of the underlying investment).

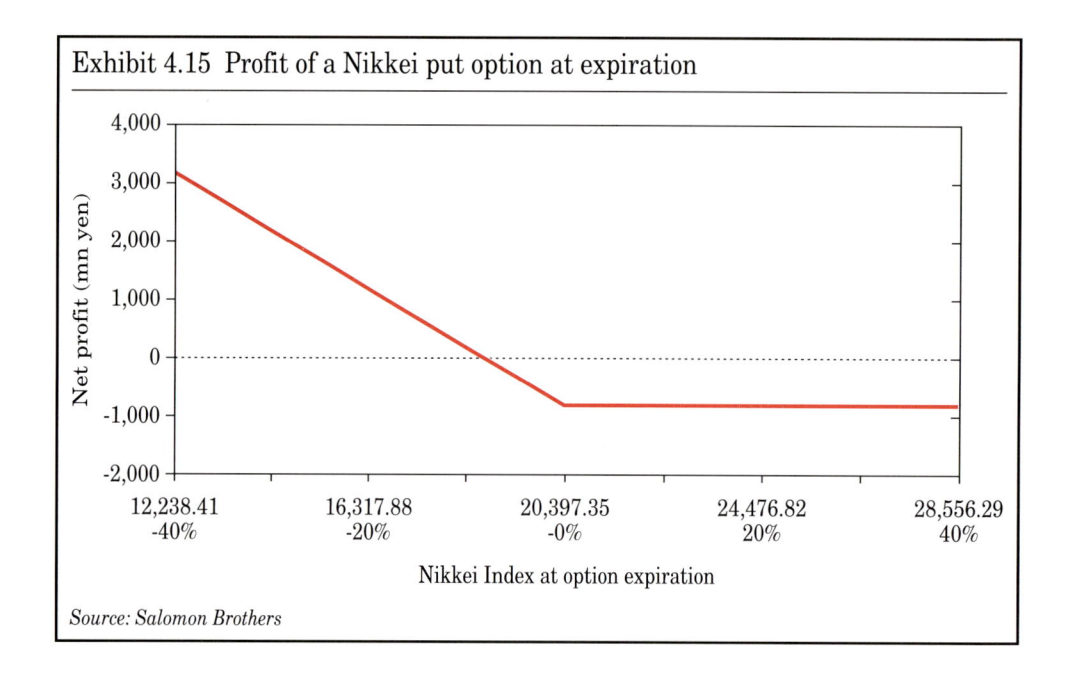

Exhibit 4.15 Profit of a Nikkei put option at expiration

[Chart: Net profit (mn yen) vs Nikkei Index at option expiration. X-axis values: 12,238.41 (-40%), 16,317.88 (-20%), 20,397.35 (-0%), 24,476.82 (20%), 28,556.29 (40%). Line declines from about 3,000 at -40% to about -800 at 0%, then flat.]

Source: Salomon Brothers

An example of an EIL option
Situation
A Japanese investor believes that the Japanese equity market is overvalued and expects the Nikkei Index to fall over the next year.

The options transactions
This investor may purchase a one-year European put option on the Nikkei Index struck at today's index level of 20,397.35 on an underlying investment of ¥10 billion. The price of this option is equal to 8.00 per cent of the underlying investment, or ¥800 million. If, in one year, the Nikkei Index exceeds 20,397.35, then the put option will expire worthless. Conversely, if the index is below the option strike, then the investor will elect to exercise his put and receive the intrinsic value of the option. For example, if the Nikkei Index falls by 20 per cent to 16,317.88, then the payment to the option buyer is equal to the following:

$$¥10,000,000,000 \times \left(\frac{20,397.35 - 16,317.88}{20,397.35} \right) = ¥2,000,000,000$$

The net profit to the investor, ignoring the cost of financing the option purchase, is equal to the payment at option exercise minus the option premium, or ¥1.2 billion. The profit of this put option versus the level of the Nikkei Index at expiration is depicted in Exhibit 4.15.

Assume that the asset manager in the above example purchased the European put option to hedge an equity portfolio that replicated the Nikkei Index. At the current level of 20,397.35, the equity portfolio has an asset value of ¥10 billion. In one year, if the Nikkei Index has fallen below the strike of the option, then the payment received from exercising the option will keep the value of the portfolio equal to ¥10 billion (or ¥9.2 billion if the cost of the option is subtracted from the portfolio value). However, the manager is still able to participate in a rise in the Nikkei Index. Exhibit 4.16 compares an unhedged Nikkei Index equity portfolio with one that is hedged with the put option described above.

Exhibit 4.16 Value of Nikkei Index equity portfolio at option expiration

[Chart showing two lines:
— Nikkei Index equity portfolio hedged with put option (solid)
⋯ Unhedged Nikkei Index equity portfolio (dotted)

Y-axis: Net asset value (mn yen), from 6,000 to 16,000
X-axis: Nikkei Index at option expiration
- 12,238.41 (-40%)
- 16,317.88 (-20%)
- 20,397.35 (-0%)
- 24,476.82 (20%)
- 28,556.29 (40%)

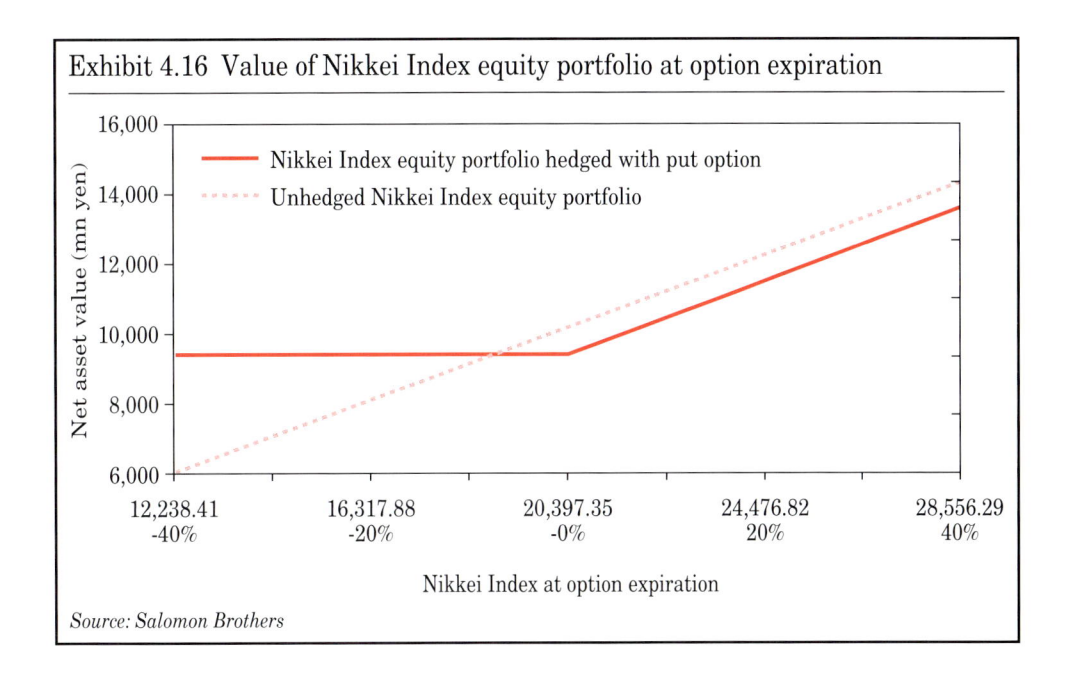

The hedged portfolio is flat at about 9,400 for index values below 20,397.35, then rises linearly parallel to (but below) the unhedged line.]

Source: Salomon Brothers

Exhibit 5.1 Bond index swap ($mn)

Period (quarters)	1	2	3	4
Swap notional principal at start of period (fixed)	$100	$100	$100	$100
Per cent change in bond index	2%	3%	2%	1%
CMB owes ASTRS	$2	$3	$2	$1
3-month Libor	6%	6%	6%	6%
ASTRS owes CMB (excl. spread)	$1.5	$1.5	$1.5	$1.5
Net payment by CMB	**$0.5**	**$1.5**	**$0.5**	**($0.5)**

Exhibit 5.2 Global basket swap ($mn)

Period (quarters)	1	2	3	4
Swap notional principal at start of period (fixed)	$250	$250	$250	$250
Per cent change in global basket value	5%	5%	(5%)	10%
CMB owes ASTRS	$12.5	$12.5	($12.5)	$25
3-month Libor	6%	6%	6%	6%
ASTRS owes CMB (excl. spread)	$3.75	$3.75	$3.75	$3.75
Net payment by CMB	**$8.75**	**$8.75**	**($16.25)**	**$21.25**

Exhibit 5.3 TOPIX equity swap (¥bn)

Period (quarters)	1	2	3	4
Swap notional principal at start of period (changes with TOPIX Index)	100.0	106.0	100.7	102.7
Per cent change in TOPIX Index	6.00%	−5.00%	2.00%	8.00%
CMB owes Trust	6.00	(5.30)	2.01	8.22
3-month yen Libor	5.00%	5.00%	5.00%	5.00%
Trust owes CMB (excl. spread)	1.25	1.33	1.26	1.28
Net payment by CMB	**4.75**	**(6.63)**	**0.75**	**6.94**

Note: In this example, Benjamin has chosen to take currency risk on the swap payments. If Benjamin had chosen a swap with no currency risk, it would pay US dollar Libor, and receive TOPIX returns translated at a fixed exchange rate.

5

Case studies

Structured Investment Products Group
The Chase Manhattan Bank, N.A.

The aim of this chapter is to provide specific examples of how equity derivative structures can be customised to meet the objectives of particular investors.

The chapter is organised into a series of case studies featuring various types of institutional investors with differing portfolio strategies and goals. In addition, each case involves special factors or problems relevant to the particular investor that need to be taken into account in customising an equity derivative structure to achieve its primary objective.

Using swaps during a manager search

The Algonquin State Teachers' Retirement System (ASTRS) wants to shift efficiently from domestic to global assets. It has decided to invest $100 million in global fixed income securities and $250 million in global equities. Funds are currently invested in US government securities with an average duration of six months.

The shift to global exposures will be delayed approximately 12 months because ASTRS is required to use a competitive bidding process.

Solution: Both a global bond index and an equity index swap
By entering into two one-year swaps with Chase Manhattan Bank (CMB) as counterparty, ASTRS can shift immediately from US interest rate exposure to global fixed income and equity exposures. ASTRS expects to have selected its global investment managers by the time the swaps terminate.

In one swap (see Exhibit 5.1), ASTRS will pay three-month Libor plus a spread and receive the return on a global bond index composed of returns on government securities from Japan, Canada, Germany, France, the United Kingdom, and several other European countries. Payments will be made quarterly and the notional principal will be fixed at $100 million. ASTRS will have the option to terminate the swap at any payment date for a small breakage fee.

In the other swap (Exhibit 5.2), ASTRS will pay three-month Libor plus a spread and receive the return on a global basket of equities covering 10 markets in Europe, Asia, Canada and Mexico. The notional principal can be fixed at $250 million throughout the life of the swap, or change with the level of the global equity basket.

Swaps to gain foreign exchange exposure

The Benjamin Family Trust's new strategic allocation strategy calls for a small shift in asset allocation to global equities. The shift will be implemented by picking a single major foreign market based on expected returns and correlations with other holdings.

The Trust does not intend to hire a foreign equity manager because its small volume and medium-term investment horizon imply a high cost of managing and holding physical securities. While it has considered using foreign stock index futures, it is concerned about the large risk of futures mispricing and trade execution, which its research indicates is higher in foreign markets than in the United States.

Solution: Three-year equity index swap
By entering into a three-year equity swap on, for example, the Japanese TOPIX Index (a Japanese market index that is more broadly based than the Nikkei 225), the Benjamin Trust can lock in substantial savings over the costs of physical investment, and avoid the risks of the TOPIX futures market.

The Trust would liquidate part of its domestic equity holdings and invest them in securities which pay yen Libor. Through the swap (see Exhibit 5.3), it would pay the yen Libor rate plus a fixed spread on the swap notional principal (which would be stated in terms of yen). It would receive quarterly payments equal to the total return on the TOPIX Index.

Swaps to reallocate assets without booking bond losses

The County Life Insurance Company wishes to reallocate assets without booking a loss on its existing bond holdings. County Life would like to reduce its portfolio of below-investment-grade bonds, some of which are trading below par, and shift funds into the equity market. The firm does not want to book the loss which would result if it sold the bonds below par.

Solution: Swaps of high yield bond index for equity index
County Life can swap the return on a generally accepted high yield portfolio index in exchange for the return on an equity index plus a fixed spread (which might be positive or negative, depending on the indices). This is illustrated in Exhibit 5.4.

Because County Life's bond portfolio is not actually sold, it will not be marked to market. At swap settlement dates, the company will receive a net payment from CMB equal to the difference between the return on the equity index (plus spread) and the return on the high yield portfolio index. At the company's choice, the notional principal of the swap can remain constant over the term of the swap, or change with either the high yield index or the equity index.

Swaps to diversify a family trust

The Haynes Family Trust is seeking to gain broader exposure to equity markets. Haynes has accumulated sizable holdings in a small group of public companies, and is looking for ways to diversify without divesting these stocks.

Reducing its existing shareholdings would trigger a substantial tax liability (because of Haynes' low basis in the shares). It would also incur significant transaction costs, and could cause the fund to lose control of some companies.

Solution: An equity basket swap

Haynes can diversify equity returns without selling its current portfolio by entering into an equity basket swap. Under the terms of the swap (see Exhibit 5.5), the Trust will pay the quarterly return on a stock basket related to the stocks in its portfolio, plus a fixed spread, and receive the quarterly return on the S&P 500 Index. The notional principal on the swap will change each quarter with the value of the basket.

Using caps and floors to protect equity gains

The Hercules Capital Fund wants to protect equity market gains after a market rally. The portfolio (which closely tracks the S&P 500) has risen in value by more than 30 per cent in the last 12 months.

The strategy of buying a floor seems too expensive and would require an upfront payment. A no cost strategy of buying a zero cost collar (buying an out-of-the-money floor and selling an out-of-the-money cap) gives up too much upside potential, and is not compatible with the fund's views on the market's trading rate for the next 12 months.

Exhibit 5.4 Index-for-index swap ($mn)

Period (quarters)	1	2	3	4
Par value of company's bonds	$100	$100	$100	$100
Market value of company's bonds	$60	$62	$58	$59
Swap notional principal at start of period (moves with high yield index)	$60.00	$62.60	$59.19	$59.62
Per cent change in high yield index	4.33%	−5.45%	0.72%	2.00%
Company owes CMB	$2.60	($3.41)	$0.43	$1.19
Per cent change in S&P 500 Index	4.00%	5.00%	−2.00%	8.00%
CMB owes company (excl. spread)	$2.40	$3.13	($1.18)	$4.77
Net payment by CMB	**($0.20)**	**$6.54**	**($1.61)**	**$3.58**

Note: Any differences between the composition of the actual bond portfolio and the high yield index will constitute basis risk and may produce "tracking error" between their respective total returns.

"S&P", "S&P 500", "Standard & Poor's", "Standard & Poor's 500", and "500" are trademarks of Standard & Poor's Corporation and have been licensed for use by Chase Manhattan.

Exhibit 5.5 Equity basket swap ($mn)

Period (quarters)	1	2	3	4
Swap notional principal at start of period (changes with basket)	$10.00	$10.50	$10.92	$12.23
Per cent change in S&P 500 Index	10.00%	5.00%	10.00%	8.00%
CMB owes Trust	$1.00	$0.53	$1.09	$0.98
Per cent change in basket value	5.00%	4.00%	12.00%	7.00%
Trust owes CMB (excl. spread)	$0.50	$0.42	$1.31	$0.86
Net payment by CMB	**$0.50**	**$0.11**	**($0.22)**	**$0.12**

Solution: Buy a floor spread and sell an out-of-the-money cap

Instead of buying the out-of-the-money floor in a zero cost collar, Hercules can buy a less expensive "floor spread" (buy an at-the-money floor and sell a floor farther out of the money). While this requires the fund to give up some protection against large declines in the index, it actually gains protection at current index levels. Because this position is cheaper, it can be financed by selling a cap fairly far out of the money, keeping more of the upside potential.

Buying the floor spread is more compatible with the fund's portfolio strategy than buying the floor in the collar. In the floor spread, all of the gains Hercules has made over the past year are fully protected unless the market drops below the strike of the floor Hercules sells. At this point, the gains begin to decline. A floor spread in line with Hercules' view was priced (see Exhibit 5.6), showing that Hercules could buy a position which expired in a year, giving it full protection for a market drop of up to 6 per cent while retaining upside growth potential of more than 10.8 per cent. A zero cost collar which would protect the fund for declines below 6 per cent would cap the upside potential at 6.8 per cent.

Earning equity returns without frequent marking to market

The objective of the Trafalgar Mutual Insurance Company is to earn equity returns without frequently marking the portfolio to market. Trafalgar holds a large fixed

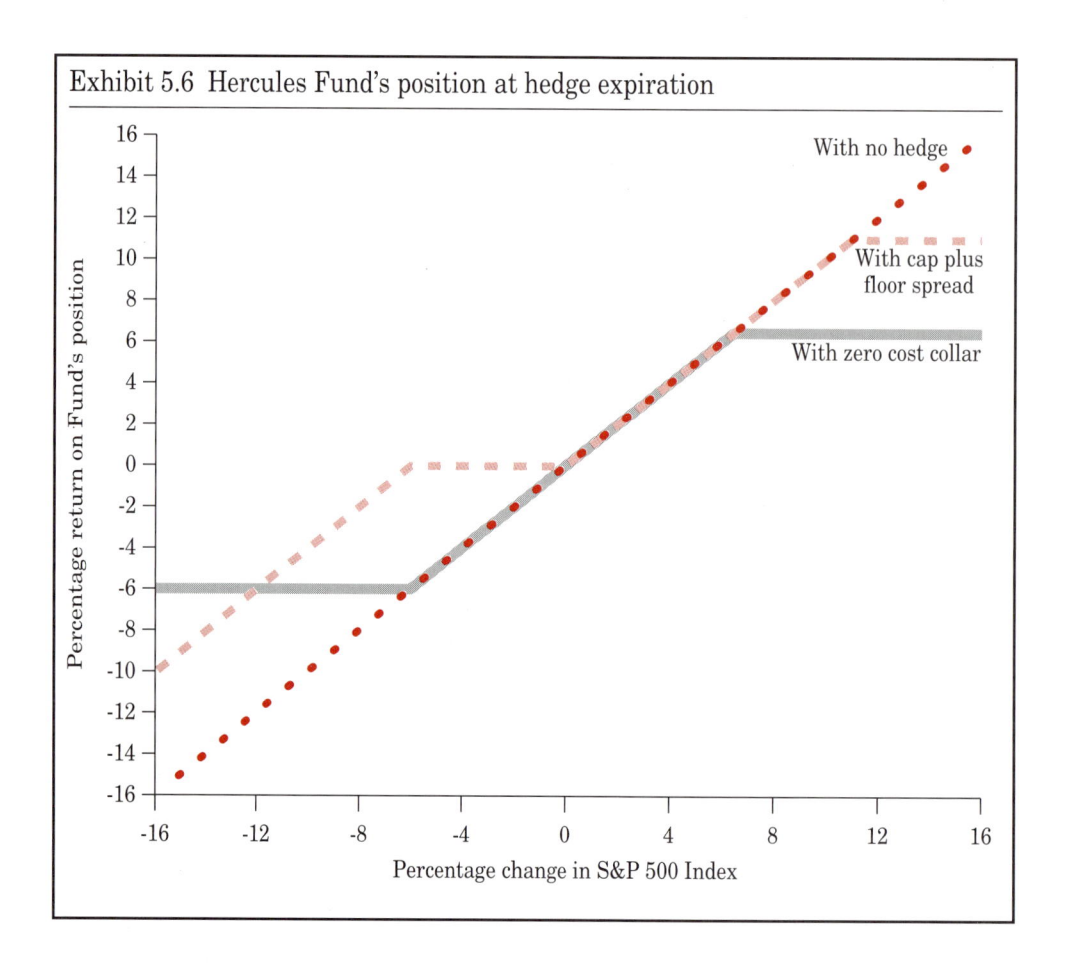

Exhibit 5.6 Hercules Fund's position at hedge expiration

Exhibit 5.7 Coupon-for-equity swap ($mn)

Period (years)	1	2	3	4
Swap notional principal at start of period (fixed)	$100	$100	$100	$100
Bond coupon rate	7.0%	7.0%	7.0%	7.0%
Trafalgar owes CMB	$7	$7	$7	$7
Per cent change in S&P 500 Index	10.0%	15.0%	2.0%	8.0%
CMB owes Trafalgar (excl. spread)	$10	$15	$2	$8
Net payment by CMB	**$3**	**$8**	**($5)**	**$1**

This example assumes certain statutory accounting treatments for the investment portfolio and derivative transactions. Interested readers should consult with their accounting advisers to ascertain the appropriateness of this treatment.

Exhibit 5.8 Equity-linked CD ($mn)

Deposit principal (3-year term)	$10.00
Per cent change in S&P 500 Index over 3 years	30.0%
Multiplier[1]	0.9
Contingent interest rate (multiplier times % change in S&P 500)	27.00%
Deposit principal returned at maturity	$10.00
Contingent interest paid at maturity	$2.70
Contingent interest, per annum yield	8.29%

[1] Multiplier is for illustrative purposes only and may be higher or lower depending on market conditions.

income portfolio and would like to enhance its expected yield by increasing its exposure to equities.

The accounting treatment for equities requires that Trafalgar mark its investment holdings to market on a regular basis. As a result, short-term negative moves in the equity market could adversely impact the firm's statutory capital position.

Solution: "Coupon for equity" swap or CMB equity-linked CD

Two different instruments can provide Trafalgar with equity returns while insulating its statutory capital position from relatively short-term equity market fluctuations.

First, it can enter into a "coupon for equity" swap (see Exhibit 5.7). Trafalgar will identify a corporate bond in its portfolio and strip the coupon from the bond. It will swap this coupon with CMB in exchange for the return on an equity index, such as the S&P 500. Trafalgar will probably receive the total return on the S&P 500 plus a spread, which depends on the bond coupon. Swap payments can be settled as infrequently as annually, at which time the change in value of the equity market will be realised.

Secondly, Trafalgar can purchase a CMB certificate of deposit (Exhibit 5.8) paying a return linked to the performance of an equity index, with a guaranteed minimum rate of interest. Full deposit principal will be returned at maturity, and early redemption is permissible with a penalty. The equity-linked return will be calculated and paid at the maturity of the deposit. Trafalgar will book deposit principal at par or at its accreted value, and any equity-linked interest as contingent interest. No mark-to-market accounting will be necessary.

Using index-linked deposits to gain global exposure

The Wolforth Foundation wishes to gain low cost foreign market exposure with limited risk. It wants to begin a global investment programme with a small equity investment in which its downside risk is limited, but the small size of the investment does not justify the cost of hiring a global equity manager to manage the portfolio.

Solution: A CMB equity-linked CD

Wolforth can purchase a CMB certificate of deposit (see Exhibit 5.9) with a term of up to five years, which will pay a return linked to the performance of equity markets in Canada, Germany, Japan, the United Kingdom, France, Hong Kong or other markets, either individually or in basket combinations. Deposit principal is guaranteed and will be returned at maturity regardless of the equity market performance. Early redemption of the CD is permissible with a penalty.

Enhancing S&P 500 returns through fixed income management

International Dynamics Retirement Plan wants to beat benchmark S&P 500 returns. The passively managed part of International Dynamic's portfolio currently generates S&P 500 returns by investing in the index stocks.

Strategies which are based on weighting the stocks differently from the benchmark index (as in a tilt fund) are incompatible with the plan's commitment to passive equity management for this portion of the portfolio.

Solution: Active fixed income management with an equity index swap

International Dynamics can capitalise on its fixed income management expertise to enhance its equity returns. Instead of investing $100 million in the basket of index stocks, it can invest the same amount in fixed income instruments and enter into an S&P 500 equity swap. In essence, International Dynamics will be substituting fixed income management risk, with which it has substantial experience, for active equity management risk.

Exhibit 5.9 Equity-linked CD ($mn)

Deposit principal (3-year term)	$10.00
Per cent change in TOPIX Index over 3 years	60%
Multiplier[1]	0.62
Contingent interest rate (multiplier times % change in TOPIX)[2]	37.2%
Deposit principal returned at maturity	$10.00
Contingent interest paid at maturity	$3.72
Contingent interest, per annum yield	11.12%

[1] Multiplier is for illustrative purposes only and may be higher or lower depending on market conditions.
[2] In this example, Wolforth has chosen to take no currency risk, so the deposit return equals the contingent interest rate in dollars. If Wolforth had chosen a deposit with currency risk, the final contingent payment would be exposed to currency rate translation.

Exhibit 5.10   S&P 500 equity swap ($mn)

Period (quarters)	1	2	3	4	5
Swap notional principal at the beginning of the period (changes with S&P 500 Index)	$100.00	$110.00	$105.60	$110.88	$115.32
Per cent change in S&P 500 Index	10.00%	−4.00%	5.00%	4.00%	
CMB owes plan	$10.00	($4.40)	$5.28	$4.44	
3-month Libor (excl. spread)	6.00%	6.00%	6.00%	6.00%	
Plan owes CMB	$1.50	$1.65	$1.58	$1.66	
Net payment by CMB	$8.50	($6.05)	$3.70	$2.77	
Investment in fixed income at start of period[1]	$100.00	$110.13	$105.86	$111.28	$115.86
Annualised fixed income yield	6.50%	6.50%	6.50%	6.50%	
Plan fixed income earnings	$1.63	$1.79	$1.72	$1.81	
S&P 500 return					**15.32%**
Plan return					**15.86%**
Enhancement					**0.55%**

[1] Investment = investment at beginning of previous period + Plan fixed income earnings in previous period + net payment by CMB in previous period. First period investment = $100.

Under the terms of the swap (see Exhibit 5.10), the Plan will receive quarterly payments equal to the total return on the S&P 500 Index over each quarter. The notional principal of the swap will start at $100 million and change each quarter, just as if the portfolio held equities. The Plan will pay Libor, set at the start of each quarter, plus a fixed spread (which might be negative, depending on the market) on the swap's notional principal. While the fixed income managers will have to maintain some liquid reserves available for the end of each quarter in case the Plan has to make a net payment, they will enhance the Plan's S&P 500 return to the extent they can beat Libor plus the fixed spread.

6

Exotic options

David Brierwood and Howard Smith
Morgan Stanley International

By imaginative use of standard options of differing strikes and maturities, the sophisticated investor can create a vast range of customised strategies with an equally varied list of names – collars, conversions, table-tops, strangles, butterflies, back-spreads, etc. All these strategies can be implemented by buying and selling conventional put and call option contracts. And they all have one feature in common – the pay-off depends only on the price of the underlying asset at the maturity (or exercise) of the component options.

In this chapter, we will be discussing so-called "exotic" options. Exotic options have developed to solve unique problems where conventional instruments have proved ineffective. In fact, just about the only feature that all these options have in common is that they cannot be created by combining regular options.

Despite the "exotic" label, these options are an increasingly common part of the armoury of investors who seek efficient solutions to the complex problems posed by today's equity markets. Indeed, their use has grown precisely because they represent elegant solutions to particular problems.

All manner of investors use exotic options. Speculators of course, but hedgers and fundamental investors will often use them better to meet one or more of the following objectives:

– *Cost reduction:* In many cases, lower upfront costs can be achieved – for example by the use of average rate options, down-and-out calls and so on.

– *Timing:* By the use of exotics, such as average strike options and lookbacks, investors can avoid making potentially costly errors in market timing.

– *Asset allocation:* Certain types of exotics (eg, outperformance options) can help to implement asset allocation decisions at the portfolio level.

– *Directional plays:* Barrier options in particular are ideal tools to benefit from very specific directional views.

– *Currency hedging:* Exotics incorporating a currency element can provide market-linked currency hedges not otherwise available.

Classes of exotic option

The scope of this chapter is to give an overview of classes of exotic option most commonly used by equity investors. As investors seek to enhance returns by isolating elements of performance or immunising others, new problems will be identified. New classes of exotic option will emerge to address the new classes of problem. The specifications of instruments described as exotic are limited only by imagination. However, there are some common formats which can be conveniently grouped as follows:

– path-dependent options;
– options on more than one asset;
– currency-linked options;
– compound options; and
– regional options.

Path-dependent options
The value of any option moves as the price of the underlying asset changes. For a regular or non-path-dependent option, knowledge of the closing price of the underlying asset at exercise or expiration translates into knowledge of final payment, irrespective of how it got there.

Often, the holder of a regular European style option may suffer (despite calling the market correctly) from sudden adverse underlying price movements close to expiry. A range of exotics has grown up which, to a greater or lesser extent, depend on the whole price history of the underlying. Many of these are naturally very appealing to the hedge player. We will discuss the following path-dependent exotics:

– average rate options;
– lookback options;
– delayed strike options; and
– barrier options.

Options on more than one asset
Another group of exotics depend for their pay-off on the price of at least two completely different assets. There are essentially two different option types commonly traded: outperformance options; and "better of" options.

Currency-linked options
Closely related to the above are options on non-currency assets which nevertheless depend for their pay-off on the movement of a particular exchange rate. Two main alternatives are available: "quanto" options; and cross-rate options.

Compound options
The ultimate in exotic options – options on options.

Regional options
Many international investors are interested in using conventional option strategies for entire regions of the world. For example, protecting a European portfolio, getting exposure to upside in the Far Eastern markets or the ubiquitous EAFE, or even the world equity market itself. This class of option does not immediately appear to have

Exhibit 6.1 Exotic options family tree

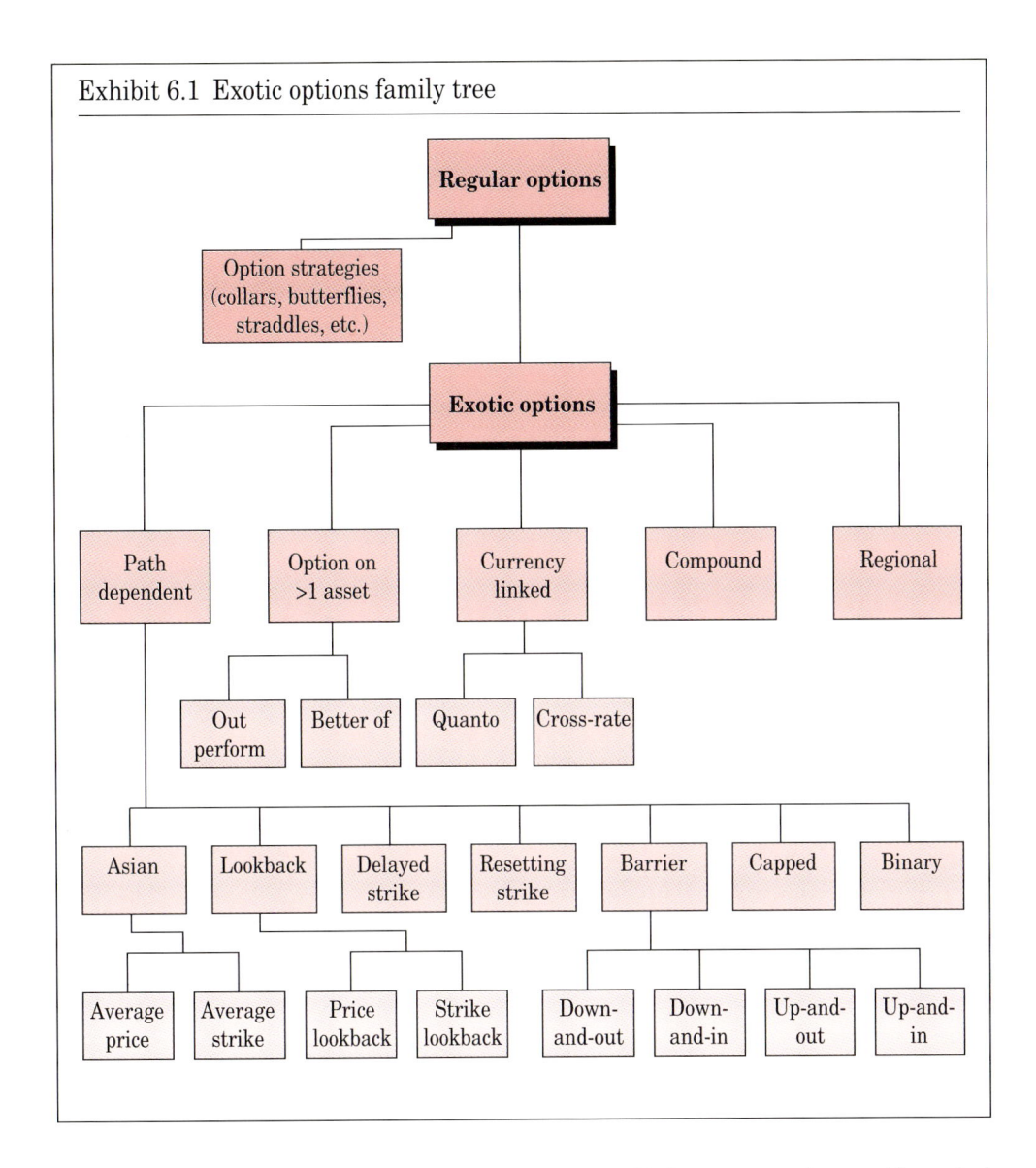

```
                         Regular options
                        /
    Option strategies
    (collars, butterflies,
    straddles, etc.)
                         Exotic options
         ┌──────────┬──────────┬──────────┬──────────┐
      Path        Option on  Currency   Compound   Regional
    dependent     >1 asset    linked
                    │           │
              ┌─────┴────┐  ┌───┴────┐
              Out      Better of  Quanto  Cross-rate
            perform
      │
   ┌──┬──────┬─────────┬─────────┬────────┬───────┬───────┐
 Asian Lookback Delayed Resetting Barrier Capped Binary
                strike   strike
   │      │                        │
 ┌─┴──┐ ┌─┴──┐                ┌────┼────┬─────┐
Average Average Price Strike  Down- Down- Up-and- Up-and-
 price  strike lookback lookback and-out and-in out  in
```

the credentials for the exotic title. But consider which currency the world market should be quoted in and the implications for hedging such an option and the exotic nature become all too obvious.

Path-dependent options

Average rate options (also known as Asian options)
The buyer of, say, a straight, one-year, at-the-money (ATM) European call may subsequently find that although the market behaved basically bullishly over the term of the option, he nevertheless suffers from bad timing either because of the time chosen to strike the option or because of the exact time of expiry. A purchase instead of an American call would mitigate the problem to some extent, but the use of an average rate option may be a much better all-round solution. There are two basic types:

1 *Average price option:* An option in which the reference price for calculating the

pay-off amount is the average of the underlying price at a predetermined number of points.

2 *Average strike option:* An option in which the strike price for calculating the pay-off is the average of the underlying price at a predetermined number of points.

The mathematical pay-off formulations for both average price and average strike options are as follows:

Average price call = max $[0, \text{average}(S_1..S_n) - K]$
Average price put   = max $[0, K - \text{average}(S_1..S_n)]$
Average strike call = max $[0, S - \text{average}(S_1..S_n)]$
Average strike put = max $[0, \text{average}(S_1..S_n) - S]$

where:

K = fixed strike price
$S_1..S_n$ = price at set of pre-specified points during life of option
S = price at maturity.

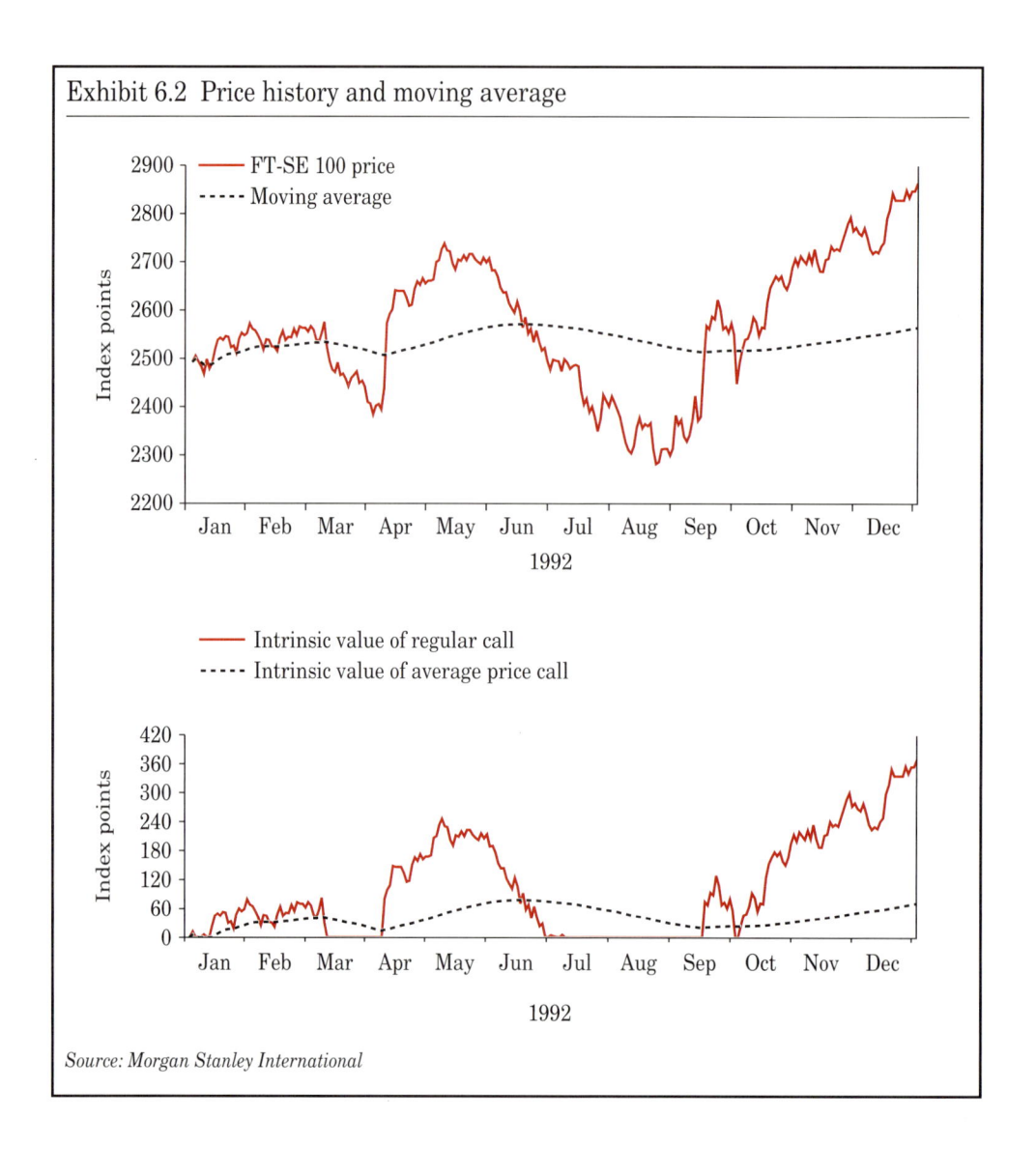

Exhibit 6.2 Price history and moving average

Source: Morgan Stanley International

The points used in determining the average always fall within the whole option period, but there may be few or many points in the average and the averaging period may be the whole life or only a small portion of the overall life. The following is an example of an average price option:

Underlying   = FT-SE 100 Stock Index;
Current level = 2,492.80;
Strike price   = 2,492.80;
Maturity   = 12 months;
Option type   = daily average price European call.

The pay-off of this option will be the amount by which, if any, the level of the FT-SE 100 averaged each day for 12 months exceeds the strike of 2,492.80. For example, if the actual price history of the FT-SE 100 was as set out in Exhibit 6.2, then this option would expire in-the-money with a pay-off of 71.68.

This option is European in the sense that the holder must wait until the final average is known after 12 months to exercise. Of course as the price moves, the average-to-date also moves. It is not possible to exercise against any interim average value although such an option could be envisaged.

The attraction of such an option is clear – the holder does not wish to be penalised if the FT-SE 100 were to rally strongly over an extended period and suffer a large collapse near to expiry causing the call to lose most (or all) of its value. A further attraction is price. Average price options are typically much cheaper than standard European equivalents. For example:

One-year ATM FT-SE 100 European call: 7.5 per cent of notional;
One-year ATM FT-SE 100 average price call: 4.0 per cent of notional;
One-year ATM FT-SE 100 average strike call: 3.5 per cent of notional.

The two fundamental reasons for the cheaper price are the reduced volatility of the average price mechanism, and the effectively shorter maturity of the option.

Of course, the fewer points in the average and the more closely bunched the averaging points, then the more that the average price option behaves like a regular European call. Conversely, the more averaging points spread evenly over the life of the option, the cheaper the average price option becomes relative to the European alternative.

The reduced sensitivity to spikes in price and the cheaper option premium are major reasons for choosing average price options. The other important reason arises where an investor has a constant level of exposure to the underlying asset. For example, a fund manager obliged to purchase $10 million of equities at the beginning of each of the next 12 months may purchase a $120 million monthly average price call option to effectively cap the average purchase price of the equities at the strike price. This would be much more effective and much cheaper than the purchase of 12 individual call options.

Options with both averaged strike and averaged reference prices are quite common in index-linked bond issues to avoid the impact of freak price movements.

Listed option contracts are also often average price options. Usually this average is taken over a period of a few minutes just prior to expiry. Examples include FT-SE 100 options traded on LIFFE where the average is taken minute-by-minute between 10.10am and 10.30am on expiration date.

Note that the behaviour of an average price option can diverge quite considerably from that of a regular option. Consider the previous FT-SE 100 example: with just

Exhibit 6.3 Price lookback call pay-off example

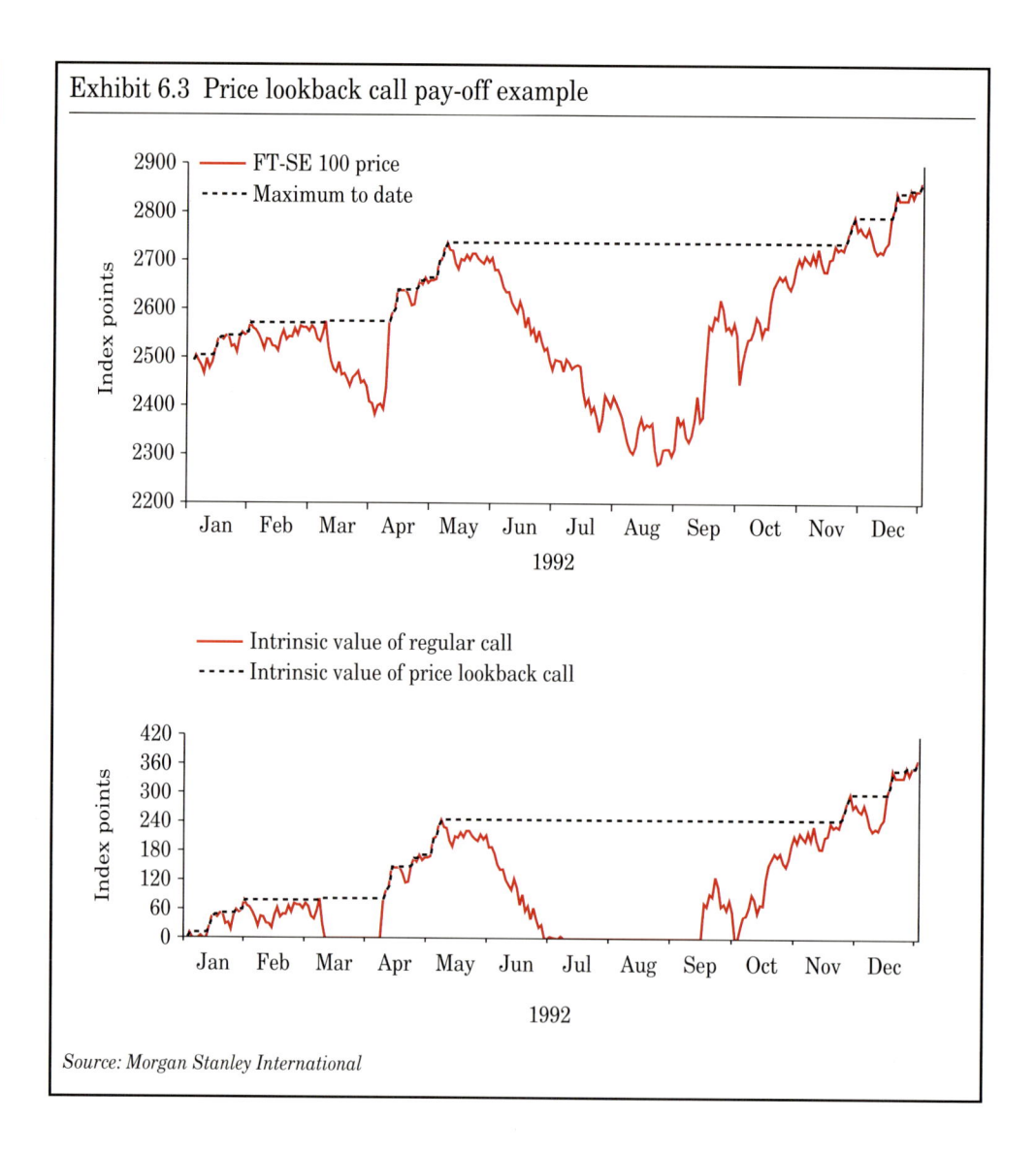

[Chart: FT-SE 100 price and Maximum to date, Jan–Dec 1992, Index points 2200–2900]

[Chart: Intrinsic value of regular call and Intrinsic value of price lookback call, Jan–Dec 1992, Index points 0–420]

Source: Morgan Stanley International

under a month to expiry, with the index at 2,792 and the average-to-date at 2,542.01 the regular call will be 12 per cent in-the-money and trading with almost 100 per cent delta. However, the average price call will expire against a price almost entirely pre-determined by the points in the average which are already known. The final points of the average will have only a minor effect, and the call will therefore have a very small delta of around 8 per cent. This is because the delta measures the sensitivity of the option price to movements in the underlying. As most of the dependence is to prices which are already known, dependence on the final values is much reduced.

Lookback options

While average rate options provide protection against wild swings in the price of the underlying asset, they do not allow the holder to capture the very best performances of the asset. Lookback options on the other hand provide the holder with the best of all worlds – 20/20 hindsight or foresight.

There are two basic types of calls and puts, depending on whether the lookback feature refers to the strike of the option or to the reference price at expiry:

Exhibit 6.4 Price lookback put pay-off example

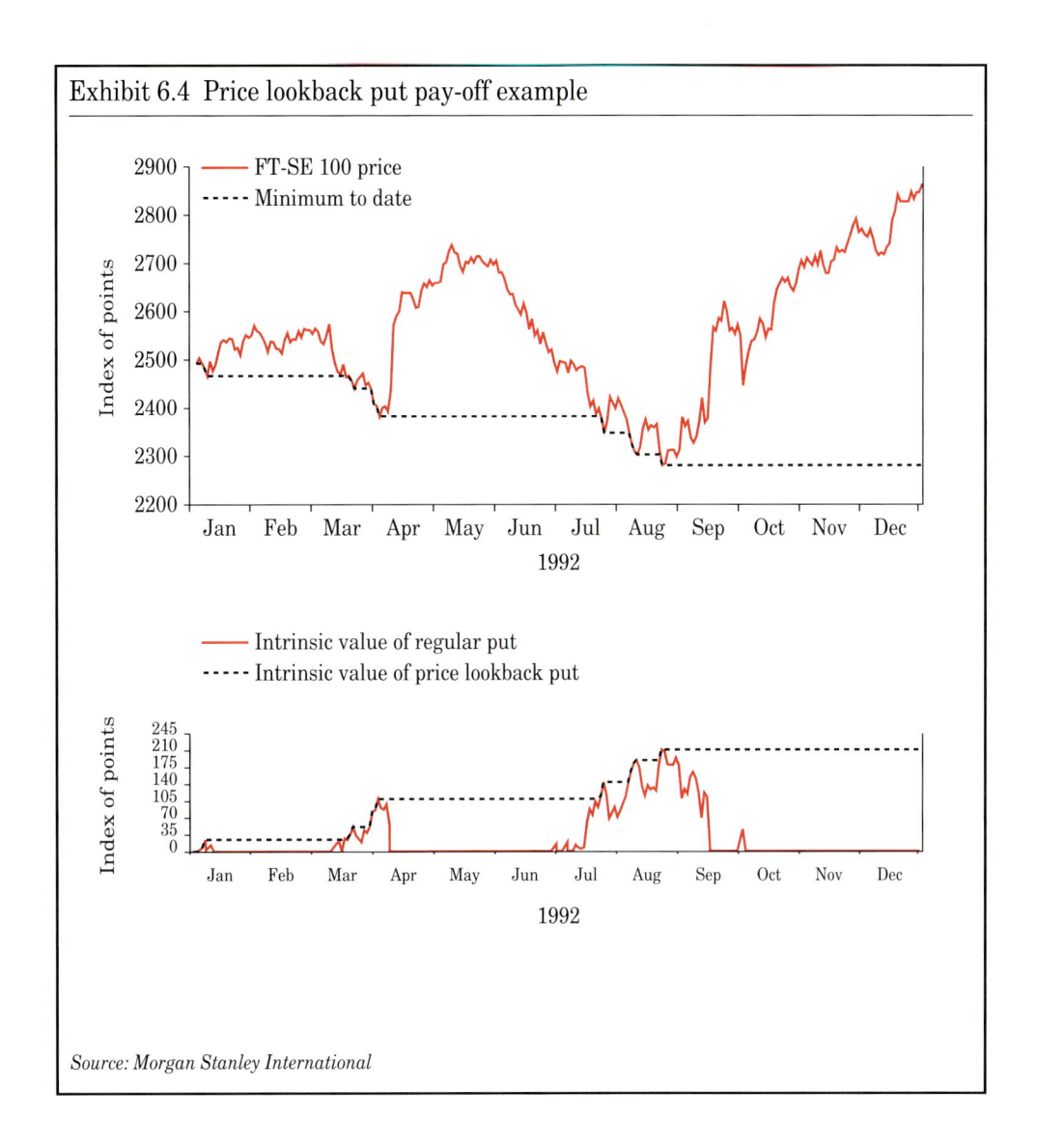

FT-SE 100 price — solid line
Minimum to date - - - - dashed line

Intrinsic value of regular put — solid line
Intrinsic value of price lookback put - - - - dashed line

Source: Morgan Stanley International

1. *(Price) lookback call:* An option paying off the amount, if any, by which the highest price reached during the life exceeds the strike price.
2. *(Price) lookback put:* An option paying off the amount, if any, by which the strike price exceeds the lowest price reached during the life.
3. *(Strike) lookback call:* An option paying off the amount, if any, by which the price at maturity exceeds the lowest price reached during the life (the strike).
4. *(Strike) lookback put:* An option paying off the amount, if any, by which the highest price reached during the life (the strike) exceeds the price at maturity.

The mathematical pay-off formulations for these options are as follows:

Price lookback call   = $S_{max} - K$
Price lookback put   = $K - S_{min}$
Strike lookback call = $S - S_{min}$
Strike lookback put   = $S_{max} - S$

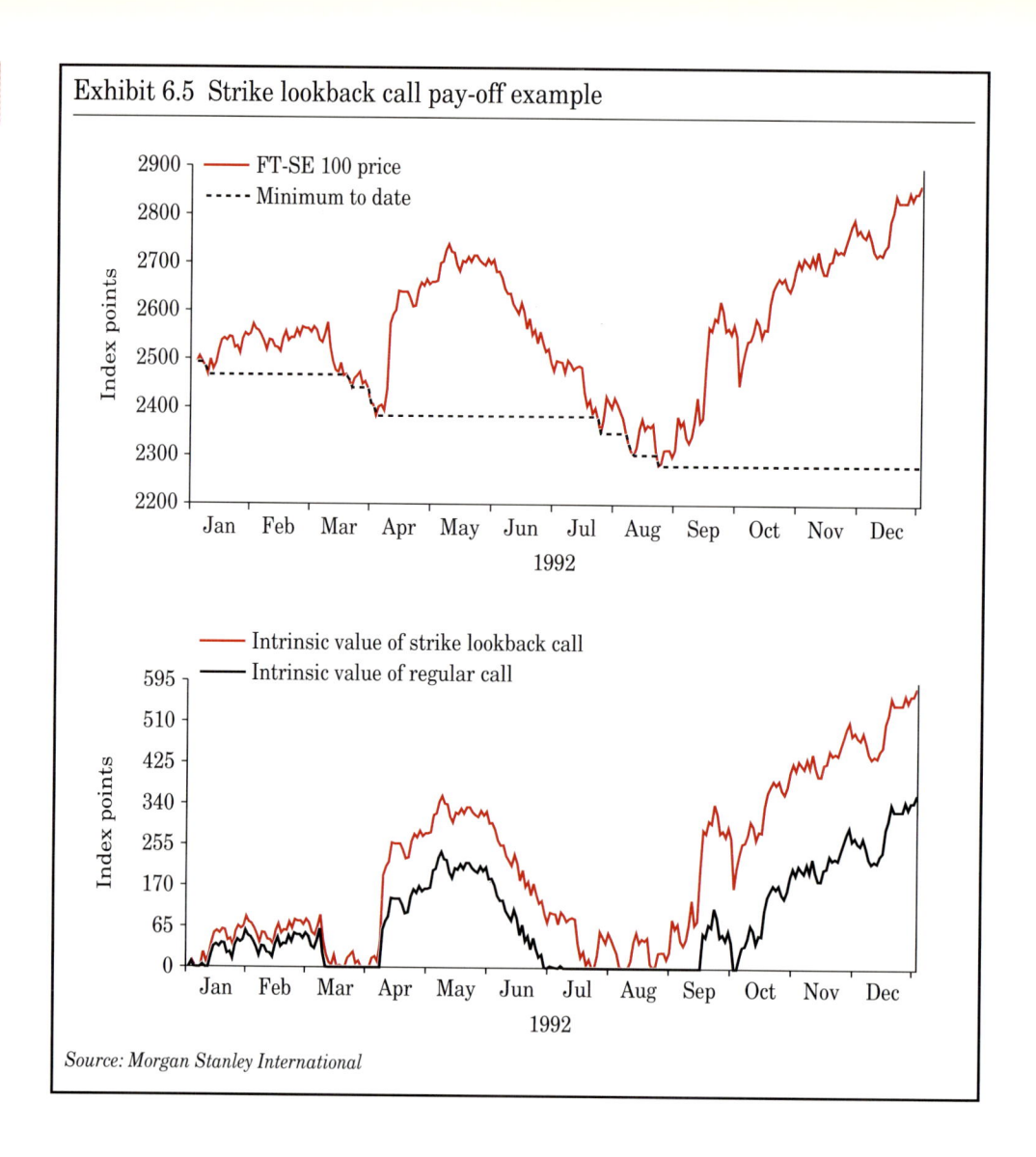

Exhibit 6.5 Strike lookback call pay-off example

Source: Morgan Stanley International

where:
- K = fixed strike
- S = price at maturity
- S_{max} = maximum value attained during life of option
- S_{min} = minimum value attained during life of option.

By referencing the highs and lows during the whole life, these options give the holder the gift of perfect timing. Holders of a price lookback call, for example, gain the same pay-off as if they bought the asset and held on to sell at the top tick over their investment horizon. Similarly, the price lookback put gives the same result as a short sale covered at the very low.

The second type of lookback is closely related. The result is the same as "looking back" over the investment horizon and then choosing the best moment to have bought (lookback call) or to have sold (lookback put).

The ultimate lookback strategy would be a long position in both the put and the call. This would pay off the difference between the highest and lowest values ever

Exhibit 6.6 Strike lookback put pay-off example

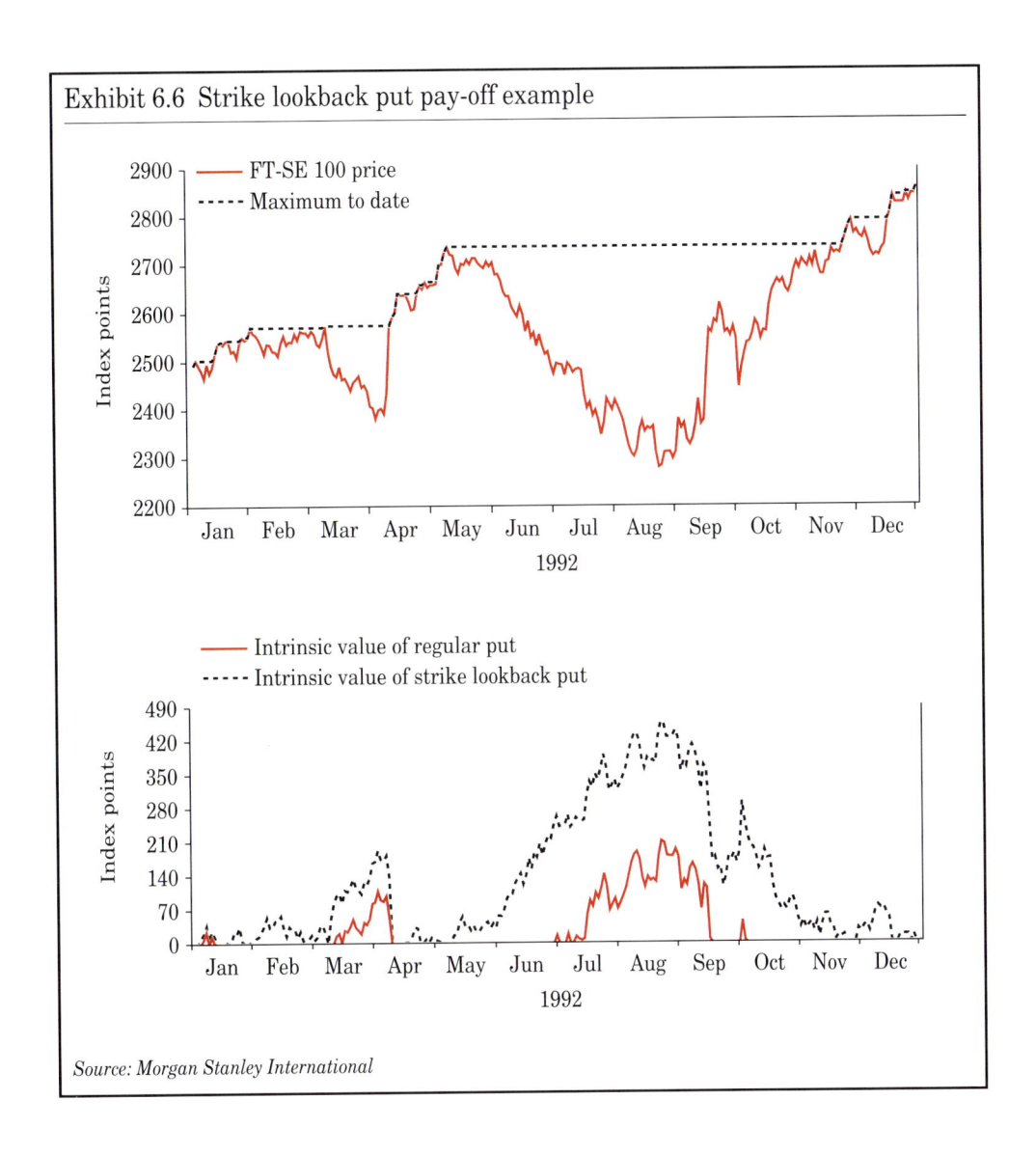

Source: Morgan Stanley International

reached and would represent the Holy Grail of investment timing – buying at the low then selling at the high or vice-versa. There is, of course, no guarantee that the profit made from buying at the low and selling at the high would cover the premium for a long lookback call and put position. All lookbacks have large premiums but, unlike most options, are virtually guaranteed to pay off something at maturity. For example:

One-year ATM FT-SE European call: 7.5 per cent of notional;
One-year ATM FT-SE price lookback call: 12.9 per cent of notional.

Often buyers of lookbacks are seeking to use them as part of a fixed term market-linked fund or index-linked bond.

Delayed strike options
Often, an investor knows that he will wish to enter a particular option strategy but does not wish to enter the market immediately or at today's level. This objective is met by delayed strike options. These are available in several slightly different forms.

One very common type is where the option is entered into today with the strike to be determined at some future date between now and the expiry date. In such a case, the buyer usually agrees to purchase, rather than a fixed number of options, options giving exposure to a specified dollar value of the underlying asset. So, for example, a fund manager wishing to allocate $10 million to US stocks over a horizon of one year but who does not wish to enter the market until, say, one month from now could buy a one-year S&P 500 call with strike to be set ATM in one-month's time. The exact number of options would be determined at the time of striking to give exposure to the full $10 million.

In other variations, the final maturity is agreed now, but the holder has the right to nominate when the strike is set. When the holder deems the timing right, he will set the strike at-the-money.

Resetting strike options (cliquet options)

One step further, and quite common particularly in the French index-bond market, are options with a strike that resets periodically to reflect the current market. So, for example, an option with overall maturity of 12 months may pay the total of the appreciation on the FT-SE 100 Index over each of four three-month periods. This amounts to a series of four three-month calls with delayed strike setting on each of the three later calls.

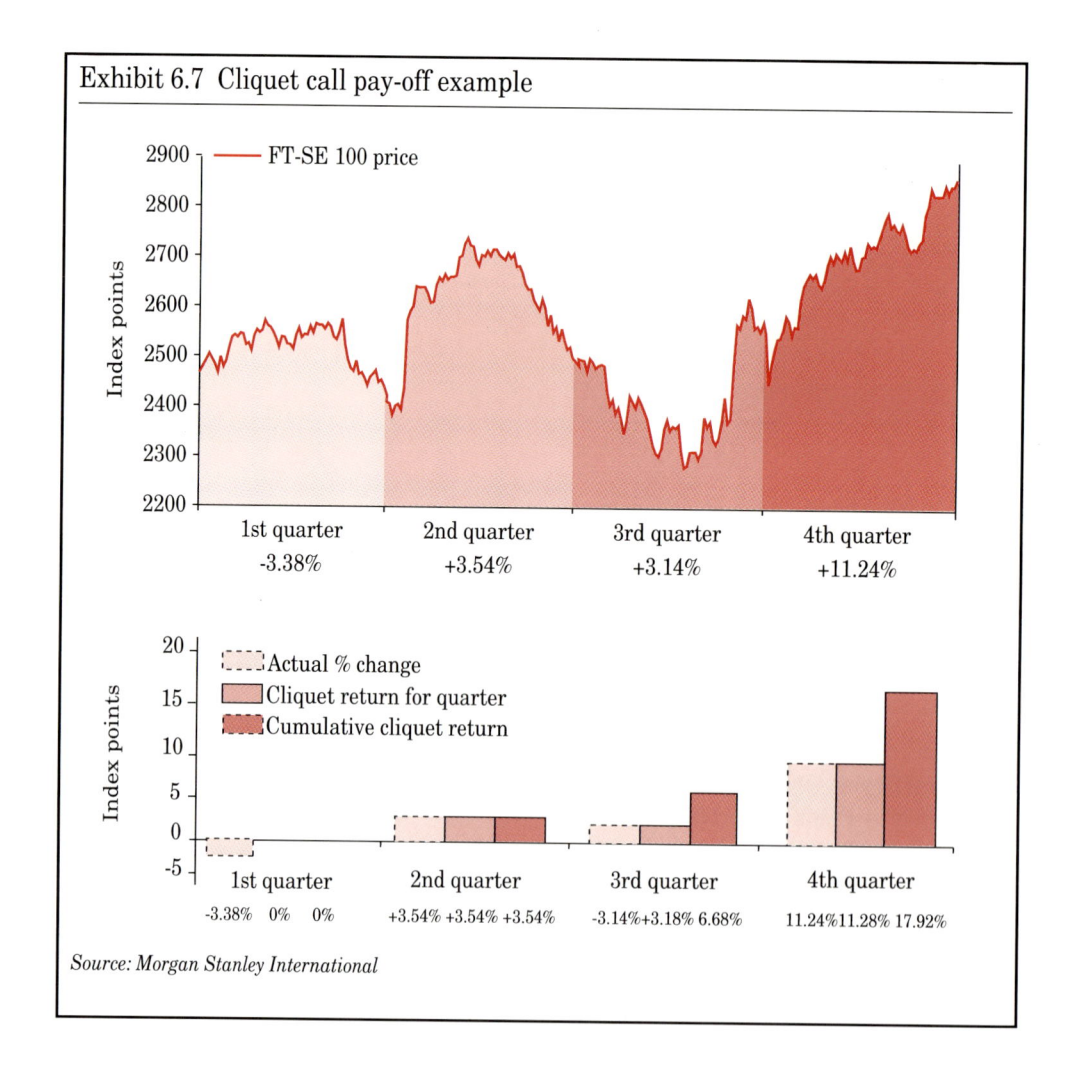

Exhibit 6.7 Cliquet call pay-off example

Quarter	1st quarter	2nd quarter	3rd quarter	4th quarter
FT-SE 100 change	-3.38%	+3.54%	+3.14%	+11.24%
Actual % change	-3.38%	+3.54%	-3.14%	11.24%
Cliquet return for quarter	0%	+3.54%	+3.18%	11.28%
Cumulative cliquet return	0%	+3.54%	6.68%	17.92%

Source: Morgan Stanley International

Barrier options

All these options have a pay-off which depends on the final value of the asset (just like regular options) and also on whether the asset ever reaches a particular level (the barrier or trigger level) during the life of the option.

There is a whole array of these options, and even more names used to describe them. The easiest approach is to use very plain language to describe accurately the various possible pay-offs. All the possibilities have their own valid uses even though some are slightly counter-intuitive at first.

There are options which expire if some barrier or trigger level is reached; these are "out" options. The converse are options which come into existence only if a particular level is reached; these are "in" options. Any of these options may be a put or a call and the barrier may be either above (up) or below (down) the current market. Thus we have eight possible basic barrier option types: put or call; in or out; up or down.

An ATM call contract, for example, which expires worthless if the underlying trades 10 per cent below its current level, is a down-and-out call. An ATM put contract which only comes into existence if the asset first trades 10 per cent higher than its level now is an up-and-in put.

The full range of possibilities is:

1 down-and-out call;
2 down-and-in call;
3 up-and-out call;
4 up-and-in call;
5 down-and-out put;
6 down-and-in put;
7 up-and-out put;
8 up-and-in put.

To really complete the list it should be mentioned that all these types can come with an extra feature – a rebate. The rebate is a specified sum of money that will be paid at expiry if the "out" option is knocked out or if the "in" option is not triggered.

By far the most common are down-and-out calls and up-and-out puts. The popularity of these option types arises because they provide the same pay-off as a regular call or put provided the barrier is not reached causing the option to disappear completely. And because there is always the risk that the option will cease to exist and pay nothing, these options are always cheaper than the corresponding regular options.

Therefore, an investor who believes that the Nikkei will fall sharply but does not wish to pay the full price for put protection may also believe that there is at most five per cent further upside and instead buy an ATM up-and-out put with the barrier five per cent above the current level. This will be considerably cheaper – the closer the barrier to today's price level the cheaper the option because of the increased likelihood of the option paying nothing.

In the past, "out" or "knock-out" options have been much more popular than "in" or "knock-in" options – partly because of a reticence to pay for something which does not yet exist and may never do so! However, they are a useful way to play market volatility. Like knock-outs, they are cheaper than regular options because they can yield no more than the corresponding regular option and may never be triggered, thus paying nothing at all.

To state the obvious, a regular call is equal to a down-and-in call plus a down-and-out call with the same strike and barrier levels and zero rebate levels. This is simply because at expiry either the barrier was reached or not. Depending on which is the

Exhibit 6.8 Barrier option pay-off formulations

Type	Pay-off if B is reached during life	Pay-off if B is never reached during life
Down-and-out call	R	Max [0, S – K]
Down-and-in call	Max [0, S – K]	R
Up-and-out call	R	Max [0, S – K]
Up-and-in call	Max [0, S – K]	R
Down-and-out put	R	Max [0, K – S]
Down-and-in put	Max [0, K – S]	R
Up-and-out put	R	Max [0, K – S]
Up-and-in put	Max [0, K – S]	R

case, one and only one of the down-and-in or down-and-out calls is still in existence and pays out the same as the regular call. Similar identities exist for other types of barrier option.

Mathematical pay-off formulations (based on a barrier option with strike K; barrier B; rebate R; and underlying value at expiry = S) are set out in Exhibit 6.8.

For example, an investor with a basically bullish view over the next year but who believes that in the meantime there could be further downside could, instead of a regular ATM call, purchase a down-and-in call which comes into existence only if the underlying asset first trades down 5 per cent.

Barrier options often behave very differently to regular options; consider, for example, a down-and-out call (knock-in options exhibit the opposite behaviour). First, the sensitivity to volatility of the underlying asset is much reduced. This is because the chance of a higher pay-off and the chance of no pay-off (due to the barrier being hit) both increase with volatility and the two effects tend to offset. Time decay is also much reduced since, all other things being equal, and if the price of the underlying does not move, then the reduced chance of the barrier ever being reached offsets the effect of time passing.

The delta or hedge ratio of barrier options can be particularly baffling – the delta of a down-and-out call exceeds that of a regular call because, as the underlying rises, then the chance of it finishing in-the-money rises while the probability that the option will be knocked out falls. On the other hand, the delta of a down-and-in call is actually negative. This counter-intuitive aspect can be understood by considering the fact that the regular call is equal to the combination of a down-and-out and a down-and-in call and, hence, the delta of the down-and-in call has to be negative to compensate for the higher delta of the down-and-out. Furthermore, as the barrier approaches, the delta of a knock-out can actually exceed one!

Capped options

This particular close cousin of the barrier option has been around for a significant period of time and has much in common (apparently) with a simple spread.

The option specifies two strike levels: if the upper strike is reached during the life of the option then the holder is immediately paid the difference between the two strikes. This is not the same as a call spread as the holder of a call spread would have to repurchase the higher strike call from the writer in order to crystallise a gain, and this value cannot be determined in advance because future volatility levels are uncertain and it is not known when, if ever, the upper strike will be reached.

Exhibit 6.9 Comparison of regular, knock-out and knock-in option parameters

	Regular ATM 1yr FTSE call	ATM 1yr FTSE call 95% knock-out level	ATM 1yr FTSE call 95% knock-in level
Price	7.50%	4.00%	3.50%
Delta	57.00%	88.00%	−31.00%
Gamma	2.20%	−0.70%	+2.90%
Kappa	0.37%	0.04%	0.33%
Theta	0.01%	0.00%	0.01%
Rho	0.50%	0.35%	0.15%

Price = percentage of spot
Delta = change in price with respect to change in spot
Gamma = change in delta for 1% change in spot
Kappa = change in price for 1% change in volatility
Theta = 1 day's time decay
Rho = change in price for a 1% change in risk-free rate

This type of spread has been referred to as a "one-touch" option, an exploding spread, a capped spread, etc. In some forms, the spread value is not paid off immediately but is guaranteed to be locked in at final maturity of the option (a deferred capped option). In fact this is simply an up-and-out call with a rebate. The strike is the lower strike with the barrier being set at the upper strike and the rebate being the value of the spread between the two strikes.

Binary options
One final set of path-dependent options – of a very extreme nature – are binary or digital options (all or nothing options).

In this type of pay-off the holder receives a fixed amount if the price is within a particular range at expiry, and nothing otherwise. This type of option is essentially nothing more than a bet. A recent Abbey National bond included this type of option on the Nikkei.

Options on more than one asset

The two assets will typically be either two different markets in the same asset class (eg, the S&P 500 and the Nikkei), or a stock and its respective market (eg, ICI and the FT-SE 100) or two different asset classes, such as equities (say the MSCI World Index) and bonds (eg, a benchmark bond index).

There are two fundamental types of two-asset option which are closely related – outperformance options and "better of" options.

Outperformance options
This is equivalent to the right to exchange one asset for another. The holder receives the outperformance of asset A over asset B, or nothing if asset B outperforms.

The mathematical pay-off formulation is as follows:

Max $[0, P_A - P_B]$

where:

P_A performance of asset A $= \dfrac{A_1 - A_0}{A_0}$

P_B performance of asset B $= \dfrac{B_1 - B_0}{B_0}$

A_0 (B_0) = price of asset A (B) at inception

A_1 (B_1) = price of asset A (B) at expiry.

The beauty is that it does not matter whether the markets move up or down in general because this is a relative measure. So, for example, one could purchase an option paying the outperformance of French equities as measured by the CAC-40 Index over Swiss equities as measured by the SMI Index. Then if, say, the CAC rose 15 per cent while the SMI was down 5 per cent, the holder of this option receives a 20 per cent pay-out.

This can be a useful asset allocation tool or may even be used to neutralise asset allocation decisions previously made. So a fund manager overweight in Switzerland might hedge out the risk in that decision with the option described above.

"Better of" options

In this case, the holder receives the return of the better performing asset or assets. So, for example, if an investor bought an option paying the better of the CAC and the SMI he would, in the previous example, receive 15 per cent – the performance of the French market.

Currency-linked options

This is an extremely popular and fast-growing area because many investors prefer to make asset allocation and currency decisions separately.

If a dollar-based investor decides to invest in Japanese stocks, then his total return does not depend only on the performance of the stocks in the local market. Any gains are enhanced if the yen strengthens against the dollar and vice versa. In fact, the investor may gain overall, even if stocks fall, if the yen appreciates sufficiently.

Often this currency dependence is accepted and is not a problem. To some extent it may be eliminated by hedging the foreign exchange forward, but the problem always remains that the required amount of hedge cannot be known because it depends on the performance of the equity market itself.

The same applies if the investor buys options on the market. Imagine that a dollar investor buys a Nikkei ATM call struck at 20,000. If he does not hedge the dollar/yen currency exposure then any gains on the call option are paid in yen and hence are worth less as the yen weakens against the investor's dollar benchmark. There are two possible alternatives – quanto and cross options.

Quanto options

This type of option is also known as a fixed exchange rate option or a percentage change option. The holder receives any gains as the percentage amount by which the option finishes in-the-money and receives this gain in the nominated currency.

So, for example, consider a Nikkei call struck ATM at 20,000 with the quanto feature into US dollars. If the Nikkei rose 25 per cent to 25,000 then the holder of such a call on $10 million of exposure would receive $2.5 million. It is clear why the name "percentage change option" is applied and it is also plain that it represents the same result as if it were possible to lock in the exchange rate throughout the life of the option.

This form of pay-off is seen on Nikkei and FT-SE futures traded on the CME and on the Japan index options traded on the American Stock Exchange. Also, this type of currency linkage is appropriate when the investor holds a view on the performance of a particular index as measured by local benchmarks. So a dollar investor may believe that Japanese equities will be strong but has no view, or a negative view, on the currency.

Cross options
Another alternative is to rebase the asset into the investor's benchmark currency. This means creating a new index such as the "Nikkei in dollars", establishing a new benchmark that reflects the value of a particular market from a foreigner's perspective.

This does not strictly eliminate the foreign exchange risk except in the technical sense that there can be no currency risk between the new asset and the benchmark currency because they are both in the same currency already! In fact, compared with a regular call the FX risk is magnified, because in the regular case only the pay-off (which may even be zero) is affected by the currency whereas here even the question of whether the option finishes in-the-money is dependent on the currency. However, it is ideal for a hedge against an existing foreign portfolio. For example, a US fund manager with $10 million in Japanese equities may wish to protect the value at $10 million for a period. The fund manager would buy a put struck in dollars on the portfolio and no matter how the equity and currency behave, the dollar value is protected. Of course he will give up any potential gains from a weaker dollar/stronger yen.

This type of option is quite common in index bonds which seek to give domestic investors exposure to foreign equities in their own terms. Consider a Nikkei ATM call (see Exhibit 6.10) with the following parameters purchased by a dollar investor: Nikkei at inception = 20,000 = NK; Nikkei at expiry = 25,000 = NK1; FX rate at inception = 125 = FX; and FX rate at expiry = 200 = FX1.

Exhibit 6.10   Comparison of regular ("unhedged") option vs. quanto option vs. cross option

	Regular ("unhedged")	Quanto	Cross
Index at inception	¥20,000	¥20,000	$160
Index at expiration	¥25,000	¥25,000	$125
Pay-off per option	¥5,000 = $25 at FX1	¥5,000 = $40 at FX	Zero
Nikkei exposure	Bullish	Bullish	Bullish
Yen exposure	Bullish on pay-off only	Neutral	Bullish on full principal amount

Indexed forward
One particular type of currency-linked strategy that has been developed to solve the problem of uncertainty over the required amount of FX hedge for an equity portfolio is the indexed forward. This takes one of two forms, analogous to the quanto and

cross options discussed above. A quanto-style indexed forward pays the percentage change in a particular index but denominated in the specified currency. A cross-style indexed forward pays the change in the index as rebased into the chosen currency.

So, for example, a fund manager wishing to gain exposure to $10 million of Japanese equities might purchase a quanto-style indexed forward at today's level, and would receive or pay the percentage upside or downside in the Nikkei on $10 million. A fund manager wishing to protect $10 million of Japanese equities could sell a cross-style indexed forward at today's level and will receive or pay an amount corresponding to the change in value of the Nikkei in dollar terms.

Compound options

This is perhaps the most exotic of all – an option to buy or sell an option. In this type of option the underlying is another option. So, for example, a call on a put is the right, but not the obligation, to purchase a put option on the ultimate underlying with specified strike and maturity at a specified premium amount.

The key rationale for this type of exotic is leverage. The premium is much reduced and the most common use is in anticipation of a major event in the market expected to have a substantial price effect and possibly a knock-on effect on volatilities as well. For example, an investor may feel that a particular outcome in a forthcoming general election may cause the stock market to fall sharply, and could purchase a regular put option and risk losing all the premium if the opposite result occurs. Instead, therefore, the investor could, for a much reduced premium, purchase a compound option – a call on the put. If the stock market does indeed tumble he can exercise into the put: given a sufficiently large fall, the payment of the extra call premium will be worthwhile, while if the expected fall does not occur, only the smaller call premium is given up.

Regional options

Many managers are benchmarked to standard measures such as MSCI (Morgan Stanley Capital International) World Index or to regional equivalents such as MSCI Europe or EAFE. The fund manager could hedge or gain exposure by buying options on indices which are commonly used in the derivatives market, such as the Nikkei, FT-SE, S&P 500, etc., but will find that it is difficult to compensate for the changing weightings in the index and the complex currency and interest rate hedge implicit in this style of replication.

Instead, the fund manager can purchase options written on the whole index, immunising all tracking and currency risk. The options can be written in the currency of the index (usually US dollars) or in the manager's reference currency. A further advantage is that the product is superficially straightforward – all the complexities of tracking, equity/currency correlations, etc. are transferred to the option seller.

Review

By no means all the possible types of exotics have been covered here. Many examples in the OTC market have been unique one-offs. And, of course, these exotics can be combined to produce yet more unusual derivatives.

While the volume in these options will never match that conducted in more conventional products, they are certainly no longer intellectual curiosities and have come to be priced by market practitioners in a much more consistent and competitive framework. There is no doubt that there will remain a growing and widening role for these instruments in the ever more sophisticated investor universe. Users have come to realise that they can have what they want – and want what they need.

Some of the options described here are already becoming near-commodity merchandise and it must be expected that the scope of products will expand further as the existing range is more vigorously explored.

7

Pricing and mathematics

Martin Vesey

Equity Derivatives
Citibank International plc

The trading and pricing of equity derivatives – instruments, the performance of which is a function of an underlying equity – is older than might be imagined. While it is true that the liquid option markets are a comparatively recent phenomenon, traditional options – individually negotiated agreements between counterparties – have traded for many years, existing well before the ground-breaking academic papers on option theory. In addition, the inevitable time lag between the publication of a paper and its ready assimilation into trading practice means that many derivative products (exchange-traded options, corporate warrants and convertibles for example) have been traded without the use of theoretical models. The ingenuity of traders and investors has consequently led to the development of specifically targeted pricing indicators for each instrument. These are still used by many to determine the value of the respective products traded.

Conventions

Interest rates and dividend yields are taken as continuously compounded throughout. In equations, the following key is adhered to:

S	current share price
F	futures price
C	value of call option
P	value of put option
K	strike price of a derivative
N.V.	notional value of one convertible bond
R	shares received on exercise of one convertible bond
t	time to expiry of a derivative
r	riskless interest rate over time to expiry
d	dividend yield of underlying share
v	volatility of underlying share price
n	number of steps in a binomial tree
ln	natural logarithm function
e	base of the natural logarithm

N( )   cumulative normal distribution function (found in any good statistics textbook)
N'( )   first differential of N( ) (found in any good statistics textbook)
PV( )   present value function (found in any good financial mathematics textbook)

Traditional product pricing

Three products that have long been traded in the official exchange-traded markets are futures contracts, warrants and convertible bonds. All have been familiar to investors in the context of traditional pricing techniques, but all are used today in sophisticated option-based strategies. A word about the methods used in the pricing of each is therefore in order.

Futures contracts

A futures contract is a standardised, exchange-traded agreement for one counterparty to buy something from the other at a fixed time in the future for a price fixed now, but paid then. A forward is much the same in theoretical terms but is an over-the-counter contract which can be traded on non-standard conditions.

Most futures and forwards have physical settlement, with the purchasing counterparty handing over cash in return for taking delivery of the underlying exchange property (commodity futures generally belong in this category). Others, including all equity index futures, operate as "contracts for differences" where one counterparty pays sufficient funds to compensate the other for the amount the market has moved away from the future value at which they had traded. This dispenses with the need to transfer ownership of the exchange property.

Pricing of futures is straightforward and is calculated based on the cost of holding the exchange property until settlement. In equities therefore, where the exchange property is usually an equity index, the buyer of the index must compensate the seller for the costs that he incurs in holding the equivalent share positions for the duration of the contract, but benefits from dividends that are paid by the shares in that period, which are reflected in the price of the contract. This is very simple on an uncompounded basis:

$$F = S(1 + (r - d)t)$$

To take account of continuous compounding the following expression is used:

$$F = Se^{(r - d)t}$$

Since all details about the contract are known with certainty in advance, apart from the dividends that are due to be paid, the market price of the future can be used to derive an "implied dividend yield" that yields the correct value when incorporated into the borrowing costs.

Example: Pricing of a futures contract
Given:
	Current share index	2000
	Length of futures contract	3 months
	Funding rate	9.00 per cent (continuously compounded)
	Dividend yield	4.00 per cent (continuously compounded)
Result:	Fair futures price	2025.16

Example: Derivation of an implied dividend yield from market futures price
Given:
- Current share index — 2000
- Length of futures contract — 3 months
- Funding rate — 9.00 per cent (continuously compounded)
- Market price of contract — 2030

Result: Implied dividend yield — 3.04 per cent (continuously compounded)

Futures traders (especially arbitrageurs) use much more sophisticated techniques than this. Individual cash flows are constructed to correspond to the projected dividends and careful note is taken of the timing of share settlement account periods, transaction costs and the bid-offer spreads in the individual components.

Futures provide a method of taking share index exposure without having to commit a large amount of capital. Trading is conducted on a margin basis, where a small commitment (initial margin) is needed at the beginning and payments are made or received (variation margin) on a daily basis, reflecting movements in the market.

Warrants (single stock or equity warrants)

A warrant is a certificate traded on an exchange that gives the holder the right to buy a fixed number of shares from the issuer, at a fixed "strike" price at or before a fixed date in the future. A warrant may be issued by:

– a company and exercisable into its own newly created shares;
– an investor with a holding in the shares; or
– a bank that will hedge its exposure using option trading techniques.

In each of these cases, the market uses the same simple measures of value and risk, partly because the investors involved in each product are largely the same but also because the instruments are intrinsically almost identical.

A call warrant allows an investor to take any upside gains in a company's share price, while providing a strictly limited exposure to downside risk. As the warrant typically costs much less than the share, it contains some measure of implied insurance as the holder can only lose the limited amount he paid for the warrant rather than the entire share value. Also, the warrant allows the deferral of the payment of the strike price until some point in the future, implying that the warrant price contains a funding benefit. However, warrant holders are not entitled to receive dividends paid on the underlying share, despite the sharp reduction in the share price when they are paid. Put warrants are rather less frequently available – usually they are only issued by investment banks. They allow gains from a fall in the share price, while being subject to limited loss if the market rises.

Premium

"Premium" seeks to measure the extra money that the investor has to pay for the comfort of being able to take advantage of the two advantages outlined above. Premium assumes that the investor wishes to hold a share position and has two natural routes to follow in order to accomplish this – he can buy the shares in the conventional manner, or he can buy warrants, immediately pay the strike price and therefore collect his shares from the issuer. Premium reflects the percentage excess that the investor must pay for taking this second route and consequently buying the extra flexibility made available. A similar computation applies for put warrants, involving money given up from the sale of shares.

$$\text{Call premium} = \frac{C + K - S}{S}$$

$$\text{Put premium} = \frac{P + S - K}{S}$$

Example: Premium calculation for a call warrant
Given: Current share price   200
        Strike price   220
        Market price of warrant   21
Result: Premium payable   20.50 per cent

Gearing

Since a warrant has similar properties to a share, but with payment of a large portion (the strike price) deferred into the future, its price today is generally much less than that of the share, but for broadly equivalent exposure. This means that the investor can either take an equivalent share exposure by spending less money, or can take a much greater exposure by spending the same amount. This potential for multiplication of effective share position is called "gearing" and is similar to the principle of trading exchange futures contracts on margin. The calculation assumes that the warrant moves on a "one-for-one" basis for absolute movements in the share price and can be used for put warrants simply by changing the sign.

$$\text{Call gearing} = \frac{S}{C}$$

$$\text{Put gearing} = \frac{-S}{P}$$

Example: Gearing calculation for any warrant
Given: Current share price   200
        Strike price   220
        Market price of warrant   21
Result: Gearing achieved   9.52 times

Breakeven share price

Warrants are a wasting asset. Should the share price not move favourably by expiry, the warrant will expire worthless. On the other hand, it is easily possible for a warrant to increase in value beyond what was paid for it. It is therefore possible to calculate a breakeven point for the warrant corresponding to the share price at which the investor has his original money returned to him. This calculation conventionally ignores financing costs, though these are easily incorporated.

$$\text{Call breakeven} = K + Ce^{rt}$$

$$\text{Put breakeven} = K - Pe^{rt}$$

Example: Breakeven calculation for a call warrant (including 10 per cent growth premium)
Given:
Current share price 200
Strike price 200
Market price of warrant 20
Return on premium required 10 per cent
Result: Breakeven share price 222

Outperformance point
Since there is a premium payable on purchase of a warrant it follows that, for sufficiently low movements in the share price, the share will outperform the warrant due to the premium paid on purchase of the warrant. On the other hand, a large move in the share price should lead to the warrant outperforming the share because of its gearing. The level at which the warrant starts to outperform an equivalent share position is known as the outperformance point.

$$\text{Call outperformance} = \frac{SK}{S-C}$$

$$\text{Put outperformance} = \frac{S(K-2P)}{S-P}$$

Example: Outperformance point for a call warrant
Given:
Current share price 200
Strike price 195
Market price of warrant 21.5
Result: Outperformance point 218.5

Drawbacks of traditional warrant pricing measures
The traditional warrant pricing measures make some assumptions that are of concern. The most widely used measure, premium, assumes that immediate exercise is always possible and will immediately be taken up, which destroys the funding and option features of the warrant. As the stock markets move around in a random fashion, this view does not adequately take into account the added value of being able to defer decisions until a later date. The gearing formula implicitly assumes that the warrant price moves up and down at the same absolute rate as the underlying share which is inconsistent, as they are not equivalent instruments. Where these measures can be useful is on a comparative basis; either between very similar issues to determine relative value or, more usefully, to determine when a warrant is historically cheap against the corresponding share based on historic data.

Convertible bonds

A convertible bond is typically a subordinated bond issue with a coupon set somewhat below market interest rates. Compensating for this is the right to exchange the entire bond for a fixed number of shares at or before a fixed date in the future. Convertible preference shares are theoretically similar, paying a fixed dividend, but are treated as equity in a corporate structure. Euro-convertible bonds are often bundled with issuer call options (used to effectively force conversion if the share price rises steeply) and holder put options (allowing the holder to sell the bond back and lock in a put yield if the share falls). Because of their hybrid nature, convertible bonds attract the attention of both bond and equity investors, each applying different investment criteria and therefore using different measures of value.

Yield to redemption/put
Yield to redemption/put tacitly assumes that the underlying share will never perform well enough to allow conversion of the bond and that the investor will hold the bond to maturity or until it is put back to the issuer, should this facility be available. The calculation is identical to that carried out for a straight bond, merely computing the internal rate of return of the cash flows involved. One problem with puttable convertibles that has been highlighted recently is that if the issuer's shares have done badly enough to make the put option attractive to investors wanting to bail out, there may well be problems with the issuer raising enough funds to pay for this effective repurchase of the bonds at or above par value. Calculations are carried out using the standard formulae for maturity date and put date (if applicable). The yield to put will generally be higher than the yield to maturity and may well have been originally set to provide an appropriate spread over a riskless yield at issue.

Running yield
The running yield is the straightforward calculation of the annual coupon yield received by the holder of the convertible bond, normally with tax corrections made to allow a straight comparison with the dividend yield of the share. This measure is usually used by equity investors, who expect a yield improvement in a switch to the convertible from the share.

Convertible bond premium
A convertible bond's premium is, in essence, much the same calculation as that involved for a warrant. If the investor buys a convertible bond and immediately converts it into shares, the shares received will have an immediate market value. This total market value for the convertible is called its parity value. The excess amount of the price of the convertible over its parity value is the premium payable.

$$\text{Convertible bond premium} = \frac{N.V. - SR}{SR}$$

A comparison often carried out by an equity investor looking to invest in a convertible is to treat the premium payable as being the cost of the bond *vis-a-vis* the share, and the excess of the running yield over the share's dividend yield as the benefit. Dividing the first by the second gives an idea of the number of years that it will take to amortise out the premium and for the bond to outperform the share.

$$\text{Premium payback period} = \frac{\text{Premium}}{\text{Running yield} - \text{Dividend yield}}$$

Example: Example of a hypothetical Euro-convertible
Details: Issued at par, notional amount $100,000, coupon 7.5 per cent annual, 10 years to maturity, 5 years to put (investors' right to redeem) at 120 per cent. Bond can be converted at any time into 333.333 shares. Share price at issue $250, dividend yield 2.00 per cent (tax at 25 per cent)

Yield to put	10.73 per cent
Yield to maturity	7.50 per cent
Running yield	5.63 per cent (tax at 25 per cent)
Premium	20.00 per cent
Premium payback period	5.51 years

After one year: Assume the share price drops to $230 and the bond trades at 95 per cent of notional:

Yield to put	13.30 per cent
Yield to maturity	8.31 per cent
Running yield	5.92 per cent (tax at 25 per cent)
Premium	23.91 per cent
Premium payback period	6.10 years

These convertible bond pricing measures suffer from many of the same problems as the equivalent warrant models. Extra complexity is added by the fact that the effective strike price of the bond is not set at issue, but when exercise takes place, because the market value of the bond is effectively used to purchase the share entitlement.

Theoretical option pricing

It is relatively simple to form a valuation structure that takes into account the funding implications of derivative products using net present value calculations. However, the problem of pricing the element of choice in an option is more difficult. The value of the "right to choose" obviously depends on the conditions that might be prevailing at the time the choice is made and these will, in turn, depend on the movement in the significant underlying variables in the interim period. The pricing models discussed below are used to evaluate not only equity warrants but, more or less appropriately, all equity derivative options including OTC index options and exchange-traded single stock options.

Theoretical behaviour of the equity market

In order to examine the more complex and complete forms of option pricing, it is therefore necessary to try to form a model for the behaviour of the share. Having accomplished this, estimates can then be placed against the possible outcomes that the market may take and a probability-weighted expected value for an option can then be constructed.

The first assumption is that stock markets are efficient, in that the share price at any point should incorporate the effects of all known data. This in turn implies that the share price tomorrow will depend on today's share price and on news as it breaks throughout the rest of today, but not on yesterday's share price as this is assumed to be already incorporated. The day-to-day movement in share prices is assumed to be governed by two factors – a constant underlying drift upwards at the risk-free interest rate and a constant element of random "noise" introduced by the uncertainty of the markets and the supply of information. These, when expressed mathematically, give rise to the reasonably simple model for share price behaviour known as Brownian motion.

If the Brownian motion of share prices is taken for granted, the distribution of possible share price returns over any predetermined time period will turn out to be lognormal in nature – ie, the (natural) logarithm of the share return is normally distributed, with the mean approximately equal to the risk-free investment rate for the period over which data is sampled. This distribution has a number of interesting properties: for example, the share price can theoretically rise to any level, but can fall no lower than zero – limited liability. Also, over a short time-scale, the probability of the share price doubling is approximately the same as it halving – and the same for other similar changes of scale. These fit in reasonably well with our perceived view of the behaviour of stock markets.

The concept of volatility
A normal distribution function is defined by two parameters, its mean and standard deviation. The mean return for share prices – namely the risk-free rate – has already been defined, but not the standard deviation, which measures the level of dispersion of returns around the mean or, alternatively, the range of values that could be taken by a sample from the distribution within certain ranges of probability. In other words, standard deviation measures the uncertainty of movements in the stock markets. If the markets did nothing except rise (or indeed fall) at a constant rate, the returns over any period would be constant and therefore have a zero standard deviation. An option on such a predictable market would naturally be simple to value, as any future share price could be calculated with certainty. Once randomness is introduced, whether it be linked to macro-economic events or just to changes in sentiment, the future evolution of share prices can no longer be absolutely predicted and the best that can be done is to put probability bounds around possible outcomes. The standard deviation of the logarithm of share price returns is conventionally referred to as the "volatility" of the share price and is essential to the pricing and trading of equity option products.

Historic volatility
Volatility is quite simple to calculate on an historical basis, given a small degree of statistical knowledge. The first step is to determine the period of interest for the calculation. Having done this, the relevant share price data must be gathered and then cleaned up to remove the effects of dividend payments and scrip or rights issues in order to reduce all data to a common basis for calculation. The clean data is then transformed into samples from a normal distribution by deriving a new series of data points, each equal to the logarithm of the return generated between two successive share values. The familiar calculations of the mean and standard deviation of the sample can be applied to this new data series to derive mean return and volatility over the time period corresponding to the sampling frequency.

The mean return on a share can be simply compounded up or down to cover any time-scale desired. Volatility is scaled by multiplication or division by the square root of the factor concerned. Those familiar with the mathematics of probability distributions will realise that this is because it is the square of standard deviation (ie, the variance) that is linearly scaled, not the standard deviation itself. For example, many practitioners calculate volatility using daily data, comparing each trading day's close to the previous day's close, but actually think of volatility on an annualised basis. Such can be converted to an annual equivalent by multiplying by 15.87 (the square root of 250, being the approximate number of trading days in a year).

Once volatility has been calculated, it can be used to gain some idea of the spread of possible returns on a share for the time period under consideration. It is known from probability theory that approximately 68.3 per cent of random samples from a normal distribution lie in the area centred on the mean and bounded by plus or minus one standard deviation. Thus, if the annual mean return is 0.00 per cent and the annual volatility is 15.00 per cent, there is about a 68 per cent chance that the annual return will lie between −15 per cent and +15 per cent. Given this methodology, the probability that the share will end up in any range desired can be calculated; for example the probability that the same share return will lie between +15 per cent and +20 per cent is the probability that a sample taken from a normal distribution will lie between 1.00 and 1.33 standard deviations above the mean – a 6.7 per cent chance. Having achieved a useful model for share price movements (both in terms of assumptions made and simplicity of analysis), the probabilities generated can then be used in option pricing.

Pricing models

Option pricing models have usually been derived on an arbitrage-free basis. This means that it should not be possible to make risk-free profits from correctly priced options by creating a portfolio of these combined with cash and share positions – a not unreasonable assumption. Were this not the case, it would be possible to arbitrage the market, or just one trader, even if his model were used consistently and correctly. Once this is taken on board, option pricing is reduced to the fundamental task of creating a mechanism for maintaining a portfolio that can replicate the behaviour of the option, with the option's value being derived as the current value of that equivalent portfolio and hedged by setting it against the hedging portfolio.

Put-call parity – a crucial relationship

Consider the situation of an investor who owns shares and wishes to sell them. He can, of course, do this immediately or he can set up the following equivalent stratagem. He first sets a common strike price K, selling a call option with strike K and buying a put option with strike K, and a common expiry date at which the options may be exercised. He knows now that, one way or the other, he will be selling his shares at expiry for the strike price K. This must be the case because, if the share rises beyond K he has written a call option which will be exercised against him (the put option expiring worthless). If the share falls below K, the call option will expire worthless and he will have his bought put option that he can exercise and force the writer to buy his shares for K. If the share finishes exactly at K, he can then sell his shares in the market at the desired level (with both options now worthless). The investor is now certain that he will receive K in hand at the expiry of the options in return for the share, so he can immediately lend out the present value of K in anticipation of the event. Since the combination of a sold call, bought put and present value of the strike has exactly the same functional characteristics as a sold share position, the two must be worth the same. Hence:

$$S = C - P + Ke^{-rt}$$

This fundamental identity, called "put-call parity" can be demonstrated to be consistent with any arbitrage-free option pricing model.

Example: Put-call parity
Given:
- Current share price: 100
- Agreed common strike: 105
- Common option expiry: 1 year
- Annual volatility: 20 per cent
- Funding rate: 10 per cent (continuously compounded)

Results: Share price   100.00
         PV of common strike   95.00
         Black-Scholes call   10.52
         Black-Scholes put   5.52

and put-call parity is preserved, since 100 equals 95.00 plus 10.52 minus 5.52.

Black-Scholes model

The first widely used option pricing model employing this technique was published by Fischer Black and Myron Scholes[1]. Their model transforms the perceived behaviour of the equity market (lognormal distribution of returns) into a straightforward normal distribution in the same fashion as the previous historic volatility calculation, then applies the arbitrage-free approach to construct a safe hedging strategy over the life of the option. Since there is a constructed equivalent position for the option at each point, and in particular at the end of the option's life, the value of this position now is the value of the option. Due to the construction of the formula, it is only suitable to value options that can be exercised on a particular date – ie, "European" options. "American" options, that can be exercised at any point up to and including the expiry date, are not handled in the original paper.

The Black-Scholes formula for a European call option is as follows:

$$C = S.N(x) - Ke^{-rt}.N(x - v\sqrt{t})$$

$$x = \frac{\ln(S/K) + (r + v^2/2)t}{v\sqrt{t}}$$

Their formula for a European put option is as follows:

$$P = Ke^{-rt}.N(-x + v\sqrt{t}) - S.N(-x)$$

x = as above

All of the parameters in the Black-Scholes model are either current or readily available from the market, with the exception of volatility and, as can be seen, volatility has a direct effect on the value of an option. It goes without saying, therefore, that an accurate estimation of anticipated volatility levels is important to accurate pricing and risk management of options. However, the only directly observable volatility data is historic volatility calculated from previous share prices, which is not generally thought to be a good indicator of future behaviour. A better alternative seems to be to take account of the market's opinion as expressed in the price of options that already exist in the market. If an existing option can be found with terms similar to the option under consideration, it is possible to calculate the level of volatility required to set the value of this benchmark option equal to the market price. This "implied volatility" can then be applied to the new option in order to calculate its theoretical price.

There is much more to using options than being able to derive the correct price at a given time. If they are to be used in hedging operations, in sophisticated products or even as a way to take exposure to the underlying share, it is important to be able to gauge their responsiveness to moves in each of the variables used in pricing. This allows the calculation of the appropriate numbers of options required and their contribution to the risk of the overall portfolio.

Share price Since the final option value is dependent on the value of the share price at expiry, the value of the share today is obviously highly significant as it directly affects the probability that the share will end up in-the-money. The sensitivity of an option's value to movements in the underlying share price is called "delta", conventionally stated as an absolute increase (or decrease) per one point move in the share price.

Call delta = $N(x)$

Put delta = $1 - N(x)$

x = as above

Delta can vary between 0 and +1 for call options and 0 and –1 for puts. Where delta is near zero, the option is deep out-of-the-money and has a low value. Where delta is near ±1, the option is deep in-the-money. Its value is largely dictated by its value if immediately exercised, or "intrinsic" value, which obviously moves in line with the share price.

Strike price The further out of the money the strike price is moved from the current share price, the less likely exercise becomes. This in turn means that the option is worth less. Since the strike price of the option is set when terms are settled, it cannot vary during the life of the option and therefore is not usually considered as a risk parameter.

Volatility One useful way to look at an option is that the premium is being paid in return for being able to take on a one-way exposure. If the share price moves in the holder's favour then he will gain in direct proportion to the move. If it moves against him, he will lose a fixed, small amount. Therefore, on balance, high volatility will be to the holder's benefit as it may amplify his gains but cannot alter his potential loss.

Specifically, if the option is at-the-money, the holder stands to gain an unlimited amount if the share moves kindly and only risks losing his premium on the downside. If the option is deep out-of-the-money, the holder's only chance of any gain is to hope for a wild swing which is more likely with a high volatility share. If an option is deep in-the-money the holder should be fairly indifferent to volatility as his exposure to swings in the share price up and down is approximately the same. In a fashion similar to delta, volatility sensitivity is measured as the absolute change in the option's price for a given change in volatility. This sensitivity, commonly called "vega" (or "kappa" for purists who prefer consistently to use Greek letters), is relatively low for options well away from the money, rising to a peak near to the strike price, where volatility effects are more pronounced.

Call and put vega = $S\sqrt{t}.N'(x)$

x = as above

Interest rates An increase in interest rates will tend to increase the value of a call option and to decrease the value of a put. This is because one of the advantages of buying a call option is the right to defer payment of the strike price until sometime in the future and this advantage is more significant in a higher interest rate scenario. Similarly, a put option holder is deferring sale of a share into the future and therefore incurring an opportunity cost in not receiving the proceeds immediately. Any increase in interest rates will make this put option less attractive and therefore reduce its price. The sensitivity of an option to movements in interest rates is called "rho".

Time to expiry On first examination, bearing in mind the flexibility an option gives in making decisions, it might appear that an option with more time to expiry has more value than one with less. However, for a European put option, this rationalisation can be incorrect, especially in the case of one that is in-the-money. It is not possible to say that more time is necessarily better than less because comparisons are then being drawn between two different potential exercise dates in the future. There is no problem with a call option, because there are no "hidden costs" in holding a call; however, holding a put option means that the payment of strike price is being deferred into the future. This opportunity cost has to be factored in and means that long-dated, in-the-money European put options will decrease in value as the time to expiry is increased beyond a certain point. This problem does not apply to American put options, where the longer expiry option is functionally the same as the shorter option plus an additional bit of time at the end that, while it may have little value, can never be a hindrance or a cost.

Dividends In its pure form, the Black-Scholes formula makes no correction for share dividends, nor does it provide for early exercise of options. As many of the exchange-traded options and warrants are into dividend-paying shares and have at least partial American exercise features, it is obviously desirable to try to amend the Black-Scholes formula to take these into consideration.

Share dividends are future cash flows, with amount and likelihood of payment varying as the time horizon for payment increases. By comparison, the currency option "dividend equivalent" – the interest rate on the foreign currency – can be hedged as a simple yield, and the bond option "dividend equivalent" – the coupon – is paid in discrete pieces, but is fully known in advance and is hedgeable. Neither timing nor amount are known with certainty for equity dividends and since equity options generally have no insulation against dividends paid, this can have a significant effect on the value of the product.

The simplest method to correct for dividends is to use a continuously paid dividend yield as an approximation. This can be simply factored into the Black-Scholes model as an adjustment to the share price in the same way as the risk-free interest rate is used to present value the strike price. This exactly parallels the adjustment for the foreign currency interest rate commonly made in the currency options market. This method is most suitable for longer-dated equity options where one feels comfortable that dividends are likely to rise and fall in line with movements in the share price prevailing at that time. However, short-dated options will have dividends that may be known with some certainty and these will definitely not move around proportionally as the share price moves. Dividend yield-adjusted call option:

$$C = Se^{-dt}.N(x) - Ke^{-rt}.N(x - v\sqrt{t})$$

$$x = \frac{\ln(S/K) + ([r-d] + v^2/2)t}{v\sqrt{t}}$$

Another commonly used adjustment is to estimate the dividends that are due to be paid during the lifetime of the option. These are then present valued back to current money terms and subtracted from the share price before it is entered into the Black-Scholes formula. This is the method used by some short-term option traders as it reflects their perceived full knowledge of declared or probable dividends. This adjustment is less suitable for long-term options as dividends become more uncertain rather quickly as one looks into the future and it becomes less plausible to say that dividends will never depend on the share price at the time. It is also strictly necessary to adjust the volatility used in the Black-Scholes formula if this correction is carried out, to reflect the factor that the share price used in the formula is artificially small and so must be made artificially more volatile to preserve the overall pattern of behaviour (Hull[2]). Discrete dividend-adjusted call option:

$$C = S'.N(x) - Ke^{-rt}.N(x - v\sqrt{t})$$

$S' = S - PV$ (discrete dividends to be paid)

$$x = \frac{\ln(S'/K) + (r + v^2/2)t}{v\sqrt{t}}$$

Early exercise   Adjustments for American exercise in the Black-Scholes model are difficult. In order to understand this problem, it is necessary to understand which conditions need be satisfied for early exercise to be sensible. If these conditions cannot be satisfied, then early exercise adds no value and an American option has the same value as the corresponding European option. Conversely, if the conditions are very likely to be met, American options will be far more valuable than their more restrictive European counterparts.

Options can be intuitively considered to be made up of three components in combination: intrinsic value, volatility and funding. Intrinsic value refers to the amount (if any) that the option is in-the-money, volatility refers to the value that the option derives from the value of being able to defer the exercise decision because of the uncertainty in the markets, and funding refers to the costs or benefits of holding the option, a call option allowing delay in paying the strike price and a put delaying the receipt of the strike price. These three components combine in a complex manner to give the actual value of the option as a net result. If an option is exercised early, the intrinsic value is immediately taken out and crystallised, at the cost of losing the value of the other two factors and the question as to whether such exercise is merited is settled by establishing whether taking the intrinsic value now is better or worse than hanging on until later.

In the case of an American call option, all three factors are normally beneficial to the holder. He is entitled to the intrinsic value on exercise and benefits from both volatility and funding considerations in the interim period. It will therefore only be worth the holder exercising if he will be recompensed for the loss of funding and volatility benefits by taking the intrinsic value at that time rather than later. Therefore, in order to find where early exercise might be profitable, the periods to be examined are those where the intrinsic value of the option is under risk from abrupt and anticipated decreases in value. This only occurs when a discrete dividend is paid, as the share price and therefore the intrinsic value of the option decreases. If this anticipated loss of intrinsic value is more than the possible loss of volatility and funding benefits on exercise, then early exercise is indicated.

Given that the decision to exercise an American call option is only ever considered just before each point at which the share stops trading with a dividend entitlement included (on each "ex-dividend" date), an approximation to the theoretical value can be generated via a series of Black-Scholes calculations that reflect values around each ex-dividend date and then, because the holder can choose on which date to exercise, take the highest value. The first option to be valued expires a fraction before the first ex-dividend date. This option reflects the value if exercised at that point and therefore no dividends are used in the calculation. The second calculation is the valuation of an option expiring just before the second ex-dividend date. This reflects the value assuming exercise then and the option value is naturally corrected for the first dividend only, as the second has not yet been paid. This process is continued for each dividend payment with the cumulative dividend subtractions increasing and the final Black-Scholes calculation assumes the last exercise decision to be at the final expiry of the option. Each of the values derived are examined and the option value is taken as the highest of these. This "pseudo-American" option correction works best for short-dated options with relatively few dividends and is viewed as a lower bound to the value of the option.

The position with respect to American put options is even more clouded. The three factors mentioned before do not now work in harmony. The option holder benefits again from intrinsic value on exercise and from volatility, but funding works against him. If a put option is sufficiently deep in-the-money, the funding costs of holding the position may become so expensive as to force early exercise. Because this phenomenon is not directly dependent on dividend payment dates (indeed dividend payments tend to mitigate this tendency), the pseudo-American correction cannot safely be used for put options.

In order to best look at the possibilities for American exercise of options, it is necessary to test the exercise decision on a frequent basis. The Black-Scholes formula allows for a one-off decision to be made while the pseudo-American construction allows for several decisions to made but independently, without considering the mutual effect that they have on each other. Unfortunately, the actual decisions to be made are not truly independent and so what is really required is a way to split down the consideration of time in the Black-Scholes formula into small discrete pieces and to construct a share price behaviour model that can show the distribution of share prices at each of these points in time. The model could then decide whether exercise was optimal at each point in time, which would work for both put and call options. A useful side-effect would be the added flexibility that this model would provide for dividend treatment and complex options.

Binomial model

In order to proceed from the continuous Black-Scholes model to a discrete time model that can cope with the requirements above, a discrete binomial distribution function can be substituted for the continuous normal function. The binomial function assumes that, at each point, the share price faces an independent decision whether to rise or to fall. If these steps are calculated on a daily basis, a 100-day option will face 100 choices, in a fashion somewhat similar to a person tossing a coin 100 times. It is therefore straightforward, in theory, to calculate the probability of each possible outcome occurring, whether one is dealing with the occurrence of heads or a possible share price at any time, not solely at expiry.

The binomial tree is constructed using the following definitions, which are designed to ensure the tree has approximately the same mean growth rate and volatility as the underlying share price. These approximations are quite rough for a small number of steps, improving in quality as the tree is constructed with more.

$$\text{Growth} = e^{t/n}$$

$$\text{Upstep} = e^{v\sqrt{t/n}}$$

$$\text{Downstep} = \frac{1}{\text{Upstep}}$$

$$P\{u\} = \frac{\text{Growth} - \text{Downstep}}{\text{Upstep} - \text{Downstep}}$$

$P\{d\} = 1 - P\{u\}$

Generation of the binomial tree is now straightforward. If the current share price is denoted by S, an upwards move in the market by u and a downwards move by d, the share can move to Su or Sd in one step. For two steps, the share price can move in one of four ways: Suu, Sud, Sdu, Sdd. From the defined formulae above, it is evident that Sud and Sdu are actually the same (perhaps equivalent to tossing a head then a tail, or a tail then a head on a coin). Similarly there are a total of eight paths that can be taken over three time steps, but when grouped they only result in four possible share prices:

Suuu	*Suud*	*Sudd*	*Sddd*
	Sudu	*Sdud*	
	Sduu	*Sddu*	

and so it continues. After n steps, there will be $n+1$ possible share prices. The value of each node can be calculated exactly along with the probability of arriving there and the expected pay-off of the product can therefore be established. The generalised formulae for the share prices and probabilities are as follows. Share price realised given i upward and $n-i$ downward moves:

$$= Su^i d^{n-i}$$

$$\text{Probability} = \frac{n!}{i!(n-i)!} \cdot P\{u\}^i \cdot P\{d\}^{n-i}$$

Example: Value of a three-day European call option on a three-step binomial tree

Given:
- Current share price — 100
- Strike price — 100
- Volatility — 20 per cent (annual)
- Funding rate — 10 per cent (continuously compounded)
- Time to expiry — 3 days
- Time per step — 1 day

Calculate:
- upstep — 1.01052
- downstep — 0.98959
- growth — 1.00027
- p(upstep) — 51.047 per cent
- p(downstep) — 48.953 per cent

Outcomes:

	Share price	Exercise value	Probability	Probability-weighted
Assuming three upticks and no downticks	103.1904	3.1904	13.30%	0.4244
Assuming two upticks and one downtick	101.0523	1.0523	38.27%	0.4027

Assuming one uptick and two downticks	98.9586	0.0000	36.70%	0.0000
Assuming no upticks and three downticks	96.9083	0.0000	11.73%	0.0000

Value: totalling the probability-weighted column and present valuing the result gives 0.8264.

Since the binomial tree as derived comes from the same assumptions as the Black-Scholes model but via a slightly different route, it should give the same results when used on the same data, although there is room for deviation in the fact that the discrete binomial distribution is just an approximation to the continuous normal distribution, especially when relatively few steps are used. The example given above is merely an illustration and would be hopelessly inadequate for serious purposes due to the coarseness of the grid. It is usually necessary to employ between 50 and 200 steps for an accurate calculation of the option price and even then there may be discrepancies of a per cent or so on the price of an option.

American exercise can be incorporated into the binomial tree method rather easily, though it will substantially increase calculation time. The possible share prices at all stages, not just at expiry, are generated using the above formulae. In the example above that would result in two prices generated after the first step, three more after the second and four after the third – nine prices in all. The intrinsic value of the option is known with certainty at each of the four possible final share prices and can be used to start to work backwards through the earlier parts of the tree. At each earlier share price, the value of the option if immediately exercised (being its intrinsic value at that point) is compared with the value of the option if it were to continue to be held unexercised, calculated by taking the probability-weighted sum of the two possible outcomes from that point (allowing for funding costs). The higher of the two values is a reflection of the correct value at that stage and can be taken back in successive steps through previous stages until the process finishes back at today. The option value is then taken to be the price finally determined at the end of this process.

Monte Carlo simulation

Monte Carlo simulation is the method of choice among practitioners for many complex instruments and portfolios which present problems that are difficult or impossible to solve using formulae or tree techniques. Rather than constructing a complex mathematical structure to capture all possible outcomes, suitably weighted by probability of occurrence, a computer program is written that can simulate the random evolution of the share price through time, actually using Brownian motion directly. This program then monitors the potential share prices generated and, once the option is exercised or expires, calculates the final pay-off that would have been made. This process is repeated many times, with different share price paths and all the resulting pay-offs are averaged out.

The only difficult part in this is to write down the expression for the relationship between yesterday's share price and today's:

$$S_{tomorrow} = S_{today}e^{(r - v^2/2)\Delta t + v\varepsilon\sqrt{\Delta t}}$$

Δt = the time difference between today and tomorrow

ε = a sample from a standard normal distribution

The main difficulties with Monte Carlo simulation are the large computation times (even on a fast computer, 10,000 possible evolutions of a share price over a year take a long time) and making sure that the random number generation used is up to scratch (Morgan[3]). All random number generators commonly used on computers are cyclical, with random numbers repeating after a certain number of iterations, and one that starts to repeat too quickly is effectively useless, potentially generating systematic patterns in the share price generation process.

Concerns

Many practitioners are concerned that the simple Brownian motion model of the market does not reflect certain important aspects of its true behaviour, pointing to two important phenomena that arise when using conventional option models. First, implied volatilities charged by the market are often relatively high for deep in-the-money options compared to the level at-the-money (the "smile" effect). Secondly, volatilities that appear to be charged for puts and calls at the same strike and with the same expiry may be very different. These are both disturbing features as the implied volatility should be telling us something about the volatility of the underlying share market, which should not vary from option to option. Consequently, the implied volatility of puts, calls, out-, at- and in-the-money options should just be windows on to the same landscape, not different pictures altogether.

The pricing and implied volatility calculations are only ever as good as the model used to generate them, and that model relies on the assumptions it makes about the underlying market. Many practitioners feel that the Brownian motion model underestimates the probability of sudden large moves in the market (the "fat tails" or "kurtosis" theory) and/or feel that the distribution of share price returns is biased in some way ("skewing"). These, and more elaborate share price models, can be developed into option pricing models that attempt to capture this perceived behaviour. These are obviously capable of explaining the phenomenon that they seek to address, but each is more complex, has more parameters to estimate and none is in as wide usage as the Black-Scholes and binomial models.

Conclusions

Forecasting movements in world stock markets seems incredibly difficult, and for good reason. Derivatives are a useful class of instruments to manage risks selectively, immunising one's portfolio against difficult or unfamiliar risk or increasing risk in the hope of higher returns.

In order to use derivatives, however, one needs to understand something of their pricing and management. The adherents of the efficient market hypotheses claim, with some common sense, that any model that can be used to predict the movements in the market will soon become obsolete if if becomes widely known, as instrument prices will react so as to take its predictions into account. Presumably there are therefore many systems under development using new techniques designed to convey an advantage, each of which may have a limited useful life before, in its turn, becoming part of common market practice. Each innovation, building on those that go before, adds value in its own fashion and each allows the user of derivatives to understand his position slightly more clearly.

Notes

[1] Black, Fischer and Scholes, Myron (1973). The pricing of options and corporate liabilities, *Journal of Political Economy*, 81 (May–June), 637–659.

[2] Hull, John (1989). *Options, futures and other derivative securities*, Prentice-Hall International. See also Hull (1991). *Introduction to futures and options markets*, Prentice-Hall International.

[3] Morgan, Byron J.T. (1984). *Elements of simulation*, Chapman and Hall, London.

8

Regulatory and documentation overview

Andrew Roberts[1]
Linklaters & Paines

Jeffrey B. Golden and Joseph P. Stevens[2]
Cravath, Swaine & Moore

Background to the UK regulatory environment

Unlike other jurisdictions (notably the US), there is in the UK no separation of the regulatory function between securities business and commodity and financial derivatives trading. Equity derivatives are treated merely as a sub-set of the large range of financial products governed by the UK regulatory system set up under the Financial Services Act 1986 (the "FSA"). In general, the system applies to equity (and other) derivatives as it does to underlying securities but there is in some instances effectively an additional layer of regulation specifically targeted at derivatives.

The FSA set up a new framework for regulation of "investment business", the definition of which covers both securities and derivatives activities. The FSA provided for the establishment of The Securities and Investments Board ("SIB"), a non-statutory body responsible, subject to the supervision of HM Treasury, for the operation of the FSA. Persons carrying on "investment business" in the UK require authorisation under the FSA. This is generally obtained by acquiring membership of one of the self-regulating organisations ("SROs") recognised by the SIB.

The SIB in its 1991–92 report stated that the role of the regulatory system as a whole is: "... the promotion of high standards of investor protection and integrity throughout the investment business industry." The report also went on to state that the SIB believes that this role should be pursued in a way which: "... is cost-effective, maintains confidence in the UK as a place to do business, has proper regard to the well-being of the financial services industry and is responsive to the public and its needs."

---

[1] Andrew Roberts wrote the first part of this chapter covering the regulation of equity derivatives in the UK and their fiscal treatment in the UK, US and France.

[2] Jeffrey B. Golden and Joseph P. Stevens wrote the concluding part of this chapter covering documentation, containing the practitioner's guide to the ISDA confirmation for OTC equity index option transactions.

General approach

In order to obtain authorisation to conduct investment business, a firm must show that it meets various prudential requirements, often summarised as "honesty, solvency and competence". The firm will also be subject to detailed conduct of business requirements in its dealings with investors. These requirements are designed to achieve the aim of investor protection and integrity, and a number of different regulatory techniques are employed, depending on the type of product, the type of firm and the type of investor concerned. The aim is to identify the main risks involved in the relevant transaction and to take appropriate steps to minimise those risks.

In relation to derivatives, the main areas of risk can be viewed as the following:

1 *Counterparty default* – the risk that the other party to a transaction cannot or will not perform.
2 *Position deterioration* – the risk that the transaction will cause substantial loss to the investor.

Most of the protective mechanisms integral to the regulatory system can be identified as falling within one of these two heads. As an illustration of this, Exhibit 8.1 sets out the principal features of the regulatory system (in conceptual terms) categorised according to the risks they are designed to safeguard against. The concepts set out in the table will be further discussed below when looking at the implementation of the regulations in the UK.

The notion of investor protection must be qualified by the extent to which particular types of investors need protection. Since "investors" can range from the smallest and most inexperienced individual investor, through large corporations, to a sophisticated securities firm, unlike the approach in the US, the regulatory system in the UK has given different levels of protection to each type of investor. The inexperienced individual is unlikely to be able to withstand large losses like a large corporation, nor understand the securities markets, particularly derivative markets, like the sophisticated securities firm. Hence the private individual investor has been given protection additional to that afforded to business investors or market professionals. In fact, it is not only private individual investors who are entitled to the additional protection – small businesses that, by virtue of their size, are not regarded as sufficiently able to

Exhibit 8.1 The regulatory system and risk

Counterparty default	*Position deterioration*
Authorisation (fitness and properness) requirements	Marketing rules – (investment and advertisements and unsolicited calls
Client money rules	Risk warnings
Capital adequacy	Marketing restrictions
Market integrity	Best advice and suitability
Disclosure	Reports and valuations
Margin requirements	
Clearing houses	
Default rules	

withstand large losses, are also often treated as private customers for regulatory purposes unless they are dealing in investments relevant to their main business (eg, a gold producer dealing in gold futures).

Derivatives – special cases?
Derivatives have three particular characteristics which the regulatory system has recognised as making them potentially riskier investments than underlying securities. They are:

1. *Complexity* – their value, and the factors that affect their value, are far more complex than underlying securities. There will be a considerable differential as between knowledge and understanding of risk as between a derivatives dealer and his customer.
2. *Potential loss* – there are two aspects to this, volatility and gearing. For underlying securities the loss will generally be no greater than the purchase price and indeed 100 per cent loss will not occur except in exceptional circumstances – typically business failure by the issuer. Additionally, while sharp declines upon the announcement of severe adverse information do occur, generally the speed of decline of a share price is slower than that of an equity derivative, giving an investor the opportunity to cut the losses. The potential loss on some derivatives, however, can exceed the initial payment made so that an investor is required to provide further funds, and the amount of loss can be unlimited.
3. *Liquidity* – although this is less the case as time passes and the derivatives markets become more widely used, there may be less liquidity in the exchange-traded derivatives markets than in the exchange-traded equity (or debt) markets, and of course even less in the customised over-the-counter ("OTC") derivatives markets. This may mean that the unwinding of positions takes longer, and the costs are higher. The ability to unwind positions may also be affected by market lock-out rules on an exchange.

Accordingly, the extra protection that the regulatory system provides as regards derivatives is based on minimising the above risks, and especially so with respect to private investors and, to the extent that they cannot be minimised, ensuring that investors are given adequate information and warnings of the risks involved. In the main, the regulation of equity derivatives *vis-à-vis* non-private investors is not significantly stricter than the regulation of the underlying equities.

As stated above, derivatives are "potentially" risky investments. It is important to note, however, that this is not necessarily the case. It all depends on the type of derivative used and the purpose for which it is used. Conventional exchange-traded futures and options utilised for hedging (rather than speculative purposes) need be no more risky to an investor than an equivalent position in the underlying security. Indeed, appropriate hedging of a portfolio with derivatives is designed to reduce the overall risk profile. For this reason, derivatives can have conflicting characteristics. The regulatory system must ensure that investor protection is given where it is appropriate but that where it is unnecessary, the efficient operation of the market is not hampered by unduly restrictive rules.

Summary
From the securities industry's point of view, regulation is perceived as stifling and costly. However, from the government's point of view investor losses are unpopular and costly. The system's early mandate tended to focus more on investor protection

without true regard to the costs of regulation. This led to a complex (and sometimes unworkable) web of regulation, in many instances restricting activities more than was probably ever envisaged. Over time, more exceptions and qualifications have been granted, regulators are now required to have regard to the cost of compliance with new rules as balanced against the benefits to be obtained and there has been an attempt to simplify the SIB and SRO rulebooks. However, these initiatives have had only very limited effects on easing the burden of regulation. Indeed over recent months, concerns have been raised that the present system is not providing enough investor protection and that more attention needs to be focused on enforcement (whether in the context of the existing system or as part of a new regulatory regime involving an "SEC-style" principal regulator as some have suggested). The fact that equity derivatives are beginning to be marketed more widely to the retail public may lead to further concerns being expressed by the regulators in the future.

The regulatory system

The UK regulatory system is based on a functional rather than an institutional approach. That is, one entity that performs different functions may need to be simultaneously regulated by a number of different regulators. Clearly there is scope for confusion and duplication, but in general there is, amongst the regulators, an attitude of co-operation. On financial regulatory matters, often they will agree on a "lead regulator" which takes primary responsibility for the capital position of the entity but which shares information with the other regulator(s). Nevertheless, on conduct of business matters a firm which is a member of more than one SRO must comply with the rules of whichever SRO's regulatory scope covers the relevant activities. It is not generally necessary to comply with the rules of more than one SRO in relation to a particular item of business.

Duplication of regulation is also avoided so far as the Banking Act 1987 is concerned, by a specific exemption which ensures that deposits taken for the purposes of investment transactions do not fall within the Banking Act. However, this does not change the fact that a financial services group dealing in equities, debt, derivatives, life insurance and accepting deposits and making loans can be subject to direct regulation under at least four financial services statutes – namely the FSA, the Banking Act, the Insurance Companies Act 1982 ("ICA"), and the Consumer Credit Act 1974 ("CCA"). Indeed, these are currently the four principal sources of regulation in the UK. As the various Directives relating to financial services adopted by the European Commission are implemented in the UK, the European Community will become an increasingly important source of law and jurisprudence in this area.

In the area of equity derivatives it is unlikely that the Banking Act, ICA or CCA will have much impact. The principal concern will be the FSA, as amended in the future by EC Directives. However, it is worth noting that some financial products which are similar in economic effect to equity derivatives may be structured so as to be regulated under the Banking Act (index-linked deposit accounts) or as insurance policies regulated under the ICA, such as a capital bond the return on which is index-linked.

In addition to the FSA regime, exchange-traded equity derivatives will attract further regulation by way of the rules of the relevant exchanges. Equity derivatives, depending upon their precise nature, can be traded on the International Stock Exchange of the United Kingdom and the Republic of Ireland Limited (the "London Stock Exchange"), or the London International Financial Futures and Options

Exchange ("LIFFE"). Equity warrants and convertible debt may be traded on the London Stock Exchange (although they are more normally traded off-exchange on the inter-dealer market), whereas all other exchange-traded equity derivatives (equity options, index-linked futures such as FT-SE contracts and other index-linked derivatives) are traded on LIFFE. Space does not permit a detailed analysis of the requirements of these exchanges, but it should be noted that, in some instances, the regulatory system under the FSA differentiates between exchange-traded and OTC products.

Of particular significance in the regulatory context are the LIFFE rules requiring LIFFE members to provide margin in respect of transactions on the exchange, and for transactions to be guaranteed by the clearing house. On a default by a LIFFE member, the default rules provide for closing out of all the member's transactions and for netting of all transactions with each counterparty, with the clearing house applying margin provided by the defaulter to cover any net balance due to the clearing house. These rules are all designed to minimise the risk of default, and to prevent the failure of one member leading to a systematic market default.

The FSA regime
Scope
The FSA was passed in 1986 and the principal regulatory provisions came into operation on 29 April 1988. The FSA is extremely complex and raises a number of difficult issues. However, the principal areas covered by the FSA are as follows:

1. The establishment of the regulatory structure.
2. The prohibition of carrying on investment business other than by authorised or exempted persons.
3. The regulation of collective investment schemes. Although these include conventional unit trusts, they also embrace other arrangements, even where underlying assets other than "investments" for the purpose of the FSA are involved.
4. The regulation of the conduct of investment business by authorised persons (and, in relation to "misleading statements and practices", "cold calling" and "investment advertisements", regulation also of the conduct of others).
5. Listing particulars in relation to admission of securities to official listing on the London Stock Exchange (Part IV) and prospectuses in relation to public offers of "unlisted" securities, including stocks listed on foreign stock exchanges (Part V). Until Part V of the FSA is brought into force, which is unlikely to be before mid-1993, the prospectus provisions of the Companies Act continue to apply to offers of unlisted shares or debentures.
6. Miscellaneous provisions dealing with organisational structure, enforcement, etc.

The regulators
Many of the powers which the FSA gives in the first instance to the Secretary of State (ie, HM Treasury) have been delegated to the SIB. These include powers to make rules and regulations, power to confer authorisation on various categories of person, power to recognise other regulators for the purposes of the FSA and various enforcement powers.

Much of the regulatory burden under the FSA falls upon self-regulating organisations ("SROs") recognised by the SIB, with different SROs regulating different types of investment business. Practitioners have a say in the scheme of regulation since the governing bodies of SROs comprise a mixture of representatives of regulated businesses and outsiders representing the public interest.

SROs are required to provide appropriate investor safeguards and to demonstrate an adequate monitoring and enforcement capability in relation to their members.

The principal SRO in relation to equity derivatives is The Securities and Futures Authority ("SFA") which is primarily concerned with dealing and advisory businesses relating to securities, futures, options and contracts for differences. To a lesser extent, The Investment Management Regulatory Organisation ("IMRO") – primarily concerned with investment management activities, including the operation of unit trusts and other collective investment schemes – and the Financial Intermediaries, Managers and Brokers Regulatory Association ("FIMBRA") – primarily concerned with the regulation of independent intermediaries, excluding market-makers and brokers or dealers in futures and contracts for differences – are relevant.

Following a review of retail regulation in the UK by the SIB, proposals are underway for the establishment of a single SRO to regulate investment products aimed at retail investors, to be known as the Personal Investment Authority.

Securities firms involved in equity derivatives will be members of the SFA. Investment managers and operators of collective investment schemes such as futures and options funds and geared futures and options funds will be members of IMRO. FIMBRA members, whose customers are predominantly private investors, are greatly restricted in their involvement with equity derivatives, but can market them to a limited degree.

Members of SROs must be fit and proper to carry on the investment business concerned. A person who is so authorised is authorised for all purposes of the FSA. However, in most cases, he will be allowed by his SRO to engage only in certain types of investment business. Individual employees of an authorised firm do not themselves need to be authorised. However, SFA requires that those who advise clients or commit the firm to dealings should be registered with SFA and to do so must demonstrate their personal fitness and properness. Various categories of registration are possible, the most relevant to equity derivatives being the General Representative Category and the Futures and Options Representative Category. Both require the representative to have passed the relevant SFA examination or to have secured exemption either by overseas qualification or continuous experience in the market pre-dating the FSA.

The need for authorisation
Section 3 of the FSA provides that no person may carry on "investment business" in the United Kingdom unless he is either an authorised person or an exempted person.

Exempted persons, who enjoy exemption only in relation to their exempt activities, include recognised investment exchanges (which include the London Stock Exchange and LIFFE) and recognised clearing houses such as the London Clearing House. The Bank of England regulates the short-term money market pursuant to Section 43 and Schedule 5 to the FSA under which market-makers and dealers whose names appear on a list maintained by the Bank of England are exempted persons in respect of their dealings in the money markets. However, this exemption applies only to certain types of investments and although some derivatives in relation to currencies and money market investments are included, equity-based derivatives are not.

If a person carries on investment business without being authorised or exempted, two consequences follow. First, he commits a criminal offence. Secondly, any agreement entered into by him is unenforceable and any money paid or property transferred to him can be recovered by the other party who can also receive compensation for losses suffered, unless the Court orders otherwise.

Under the FSA, "investment business" means carrying on the business of engaging in one or more of certain specified activities. A person has to ask himself four questions:

1. Do his activities involve FSA "investments"? Equity derivatives fall within the definition of investments.
2. If so, are those activities FSA "investment activities"? Buying, selling or granting options, futures or rights would generally constitute investment activities.
3. If so, are there any applicable exclusions? See below.
4. If not, do they constitute the carrying on of a business in the United Kingdom?

FSA "investment activities" (question 2) are dealing in investments (ie, buying or selling, or granting any rights – eg an option – whether as principal or agent), arranging deals in investments, managing investments, giving investment advice, and establishing, operating or winding-up collective investment schemes. The definitions are rather wide, so that it is often more important to look at the exclusions as well as the interpretation provisions in Part V of Schedule 1.

The exclusions (ie, question 3) are relevant for determining whether or not a person carries on investment business but they are not necessarily relevant in determining whether other provisions (misleading practices and statements, cold calling and investment advertisements) of the FSA apply. The exclusions are complex and different exclusions apply to different investment activities. None of the exclusions apply to establishing, operating or winding-up collective investment schemes in the United Kingdom.

The exclusions, as relevant to equity derivatives, include dealing as principal (but not in the case of professional dealers), activities within corporate groups, and activities by overseas persons (ie, persons carrying on investment activities into the UK from overseas and not from a permanent place of business in the UK) with or for professionals or large institutions. However, as with other parts of the FSA, there are many complex conditions which need to be satisfied before an exclusion can apply.

It is, perhaps, worth noting that the FSA's terminology does not, in all respects, accord with terminology used in the market. The SFA Rules define "derivatives" as those investments falling within paragraphs 7, 8 or 9 of Schedule 1 to the FSA (entitled respectively "options", "futures" and "contracts for differences"). The term does not, therefore, include convertible bonds although anomalously it seems to cover exchangeable bonds (since these would fall within the definition of an "option"). Similarly, it does not cover an equity warrant entitling the holder to subscribe for the issuer's equity but does include a covered warrant which, in FSA terms, is an option. It should also be noted that contracts which either by agreement or by their very nature are to be cash settled will normally amount to "contracts for differences" irrespective of what they are called. Accordingly, an index option is not, in FSA terminology, an option at all but rather a contract for a difference. Similarly, whilst, as mentioned above, an equity warrant is not generally a derivative, if that warrant is to be cash-settled rather than settled by physical delivery, it becomes a contract for differences and hence a derivative. The regulations do, therefore, present ample opportunity for confusion. Indeed it is very difficult to see why the FSA treats equity warrants as not being derivatives in the first place. They exhibit most of the characteristics of other derivative instruments in terms of volatility and gearing, and similar risk warnings are required in respect of them under the SRO rules. Fortunately, the only distinction of major relevance is that between derivatives and non-derivatives. If an instrument is a derivative (ie, within paragraph 7, 8 or 9 of Schedule 1 to the FSA) it generally does not matter in terms of regulation which of those paragraphs it falls within.

Implementation of the regulations

Persons authorised by the SIB or through membership of an SRO are required to comply with the rulebook of the SIB or the relevant SRO, which rulebooks must comply with certain statutory requirements. The FSA regime contemplates three tiers of regulation of authorised persons. First, there are "statements of principle" issued by the SIB which apply to all authorised persons. Secondly, there are "core rules" issued by the SIB designated to apply to members of all the SROs. These cover conduct of business, financial resources, safeguarding of clients' money and unsolicited calls. Such core rules are supported by "third tier" rules issued by individual SROs adapting and supplementing the core rules in the context of business regulated by those SROs. The rulebooks as a whole are required to provide "adequate" investor protection.

Breach of the core rules and third tier rules, like breach of the SIB statements of principle, has disciplinary consequences (including, in an extreme case, loss of authorisation). Contraventions of such rules (but not the principles) may also be actionable at the suit of persons who suffer loss as a result of the contravention but, with limited exceptions, rights of action are confined to private investors. A more detailed discussion of the rules relating to derivatives is contained in the "SRO rulebooks and equity derivatives" section below.

The SIB has also established an Investors Compensation Scheme ("ICS") funded by levies from authorised persons. The ICS provides compensation of up to £48,000 for private investors who suffer loss as the result of the insolvent default of an authorised person. Rules have also been made by the SIB conferring cancellation rights on certain investors who acquire, amongst other things, units in publicly marketable collective investment schemes. These rules apply both to persons directly authorised by the SIB and to members of SROs.

There are three important regulatory safeguards in the FSA which apply not only to authorised persons, but to everyone. These are:

1 *Misleading statements and practices*: Section 47 of the FSA creates criminal offences designed to catch misleading inducements to deal in investments, and market manipulation. (Note that because "market manipulation" could catch stabilisation carried out in relation to offerings of investments, the SIB has made rules governing the conduct of stabilisation activity which provide a safe harbour for stabilisation in conformity with the rules. The provisions are an attempt to ensure that adequate disclosure is made before investment decisions are made. However, only certain types of issue may be stabilised. These include equity warrants and convertibles but other equity derivatives are largely excluded.)

2 *Cold calling*: except as permitted by the Unsolicited Calls Regulations ("UCRs") made by the SIB, no person may in the course of or in consequence of an unsolicited call made in or from the UK induce the person called to enter into an agreement relating to FSA investments. Authorised persons are normally also subject to SROs' rules governing the conduct of permitted calls on private investors. There is no general ability to make unsolicited calls on private investors in relation to equity-derivatives although authorised persons can in certain circumstances make such calls on their existing private customers.

3 *Investment advertisements*: by Section 57 of the FSA, no person other than an authorised person may issue or cause to be issued an investment advertisement

in the United Kingdom unless its contents have been approved by an authorised person or unless some exemption applies. Broadly, an investment advertisement means any advertisement inviting persons to enter into an agreement relating to FSA investments, to exercise any rights conferred by an investment or containing information calculated to lead directly or indirectly to persons doing so. Advertisement" includes any form of advertising, for example, screen-based advertising.

Looking in more detail at the investment advertisements safeguard, breach of Section 57 is a criminal offence, the agreement is unenforceable by the guilty party and the other side can recover any money or property transferred under the agreement, plus compensation (subject to the court ordering otherwise). An overseas person which is in breach of the restrictions on advertising may thereby forfeit its exclusion from the need to be authorised.

A number of exemptions from Section 57 are contained both in the FSA and in statutory instruments made under it. In the context of equity derivatives, the most important exemption is for advertisements issued to specified types of investors who are regarded as sufficiently expert to understand the risks involved. This applies to advertisements issued to authorised persons, exempted persons and large companies which are non-private investors for the purposes of the FSA. There is also an exemption for advertisements which are directed only at informing certain types of person (primarily those involved in the investment industry rather than end-investors).

Prospectuses and listing particulars, being subject to regulation in their own right, are also exempt from the advertising rules. Generally, where an advertisement is exempt and so could be issued by an unauthorised person, if the person issuing it is actually an authorised person, the advertisement will not be subject to the advertisement content requirements of that person's SRO referred to below.

Authorised persons who issue or approve investment advertisements are generally subject to detailed conduct of business rules, imposed by their SROs. Generally, the Rules specify certain types of advertisement which may not be issued and, for those types which can be issued, impose obligations of due diligence and verification as well as requiring that certain mandatory contents are included in the advertisement – for example, in the context of equity derivatives, risk warnings as to the volatility of the product.

Collective investment schemes
The FSA provisions dealing with collective investment schemes are principally directed at mutual funds such as unit trusts and other similar collective investment vehicles (including open-ended investment companies but not conventional closed-ended investment companies). Although funds investing in equity derivatives exist, detailed consideration of the regulation of mutual funds is outside the scope of this chapter.

SRO rulebooks and equity derivatives
Introduction   As mentioned above, the main SRO relevant to equity derivatives is the SFA. Its rules contain a number of provisions relating specifically to derivatives, some of which are SIB core rules and are therefore reflected also in the rulebooks of the other SROs. Generally, the rulebook does not distinguish between "equity derivatives" and other types of derivatives. The only relevant distinction between derivatives is between those which are, and those which are not, "contingent liability transactions" – that is to say a transaction under which the investor is, or may be, required to

pay an additional amount at settlement (other than charges). Accordingly, futures transactions and written options are contingent liability transactions as are most contracts for differences (such as equity index options or equity swaps). However, a purchased option would not be a contingent liability transaction since the holder is not obliged to exercise it and will only do so if he considers it profitable at the time. He is therefore not bound to pay any sum over and above the initial premium paid.

In addition to the distinction between private and non-private investors and between contingent liability and other transactions, SRO rules are also specifically tailored to the particular degree of investor protection required by distinctions between contracts traded on recognised investment exchanges and those not so traded (ie, OTC options and those traded on unrecognised exchanges). This is because the requirements for recognition as an investment exchange themselves require certain investor protections to be built into the rules of that exchange. Margined and non-margined contracts are also distinguished, those undertaken on a margined basis requiring much greater disclosure – although it is arguable that the key issue ought not to be margin but rather gearing. Hedging transactions and purely speculative transactions are also distinguished in some cases given that hedging implies a lesser degree of risk.

Conduct of business rules   The rules applicable to conduct of business are, broadly, as follows:
– Direct offer advertisements (those where the reader can invest by completing and tearing out the application form and sending in the appropriate funds) cannot be issued to private investors in relation to derivatives. The purpose is, essentially, to ensure that such investors cannot commit themselves to riskier, more complex products on the basis of a one-way document and without the benefit of further advice.
– Before a firm begins making unsolicited calls on private investors in respect of riskier products such as futures and options funds, geared futures and options funds (but not other types of derivatives) it must satisfy the SFA as to various compliance and supervision matters.
– In general, a firm intending to provide services to a private customer in relation to contingent liability transactions must do so under a two-way customer agreement – ie, one which the customer has signed and sent back (as opposed to merely notifying the customer of the terms of business, which it can do in other instances) and which the firm is satisfied the customer has had a proper opportunity to consider.
– Firms must not effect margined transactions for private customers unless the firm reasonably believes that the customer fully understands the concept of margin and the consequences of failure to meet margin calls and the circumstances in which the customer's position may be closed out other than on failure to provide margin.
– Before a firm provides any services to most private customers in relation to warrants or derivatives, it must send to the customer specified risk warning notices, and receive signed copies back, and be satisfied that the customer has had a proper opportunity to consider their terms.
– There are various specific confirmation details that must be sent to customers after derivatives trades have been effected for them, or options have been exercised for or against them. These aim to ensure that the investor is kept apprised of his open positions.
– Periodic valuation reports must be sent to customers for whom the firm acts as investment manager, and for derivatives, the required frequency of and details in such reports are greater than for other securities.

- Firms may only effect, arrange or recommend OTC contingent liability derivatives transactions for private customers if the firm reasonably believes that the purpose of the transaction is to hedge the currency risk of a customer's position. Otherwise, all derivatives deals for private customers must be on-exchange.
- In addition, the SIB's rules on the holding of client money, and the capital requirements of firms, are incorporated into the SFA rulebook. There are special provisions in each case in relation to derivatives. In the case of client money, there is a requirement that special accounts be set up and used for margin transactions, and OTC margin transactions (because they are not subject to the margin rules of exchanges in the way that on-exchange transactions are) are subject to a stricter regime than on-exchange margin transactions. In the case of capital requirements, there are varying and complex calculations required to ensure that sufficient capital is held in relation to counterparty and position risks inherent in equity derivatives.
- Certain transactions must be reported to the SFA by the end of the next business day through an approved reporting system. Most equity derivatives transactions are subject to the reporting requirement. Reports to the SFA are not required, however, where the transaction has been reported to a "qualifying exchange" such as the London Stock Exchange, LIFFE, LME, London FOX and many other derivatives exchanges both in the UK and abroad.

The above summarises those conduct of business rules which apply specifically to derivatives (including contingent liability transactions). However, a number of rules of more general application are nevertheless of particular importance in the case of equity derivatives. These include the requirement that a firm must not recommend a transaction for a private investor unless it believes on the basis of the information which it knows or ought to know about the customer concerned that it is suitable for his investment objectives. It follows that before a firm can recommend a speculative transaction, it must be satisfied that the investor understands the risks involved, is prepared to take the degree of risk involved and has the financial resources and ability to absorb any losses which may be incurred.

As has been seen, a number of rules apply only in the case of private investors. In some circumstances, a person who would normally be a private investor can be treated as an expert (and hence non-private) investor. Broadly, a firm will need to demonstrate that the investor has sufficient experience to understand the risks involved in the transaction and, having been warned of the loss of protection under the rules, that customer has consented to be treated as a non-private customer. It can readily be seen that classifying a customer as an expert will radically reduce the compliance burden. Nevertheless, the risks of doing so should not be underestimated. When individual investors lose money they are likely to claim that they should never have been classified as an expert in the first place. A firm which proposes to treat a client as "an expert" should maintain a careful record of the classification process and details demonstrating the customer's experience of the types of instrument or types of risk involved.

Financial regulations Firms are required to meet certain financial supervision requirements under SFA rules. The core of these requirements is the requirement to have adequate capital to support the level of business being undertaken. The rules require that financial resources must at least equal the financial resources requirement.

The calculation of available financial resources is complex but in essence comprises capital and reserves adjusted by deducting intangible assets and adding, subject to certain limits, eligible capital substitutes (ie, subordinated loans, approved bank bonds and approved undertakings).

The financial resources requirement is even more complex and consists of three separate elements:

1. a primary requirement, representing a basic minimum capital for any business;
2. a position risk requirement (PRR) to reflect the risk of the market value positions held by the firm fluctuating to the detriment of the firm; and
3. a counterparty risk requirement (CRR) to reflect the risk that counterparties may default on their obligations to the firm.

The primary requirement consists of a base requirement (being the greater of an absolute minimum requirement of between £10,000 and £100,000 depending on the firm and an expenditure-based requirement of three months' expenditure). The base requirement is then increased by the amount of illiquid assets, charged assets, deficiencies in subsidiaries and, if the SFA so requires, contingent liabilities.

The PRR calculation is, again, complex although a simplified method is available which, however, normally produces a higher figure. The basic methodology is to calculate a value for the position concerned (or the equivalent position in the underlying security in the case of derivatives) and attribute to it a percentage risk addition (PRA) which is a figure derived from empirical research and intended to reflect the degree of risk of the position concerned. Under the full PRR calculation positions are allocated to a particular "method" of calculation and the total of all methods aggregated. For present purposes the relevant methods are the equity method, the equity derivatives method and the equity warrants method. In some cases, allocation to a particular method is mandatory, in others it is optional so that firms have the choice of the most favourable method. Sub-methods may be available within the main methods to take account of such matters as hedging positions and the net effect of long and short positions, to relate the requirements to an exchange's margin requirements or to make provision of special methods for significant traders in the particular market.

The CRR requirement depends on the settlement method of the transaction concerned, the nature of the counterparty (and the existence of any credit management policy for that client) and the time by which settlement is overdue. A percentage is specified to be applied to the mark to market value of the position.

Monitoring and enforcing compliance with the regulations   SFA members are required to have compliance and finance officers who, subject to the ultimate responsibility of the nominated senior executive officer, are responsible for monitoring compliance within the firm. Specifically an annual compliance review must be undertaken and the results reported to the SFA.

The SFA has power to make periodic inspection visits and to mount investigations where appropriate. It can also issue warnings, direction notices and intervention orders. Disciplinary action may also be taken before the SFA's disciplinary tribunal in the case of misconduct, including rule breaches. The penalties imposed include fines, reprimands, severe reprimands and, in extreme cases, suspension or expulsion.

The future

As ever, it is difficult to predict the future. However, two developments already on the horizon are the implementation of the EC Second Banking Co-ordination Directive and, within the next few years, the EC Investment Services Directive and Capital Adequacy Directive. These Directives will entitle institutions with a head office in an

EC member state (its "home state") to operate throughout the Community on the basis of a single "passport" obviating the need for separate authorisation in each state. However, the host state will, to some extent, be entitled to impose rules on the conduct of business in its own territory. Although some amendments to UK law will be necessitated in implementing these Directives, they alone do not imply any need for a complete overhaul of the regulatory system. Nevertheless, those Directives, and the Investment Services Directive in particular, may still prove a catalyst for significant change to the regulatory system.

At present, there are different pressures for change in relation to the retail financial services sector and the professional sector. As far as professionals are concerned, while the need for capital requirements is accepted, the level of detail of conduct of business regulation remains a source of criticism. The implementation of the EC Directives may result in firms from other EC member states doing business in the UK under a less onerous regulatory regime, putting UK-based firms at a competitive disadvantage and leading to businesses migrating to other jurisdictions.

On the other hand, where retail investors are concerned, there is criticism of the effectiveness of the current system of practitioner-based regulation within a statutory framework. Certainly business failures and scandals continue – many of which have some element of fraud attached to them. This may imply that the problem is not so much with the regulations themselves but rather with their enforcement. The enforcement authorities are currently rather fragmented – for example, the SROs police their own rulebooks, the Serious Fraud Office conducts criminal investigations into cases of serious fraud and the Stock Exchange investigates cases of alleged insider dealing. Moreover, HM Treasury retains the power to prosecute cases of misleading statements and conduct (although that power is collaterally exercisable by the Serious Fraud Office and the DPP). It has been suggested in some quarters than an SEC-style enforcement agency is required, although whether that is a role which the SIB, in its current form, could undertake may be doubted.

The concerns noted in the previous paragraphs relate to the regulatory system generally. Of specific relevance to the derivatives market, however, is the growing concern in some quarters as to the size and inter-dependence of the derivatives market and the risk of defaults precipitating a systemic failure. This may be an area which will become more specifically regulated in the future. Some derivatives firms have sought to guard against the risk of default through the establishment of "bankruptcy-remote" subsidiaries which through various techniques seek to ensure that the group company undertaking derivatives business is not at significant risk of bankruptcy. These techniques go some way to replicating the clearing house guarantees which exchange-traded contracts offer. The techniques used vary but include such things as full collateralisation, back-to-back contracts with other group companies, the use of market-neutral balanced portfolios and, ultimately, the back up of a financial insurer.

In view of the above, it is clear that the immediate future holds a number of changes in store for the equity derivatives industry although, as always, it is difficult to predict exactly when and how those changes will be implemented.

Taxation of derivatives

The section considers the basis on which derivative products (principally options and financial futures) are taxed in three jurisdictions: the UK, the US and France.

Although each of these jurisdictions has developed legislation to deal with such taxation in differing ways and in varying levels of detail, it will be seen that there are common concerns. First, in each case the tax treatment will depend to some extent on the use to which the derivative is put. In particular, where a derivative has been used as a hedge its tax treatment will often be different from that which applies where it is held for investment, speculation or trade. Secondly, each jurisdiction has adopted to some extent or is intending to adopt a mark-to-market regime under which unrealised gains and losses on instruments which are traded are taken into account each year:

1. in the UK this regime currently affects only financial traders which prepare their accounts on a mark-to-market basis, but may in future be extended to interest-rate-related instruments held by other companies;
2. in the US the scope of a limited mark-to-market regime is being extended to financial traders who normally prepare accounts on such a basis;
3. in France it is not always the case. There are rules under which any company (whether or not a financial trader) will be taxed on this basis in relation to marketable or market linked instruments.

The United Kingdom

What are financial futures and options?
No comprehensive definition of either futures or options exists for tax (as opposed to regulatory) purposes. However, the UK Inland Revenue has provided some guidelines in a statement of practice. Accordingly, for tax purposes a "financial future" includes, *inter alia*, contracts for future delivery of shares, securities, foreign currency or other financial instruments. It may also include a contract settled by payment of cash differences determined by reference to movements in the price of those instruments (including a contract where settlement is based on the application of an interest rate or a financial index to a notional principal amount) and a contract settled by delivery. Both exchange-traded and over-the-counter (OTC) contracts are included in this definition.

An option (or warrant) includes both exchange-traded and OTC options and options that provide for cash settlement between the parties as well as those which provide for delivery.

There is also currently very little tax legislation in the UK that deals specifically with these kinds of financial instruments. The general approach to date has been to try to fit the instruments within the existing framework. This has caused a number of difficulties and anomalies which are discussed below. In some cases legislation has been enacted but regrettably the approach has been somewhat piecemeal.

Basic taxation framework
The taxation treatment in relation to equity derivatives depends on the context in which dealings in the relevant instrument are carried out. The UK Inland Revenue recognises that derivative instruments may be employed in the context of a financial trade, on capital account as a method of hedging some other exposure, or as a means of speculation. The taxation consequences of any particular transaction in equity derivatives will depend on the manner in which it is used and by whom it is used. This can mean that the taxation treatment can differ widely between differing users even where they are party to the same transaction. Similar questions arise in relation to the US regime.

Financial trader
The position of a financial trader is the simplest to deal with. Profits or losses realised on equity derivatives dealt within the course of a financial trade will be taxed under trading rules. This broadly will mean that the taxation consequences will follow the economic results of the transaction. Thus, any upfront fee or premium will be deductible (as will the finance costs of any margin), and there will be relative symmetry of taxation of profits and losses.

The position where the investor does not carry on a financial trade is more complicated. The transaction may be a speculative or a trading transaction or it may be entered into to hedge an existing position. The taxation consequences differ significantly. Thus it is important, even for financial traders, to have an understanding of the issues that face non-financial trade customers.

Non-financial trader – hedging transaction
In the case of financial instruments generally, a distinction is drawn between transactions which hedge a trading transaction or position (for example, a copper trader buying a future to hedge against a future price fluctuation) and those which hedge transactions on capital account such as an investment company entering into a futures contract to hedge its portfolio. It is, however, difficult to see circumstances in which a *non*-financial trader would use *equity* derivatives, such as options or futures, to hedge trading transactions. This section therefore deals only with hedging a capital exposure. Gains (or losses) on instruments used for this purpose will be taxed under capital gains tax rules.

A derivative instrument will in general be regarded by the UK Inland Revenue as hedging another transaction where:

1. there is another transaction, which has either already been undertaken or which will be undertaken in the future;
2. the financial futures or options transaction is intended to eliminate or reduce risk or reduce transaction costs; and
3. the futures or options transaction is economically appropriate to the elimination or reduction of risk, or transaction costs.

These requirements are similar to the requirements under the (more limited) French hedging regime.

Whereas this will be relatively easy to demonstrate with, for example, an option or future to hedge a particular equity investment or basket of investments, it may be more difficult with an option or a futures contract based on an index. However, the Inland Revenue accepts that such a contract can be economically appropriate as a hedging transaction. An example of this could be where the investor has a broadly based equity portfolio.

The capital gains tax rules differ in one material aspect depending on whether futures or options are used. These are therefore dealt with separately.

Futures
The capital gains tax rules discussed below apply only to commodity or financial futures. These are defined as futures contracts which are dealt in from time to time on a recognised futures exchange or are entered into with, or closed out by entry into a contract with, an authorised person or listed institution (as defined in the FSA).

Where a person enters into a futures transaction, the futures contract may either be closed out (by entering a reciprocal contract) or may run to maturity. On maturity, settlement can be either by delivery of the underlying equities (which is unusual) or by cash settlement.

Where the contract is closed out by entry into a reciprocal contract, the entry into the second contract will be regarded as a disposal of the first. Any payments of money or money's worth made or received will be treated as incidental costs of disposal of the contract or, as the case may be, consideration for the disposal, creating either a capital loss or a gain.

Where the contract is closed out by cash settlement, this is also regarded as being a disposal of the futures contract and any payment made or received will be treated as incidental costs of disposal (which may give rise to a capital loss) or, as the case may be, proceeds of disposal.

The position where a futures contract runs to delivery is not entirely clear, as the legislation makes no mention of it. The better view is that such a contract is no more than an agreement to purchase or sell the underlying asset or commodity. On this basis any costs or expenses associated with the expiry of the contract, where the underlying shares are received, are part of the costs of acquiring the shares (similar to the approach with options) or, where the underlying shares are disposed of, possibly deductible as incidental costs of disposal of those shares. However, in the absence of specific provisions similar to that where the contract is closed out or settled in cash, uncertainties can arise.

Uncertainties can also arise in relation to contracts which are not dealt in on a recognised futures exchange, or entered into with or closed out by entry into a contract with an authorised person or listed institution. This is particularly so if the transaction could be regarded as speculative, but outside of normal trading rules. Transactions which fall within the legislation mentioned above and are not on trading account are *automatically* taxed under capital gains tax rules. Those which are not, could, for non-corporates at least, be taxed under Schedule D Case VI rules (miscellaneous income) as income. This can be disadvantageous where losses arise.

Futures relating to gilts or qualifying corporate bonds (broadly sterling debt instruments) fall outside the capital gains tax net in the same way as do the underlying instruments.

The question of whether relief is available for any upfront costs of entering into a futures contract is also difficult. The Inland Revenue has indicated that it regards futures as wasting assets (ie, assets with a predictable life of less than 50 years). This means that the premium and upfront costs paid (if any) are deemed to amortise to the residual value over the life of the contract on a straight-line basis. Residual value is determined at the time the contract is entered into. The Inland Revenue view appears to be that such value is nil and that consequently no relief is available for the upfront costs or premium where the contract runs to maturity. This view is, however, debatable as the precise value of the contract on maturity, whilst uncertain at the outset, is unlikely to be nil, although it could be negative. A contrary view to that taken by the Inland Revenue could therefore be argued, although its success cannot be guaranteed.

Options

There are tax consequences both on the grant of the option and also on its expiry or exercise. An option can expire unexercised, be settled by cash payment (which will almost certainly be the case for index-based options or options over baskets of shares), by delivery of the underlying equities or other instruments or, in the case of certain traded options, by acquiring a traded option of the same description.

Where the option expires unexercised, the taxation consequences will depend on whether the option is, *inter alia*:

1. a quoted option to subscribe for shares in a company;
2. a traded or financial option – which is defined in the tax legislation and broadly covers exchange-traded options and options entered into with an authorised person or a listed institution (as those terms are defined in the FSA); or
3. an option over a gilt or qualifying corporate bond. As for futures relating to such instruments, such options fall outside the capital gains tax net.

If the option falls within either of the first two categories, then the abandonment of the option will be a disposal of an asset (by the person by whom the option is exerciseable). This may give rise to an allowable loss for capital gains tax purposes, equal to the amount paid to acquire the option plus indexation relief where appropriate (depending on whether the option is regarded as being a wasting asset).

Quoted options to subscribe for shares in a company are not wasting assets, nor are traded or financial options. However, certain other equity-based options will be wasting assets, which means that where such options expire unexercised, no relief is available for any upfront premium.

Where the option is settled by delivery, the acquisition of the option and the acquisition or (as the case may be) the disposal of the underlying asset will be looked at as a single transaction. Therefore, the option premium will, for capital gains tax, either be added to the base cost of the asset acquired or will be treated as an incidental cost of disposal of the underlying asset. Where the option is a call option for indexation purposes, the option premium and the consideration paid to acquire the underlying securities are treated separately and, in effect, are indexed from the respective dates of payment.

If a non-financial trader grants the option, there is an immediate disposal of an asset, and the grantor is taxed under capital gains tax rules on any premium received. However, if at a later date the option is exercised, the computation is reopened and tax is calculated on the basis that the grant of the option and any acquisition or disposal of the underlying asset were a single transaction. Thus, any premium received for granting the option will be added to the sale consideration received or, as the case may be, deducted from the consideration paid. Any tax paid on the grant of an option will be refunded together with repayment supplement (interest) where applicable.

Where an option to subscribe for shares is exercised, because the issue of shares is not the disposal of an asset for capital gains tax purposes, there will be a refund of any tax paid on the grant of the option. In practice, repayment supplement will also be paid if applicable.

The Inland Revenue is sometimes willing to operate a "wait and see" policy where such an option is of a relatively short duration (no more than two to three years) and in those circumstances will not seek to tax the premium paid for the grant of the option until it is clear whether the option will be exercised.

Cash difference options
Options based on an index or basket of shares are normally settled by a cash payment. The tax position of such options can be complicated as there are arguments that such options are not strictly options and do not fall within the legislation. In practice, however, the Inland Revenue treats most cash difference options as falling within the option rules provided that they are capable of exercise on more than one day. Where a cash difference option is capable of exercise on one day only, the Inland Revenue

view appears to be that these are not options but contracts for differences which are likely to be taxed in much the same way as sterling cash difference options. In practice, the only real difference this will make is in relation to any premium paid, as a contract for difference may not escape the wasting asset rules, consequently, it may not be possible to obtain any relief for the premium.

Even so, the tax analysis will depend on whether the cash payment is in a currency other than sterling. Foreign currency is a chargeable asset and, consequently, the provisions outlined under "Options" above apply.

Sterling is not, however, a chargeable asset and therefore the rules are difficult to apply. It is probable, however, that for the person entitled to exercise the option, the cash proceeds will be taxed under general capital gains tax principles as a capital sum derived from an asset. There are, however, views to the contrary. The position of the grantor is equally unclear. In making a sterling payment, the grantor has not disposed of any asset, and it is therefore difficult to see how relief would be available for the payment made under capital gains tax rules.

Speculative transactions
There is, in theory, a class of transactions which are not on capital account but do not qualify as trading transactions or adventures in the nature of a trade. Any profits or losses from such transactions fall within Schedule D Case VI. The scope of this class of transactions is limited because the Inland Revenue takes the view that a company cannot speculate – its activities are either trading or on capital account. Furthermore, where the derivative used is a commodity or financial future, or a qualifying option as defined, and where the transaction is not a trading transaction, capital gains tax rules apply.

Stamp duty
The stamp duty and stamp duty reserve tax consequences in relation to options depends on the type of option involved. For this purpose options can be categorised into cash difference options (eg, options over an index or basket of shares where settlement will be in cash) and options over specific shares.

Stamp duty can arise on the grant of an option either under legislation or under the principle in *George Wimpey & Co Ltd* v *IRC*. This case broadly held that the grant of an option over property was itself an instrument which transferred property and that therefore the option instrument was stampable.

An option which settles by payment of cash differences does not involve an option to buy or sell property, and therefore no charge should arise on *Wimpey* principles on grant of the option. However, there is an argument that a charge arises under general legislation, although the merits of this argument are open to doubt. In practice, the point does not appear to be pursued, but where it is a material concern, it may be safer to execute and hold the document offshore. Stamp duty is not generally charged on traded options. Technically, depending on if and where a document of transfer is exercised, there is a charge to stamp duty on a transfer of an option.

There is also a potential charge to bearer instrument duty on issue where the option is in bearer form (although, in practice, it is not clear how often the charge is paid). This charge does not apply where the option relates to non-sterling denominated shares.

No stamp duty reserve tax (SDRT) is payable on agreements to transfer cash difference options, as they are not chargeable securities.

Where the option is to be settled by physical delivery of the underlying equities, the position is more complicated. There could be a technical charge to stamp duty on grant of the option under the *Wimpey* principle, unless the underlying shares are bearer and non-sterling denominated. There may also be a charge to bearer instrument duty, which will be reduced by any stamp duty paid.

VAT
The issue and dealing in futures and options will, in general, be either exempt or zero-rated depending on the identity of the counterparty.

Future developments
In August 1991, the UK Inland Revenue published a consultative document on the taxation treatment of financial instruments. This proposed that all payments and receipts arising on financial instruments (calculated using a normal accruals policy) should be assimilated to income. Where the transaction was not on trading account, this would mean that any payments should be offset against total profits (or carried forward to subsequent years if profits were insufficient) and gains would be taxed.

However, the changes proposed relate only to instruments used to manage interest rate exposure. The Inland Revenue does not currently intend to extend the regime to equity derivatives as it considers that to do so could cause greater problems than it would solve, particularly in relation to derivatives relating to gilts or qualifying corporate bonds. It has, however, left open the possibility that the regime may be extended to equity instruments at a later date. It is not clear whether such a change, if it were to occur, would be after a further period of consultation.

Conclusion
It can be seen that material differences can arise depending on how an instrument is structured and who the counterparties are. At present, there is no indication that the position will be simplified.

The United States

Futures and options: basic US tax issues
US taxation rules in this area are more developed, and more complex, than the existing UK tax law. The following discussion highlights some of the principal US federal tax issues, in outline only. State taxation issues are not considered. The instruments considered are the financial futures and options considered in the earlier discussion of UK tax. Although not discussed here, it should be noted that the US has also developed rules for taxing instruments such as equity and commodity swaps, whose UK tax treatment is currently less well defined, and which have some similarities to financial futures and options.

Profit characterisation: ordinary income vs. capital gain
General rules
The starting point is that gains or losses on inventory of dealers (ie, generally those who hold themselves out as carrying on a business of entering into futures and options transactions with customers) are taxed as ordinary income. Gains or losses of other investors from the disposition, lapse, closing-out or termination of futures and options are taxed as capital gain or loss, if the underlying property would have been a capital asset in the hands of the investor.

The distinction between capital or ordinary treatment of gains and losses has several consequences. Because capital losses cannot be set against ordinary income, a tax mismatch can arise where a non-dealer enters into a futures contract or an option in order to hedge a risk arising in the ordinary course of its business activities (eg, a risk of a variation in commodity prices). In addition, a lower rate of tax is imposed on individual taxpayers if their gains are long-term capital gains (ie, they stem from positions held for more than one year).

Foreign currency gain or loss
The US has special tax rules which generally treat gains and losses on foreign currency forward contracts, futures contracts, options and similar instruments as ordinary income or loss. However, it is possible to elect to have foreign currency gain or loss on such transactions taxed as capital gain or loss if the taxpayer holds the futures position or the option as a capital asset, and not for dealing purposes. Certain foreign currency hedging transactions may be taxed under the foreign exchange taxation rules as if they were one integrated transaction.

Recognition of gain or loss: timing issues
Generally, gain or loss on futures and options is recognised when the relevant transaction is completed or closed out. In the case of an option (including a cash settlement option), this will be when the option lapses or is exercised and not when it is granted. The option premium will be taken into account when gain or loss on the lapse or exercise of an option is being calculated. For example, a purchaser of a call option is entitled to add the premium to his basis in the underlying property if he exercises the option, while the grantor of the call option must add the premium to the sale proceeds which he realises.

This general timing rule is subject to special rules which require gain or loss on certain futures and options to be accounted for on a "mark-to-market" basis. The scope of mark-to-market tax accounting is likely to be extended by the Revenue Reconciliation Bill which is currently before Congress. The Bill envisages that, in most cases, securities dealers (including dealers in options and futures other than commodity options and futures) will have to mark their inventory to market. At present, the mark-to-market rules only affect certain traded futures, foreign currency contracts and certain types of quoted option. In particular, equity-related or equity-linked options which are purchased or granted by options dealers are the only equity options currently subject to the mark-to-market rules. The overall aim to date has been to ensure that these tax rules only affect futures and options transactions on exchanges where mark-to-market accounting for profit and loss is the norm anyway.

As in the French regime, certain hedging transactions (notably, certain foreign currency hedging transactions) are not affected by the mark-to-market rules. Transactions which are taxed on the mark-to-market basis are not subject to the separate rules for taxing foreign exchange gains and losses unless the taxpayer elects that foreign exchange gains and losses should be taxed separately under those rules.

If a transaction is subject to the mark-to-market rules, then any resulting gain or loss to a non-dealer is generally treated as 40 per cent short-term capital gain or loss, and 60 per cent long-term capital gain or loss. This capital gains treatment will moreover apply to any foreign exchange gain or loss on the transaction unless, of course, the taxpayer has elected that foreign exchange gains and losses should be separately taxed as ordinary income and loss (see the preceding paragraph).

Taxpayers who are not dealers in stock or securities, or in futures and options relating to stock and securities, may find their allowable losses restricted where they enter into separate transactions, within a specified period of days, in relation to substantially identical shares, securities, equity futures or equity options. These rules restrict the availability of losses which might otherwise on "bed-and-breakfasting" transactions, eg, where stock carrying an unrealised loss is sold shortly before a year end in order to trigger the loss and is then bought back shortly after the year end.

Finally, there is a separate set of rules which restrict allowable losses where a taxpayer holds separate offsetting positions in, for example, shares, securities, futures or options. Offsetting positions are interests in actively traded personal property (including futures and options) where the risk of loss on one interest is substantially reduced by holding one or more other interests of this nature. The rules (which do not apply to certain identified hedging transactions) are designed to prevent a taxpayer accelerating loss by terminating a loss-making position without at the same time recognising gain on a matching profitable position.

France

The tax treatment of financial futures and options may differ according to whether the holder is an individual or a company. Individual taxation issues are not considered in the following discussion.

The corporate taxation of financial futures and options is characterised by the distinction between instruments traded on "organised" markets (which in this section we term "Market Traded Derivatives") and those traded on "non-organised" markets.

Financial instruments traded on organised markets
Definition of "organised" markets
In an administrative circular issued by the French tax authorities (which is binding as against the tax authorities but not binding on the courts in interpreting the law), an organised market must combine three elements:

– liquidity, ie, counterparties must be immediately available;
– no counterparty risks, ie, a clearing house must intervene in each contract;
– objective valuation, ie, the financial instruments must be sufficiently standardised.

Accordingly, "organised markets" include the "MATIF" (Paris Financial Futures Market), "MONEP" (Paris Negotiable Options Market), LIFFE (London International Financial Futures Exchange) and any other French or foreign organised markets or by reference to such markets.

In addition, an administrative circular indicated that the French Revenue treat the following as Market Traded Derivatives: financial instruments which are traded in sufficient volume to consider their liquidity as certain and financial instruments in relation to which underlying assets are quoted on organised markets. On this bases the following are treated as financial instruments traded on an organised market:

– currency options, futures and swaps (since such contracts can be valued by reference to the FOREX market);
– option contracts on quoted shares, indexes, etc.

When a financial instrument is traded, or treated as traded, on such an organised market, the mark-to-market and hedging rules described below will apply. In addition, the Symmetrical Position rules will apply as they apply to other derivative transactions (see below).

The mark-to-market rule

Article 38.(6).(1) provides that unrealised profits and losses on Market Traded Derivatives are taxable on a mark-to-market basis.

The French tax authorities used to consider that interest rate swaps could not be treated as Market Traded Derivatives because of the counterparty risk. As a result of recent tax law changes, however, the mark-to-market rule now applies to some swaps entered into by financial traders (*etablissements de crédit*), particularly if these swaps are aimed at hedging other financial instruments subject to the mark-to-market rule.

There are two exceptions from the mark-to-market regime. The first deals with hedging and the second with Symmetrical Positions. The hedging exemption is specific to market-traded derivatives, but the rules dealing with Symmetrical Positions are anti-avoidance rules and apply to both market-traded and to over-the-counter derivatives.

Hedging

The hedging regime is severely limited by Article 38.(6).(2). It applies only to marketed derivatives and (with the exception relating to foreign currency described below) only to hedges which will mature in the next accounting period. This rule applies if the hedged transaction is not subject to the mark-to-market rule. When the derivative and the hedged contract are both marketable, the mark-to-market regime gives a natural offset. The hedging regime applies only where there is not such an automatic offset – for example, where a currency option hedges a future obligation to pay foreign currency on a purchase.

Where hedging applies, the mark-to-market rule is not applied in the relevant accounting period, but profit and losses are realised on termination of the hedge in the following accounting period.

The hedging rule is extended where the derivative contract is aimed at heding a foreign currency obligation, whatever the term to maturity of the hedged contract. In such a case, latent gains on the hedging contract are taxable only at the time the losses on the hedged transaction occur.

In general, the rule does not affect the deductibility of provisions for losses made at the end of the first accounting period but such provisions may not be deductible in the year they are made as a result of the Symmetrical Positions rules (see below).

Symmetrical Positions

Article 38.(6).(3) operates as an anti-avoidance provision whereby the loss incurred on certain positions is not fully deductible if such position has been hedged by another position which has generated an unrealised gain. For the purpose of this rule, a position is defined as a direct or indirect ownership of financial futures, securities, currencies, debt instruments, loans or borrowing and any commitment relating to such items.

Two positions are symmetrical where their values vary in an inverse and correlated manner (either in value or in yield). Most of the difficulties arising under this rule relate to the wide interpretation given by the French Revenue. In an administrative circular, the French tax authorities have given the following examples of symmetrical positions:

- transaction on the MATIF and bonds to be issued;
- currency option and debt or liability in the same currency;
- interest swap and loan or debenture
- currency options covering future income or expenditure likely to be incurred;
- bull and bear securities.

Under the regime a loss will be deductible only to the extent that it exceeds latent gains which have not yet been taxed on matching positions.

The hedging and symmetrical regimes are similar but different. Their similarity is that they both deal with matched positions: to the situation where the risk of gain on one asset or liability is matched by the risk of loss on another. However:

1. the hedging regime only applies to market-quoted instruments (but there is an exception in the case of swaps between *etablisements de crédit*);
2. with the exception of currency hedges, the hedging regime only applies where the hedge will be closed out or realised in the following accounting period. The Symmetrical Position regime, on the other hand, applies whatever the period matching;
3. the Symmetrical Position regime prevents a loss being recognised. It does not prevent a gain arising. The hedging regime on the other hand prevents a gain arising but does not prevent a loss being recognised (although the Symmetrical Positions regime may apply to the hedged loss and prevent its recognition); and
4. the provisions of the Symmetrical Positions rules are very broad and may extend beyond derivative instruments.

Note that there is a need for these special provisions under the French tax rules without any corresponding proviso in the US or UK code since the making of a provision in the accounts of a French company may give rise to a deduction in computing taxable income where such a deduction would not be available under the UK/US tax rules.

Other Financial Instruments

Other financial instruments (Non-Market-Traded Instruments) will include those on markets where the liquidity is not certain, counterparty risks exist, and the contracts are not standardised. According to a French Revenue's administrative circular, future rate agreements, interest rate swaps, caps, floors, collars and more generally non-standard contracts should be deemed as OTC transactions since the value of such contracts is influenced by the counterparty risk.

However, financial contracts where the underlying assets are traded on an organised market (such as listed shares or bonds, foreign currencies, etc) would be necessarily deemed as traded on an organised market for tax purposes.

Where the special Article 38.(6).(1) and (2) regime does not apply, profit and losses are taxed under general tax principles. A gain is taxed at the time when the gain is realised (ie at the end of the contract or at the time when the contract is sold) and losses are deductible in the year in which a loss is made, ie, at the time of termination or sale of the contract or, to the extent that provision is made in the accounts, for an unrealised loss to the extent of the charge made in the accounts in respect of that provision. However, since the Symmetrical Position rule applies to OTC transactions, the deductibility of this provision may be denied or limited to a certain amount.

The ISDA confirmation for OTC equity index option deals

The International Swaps and Derivatives Association ("ISDA", formerly the International Swap Dealers Association) has recently published a form of confirmation for over-the-counter option transactions based on equity indices (the "Confirmation"), and this section is planned as a "practitioner's guide". The full Confirmation is set out at the end of this chapter.[3] Publication of the Confirmation reflects the continuing effort to standardise and simplify documentation for derivatives, which had earlier led to the publication by ISDA of standard form contracts and related definitions and provisions.[4]

At the time work began on the Confirmation, it was apparent that the burgeoning market in equity index options was in need of standardisation. Documentation for such transactions varied across the market-place, and in some cases trades were not being documented because the parties were unable to agree on the form the documentation should take. It would be easy to underestimate how far apart parties have been in the approaches taken in their documentation for equity derivatives in the past, very often for no good reason and only because they chose different starting points. It would also be easy to underestimate the difficulty faced in attempting to resolve the resulting "battle of the forms" in two-party negotiations. To remedy this situation, the working group met repeatedly during an eight-month period to produce the Confirmation, which was published in June 1992.[5]

The Confirmation attempts to codify market practice whenever possible. During the course of the group's work, however, it became apparent that market practices in some cases had been arbitrary at best and scope for improvement existed in several key respects. Resulting changes are reflected in the Confirmation and discussed below.

Methodology of the Confirmation

The Confirmation is intended to be used either as a confirmation under the 1992 ISDA Master Agreement, or any other master agreement, or on a stand-alone basis. It is anticipated that parties would put the form of the Confirmation on to their own systems and simply fill in the economic terms of the particular transactions they wish to document.

The Confirmation is designed to document OTC options on sponsored equity indices from around the world, such as the Nikkei 225 Index, the DAX Index, the Financial Times Stock Exchange 100 Index and the Standard & Poor's 500 Index.[6] The Confirmation addresses several issues unique to cash-settled equity index options and lacks certain provisions which may be required to document adequately other equity derivative transactions such as options on the shares of a single issuer whether settled for cash or by physical delivery of those shares.[7]

The Confirmation breaks down into seven principal sections: the introduction, general and economic terms, the procedure for exercise, valuation of the option, cash settlement terms, account details and the closing of the Confirmation. Generally, the Confirmation describes the kind of option the buyer has purchased, the amount paid for the option, when the buyer of the option may exercise the option, how the "Calculation Agent" determines the "Cash Settlement Amount" (ie, the amount, if any, that the seller must pay to the buyer following exercise of the option) and where and when the Cash Settlement Amount gets paid to the buyer.

On those points where custom would seem to warrant it, the Confirmation creates a presumption to apply in the absence of any express provision by the parties. For example, the Confirmation provides that unless the parties to an equity index option state otherwise in their agreement, a premium payment will be delayed rather than accelerated to permit it to be paid on a business day.

On some points, either because of the need to preserve flexibility or because a consensus appeared lacking as to appropriate market practice, the Confirmation creates a menu of choices and leaves the matter to be decided by the parties selecting among the choices permitted (for example, the pay-out on an option may be determined by reference to the level of the chosen index either as at the close of trading on the relevant stock exchange or as at such other time or fixing as the parties agree and specify). On other issues, matters are left entirely to the parties, without any discussion in the Confirmation, usually with a view to permitting parties to structure as they see fit certain aspects of their transaction. As to certain of these issues, the Confirmation's method is to create a framework, with the details to be supplied by the parties. For example, if the parties include certain bracketed language that appears in the Confirmation and specify a relevant exchange, the valuation of an OTC transaction may be affected by a disruption that does not affect trading on the principal securities exchange for the index but does affect the trading on another exchange of options or futures contracts on that index. In other cases, annotations in the footnotes to the Confirmation simply alert parties to other issues to which they may wish to give further thought. Thus, the parties are advised to consider issues relating to the accounting or tax treatment for the relevant transactions, regulatory issues and other requirements such as any necessary licences or approvals. Such issues have not been addressed definitively in the Confirmation because they are subject to varying local law treatment or may be specific to a particular party or type of trade.

A few basics
This "practitioner's guide" attempts to explain the principal provisions of the Confirmation. A number of those provisions derive their meaning from choices that the parties make and record at the time they enter into a trade.

Alternative headings (and closings) are provided in the Confirmation in recognition of the fact that parties may wish to confirm their transaction by exchanging either counterparts of a letter agreement (including facsimiles) or telexes. The introductory language in the Confirmation that follows after the selected heading will acknowledge the choice made in this regard, and it is here that the parties specify if they are intending the Confirmation to be used in connection with an ISDA Master Agreement or any other master agreement.[8]

General terms
Parties must specify the "Trade Date" for the transaction – that is, the date on which the transaction was agreed. They must also specify an "Option Style" – whether the option is an American one (permitting the buyer to exercise it over a period exceeding one day) or European (providing for exercise on one specified date only).[9] If an option is American style, parties should stipulate whether multiple exercise is permitted. If so, the Confirmation can set out any requirement that a minimum number of options must be exercised, or that no more than a specified maximum number of options may be exercised, on any "Exercise Date". In such cases, the parties may also specify that the options must be exercised in integral multiples of a specified number.[10]

Next, the parties specify the "Option type" – that is, whether the option is a put, in which case the buyer is in-the-money when the chosen stock index falls below the strike price, or a call, in which case the buyer is in-the-money when the stock index rises above the strike price. The parties also must identify which party is the seller of the option and which party is the buyer of the option.

The parties need to specify the particular equity index on which the option is being written, which is called "the Index". An "Exchange" (ie, the principal securities exchange for the Index) must be given. For example, if the option was based on the Nikkei 225 Index, the parties would specify the Tokyo Stock Exchange and if the option was based on the S&P 500, the parties would specify the New York Stock Exchange and the American Stock Exchange. The parties must specify the "Number of Options", which establishes the overall size of the transaction and is relevant to the calculation of the settlement payment (if any) to be made in respect of the transaction. The parties then must specify the "Strike Price" for the transaction – that is, the price over which the Index level must be on the relevant "Valuation Date" in order for the holder of a call option to receive payment of a Cash Settlement Amount or under which the Index level must be in order for the holder of a put option to receive payment of a Cash Settlement Amount. The Strike Price can be a pre-determined fixed amount (eg, 1000) representing an Index level or a formula from which the Strike Price will be determined (eg, 110 per cent of the Index level two weeks from the trade date).

Premium

The "Premium" must be specified, which is the price the buyer of the option pays for that option.

The parties must specify the "Premium Payment Date". The date specified will be subject to adjustment in accordance with the business day convention discussed below so that, if a Premium Payment Date would otherwise fall on a non-business day, the date will roll forward to the next business day.

The role of the Calculation Agent

Parties should always designate a "Calculation Agent" to make the necessary calculations in respect of the transaction. In cases where one party can be expected for the foreseeable future to have immediate access to all information necessary for, or otherwise be in a better position to make, these calculations, it may be efficient to name this party as Calculation Agent, but third parties may also be appointed to serve in this capacity. In a dealer market where both parties are well positioned to serve as Calculation Agent and anticipate that each will in some cases be a buyer and in other cases a seller of options with the other, it may be that a convention will develop by which one (eg, the seller) will be presumed to be the Calculation Agent for a transaction.

The Calculation Agent's responsibilities will include, among other things, calculating the Cash Settlement Amount, if any, that the seller must pay to the buyer following exercise of the option. The Calculation Agent may also have a potentially important role following the occurrence of a Market Disruption Event (as discussed below).

The relevance of Business Days

The general terms also set out several important business day definitions. First, "Index Business Day" is defined to mean a day that is a Seller Business Day (as described below) and is, or but for the occurrence of a Market Disruption Event would have been, a trading day on the principal exchange or exchanges of the shares comprising the Index (and any other specified options or futures exchanges) other than a day on which trading on any such exchange is scheduled to close prior to its regular weekday closing time. For example, if a French bank sells an option on the Nikkei 225 Index, an Index Business Day for that transaction will be both a Seller Business Day in Paris and a scheduled trading day for the Tokyo Stock Exchange. Subject to the relevant markets not being disrupted, amounts payable on exercise of an option will always be determined by reference to the level of the Index on an Index Business Day.

"Seller Business Day" is defined as any day on which commercial banks are open for business in the city in which the seller is located for the purpose of receiving notices. The Confirmation also notes that if the seller is not a commercial bank and is located in a city in which commercial bank holidays may differ from local stock exchange holidays (for example, on Columbus Day banks are closed in New York while the New York Stock Exchange remains open; conversely, on Good Friday New York banks are open while the New York Stock Exchange is closed) it is suggested that parties add to that definition the requirement that such day also be a scheduled trading day on local stock exchanges. The expectation is that a seller of an option reasonably can be expected to be open on a Seller Business Day and this has relevance in several contexts, including when notice of exercise may be given. Accordingly, notice may be given on a day when the city where the seller is located is up and running but the relevant exchange is not, because the necessary valuation will occur on the first following day on which it can be presumed that both the seller and the exchange are functioning.

"Currency Business Day", which has relevance for the determination of when a Cash Settlement Amount gets paid, is defined as any day on which commercial banks are open for business in the principal financial centre for the relevant currency.

How to exercise an option

When an option can be exercised and the way in which it gets exercised depend on whether that option is European or American. The "Expiration Date" is, in the case of a European style option, the only day on which an option can be exercised and, in the case of an American style option, the day after the last day on which an option can be exercised. In other words, the "Exercise Period" for an American style option runs to, but excludes, the Expiration Date.

The Expiration Date is specified by the parties in the Confirmation, but if that date is not an Index Business Day (in which case the Calculation Agent would be unable to obtain an Index level on that date), then the Expiration Date will be the first following day that is an Index Business Day.

If the option is European style, the option is automatically exercised on the Expiration Date, and no exercise notice is required to be delivered. If the option is American style, the option will be automatically exercised on the Seller Business Day immediately preceding the Expiration Date (ie, the last Seller Business Day in the Exercise Period) if not previously exercised at that time.

If the option is American style, the buyer may also exercise on any other Seller Business Day during the Exercise Period. In such case, the buyer is required to submit an exercise notice on any such Seller Business Day prior to the time specified in the Confirmation. It is presumed that the "relevant" time for this purpose will be the local time in the city where the seller of the option is located for the purpose of receiving notices, and, accordingly, the Confirmation contemplates that the parties will specify that city in the definition of Exercise Period. If a notice of exercise is received after the cut-off time, then it will be deemed delivered on the next following Seller Business

Day, if any, in the Exercise Period. If the parties have incorporated the 1991 *ISDA Definitions*, they may simply specify that Notice of Exercise and Written Confirmation are applicable. Otherwise, the parties must include the exercise provisions. Notice may be delivered orally, including by telephone, but must be followed up with a written confirmation confirming the substance of the notice within one Seller Business Day of the notice. Failure to provide the written confirmation, however, will not affect the validity of the oral notice.

To facilitate exercise procedure, the seller's telephone or facsimile number and contact details for the purposes of giving notice should be provided in the space indicated in the Confirmation.

Relevance of valuation
The Confirmation contemplates that the level of the relevant equity Index will be assessed as of a "Valuation Time". The Valuation Time may be a specified time in a specified locale, as stipulated by the parties, or it may be determined by reference to a particular event or fixing, such as the close of trading on a designated exchange.

The valuation of the Index is relevant in order to determine the Cash Settlement Amount, if any, that becomes payable to the buyer of the option.[11]

Determining the level of the Index is straightforward enough when the relevant markets are behaving normally and the Index is calculated and announced by its sponsor in the usual way. In that case, the Calculation Agent will look to the Index at the Valuation Time on the Valuation Date to fix the Index level for the purposes of determining the Cash Settlement Amount. In the case of a European style option, the Valuation Date will be the Exercise Date, and in the case of an American style option, the Valuation Date will be the Index Business Day immediately following the Exercise Date.

What happens if something unnatural is occurring in the market-place on a date that would otherwise be the relevant Valuation Date? What if the shares of several of the constituent companies reflected in the Index are suspended or otherwise not trading on that date? If the Index is capitalisation weighted, does it matter that the affected companies happen to be the biggest companies in the Index or the smallest? If the parties have agreed to value the Index at the close of business, does it matter that a particular market disruption occurred at the open of business but by the close the markets were in fact functioning smoothly? What if the Index as published is wrong? What if there is a timely correction of the mistake? What constitutes a timely correction? What if the sponsor suddenly moves to publication of the Index on a 24-hour basis so that there is no "closing time" as such? What if the sponsor ceases to publish the Index?

These and other issues like them were aired and discussed at length by the working group (and without the pressure of a two-party trade which invariably gives rise to time and other considerations that make it difficult to address and resolve such issues). The conclusions reached for the sponsored OTC equity index option market are reflected in the provisions relating to "Valuation" in the Confirmation and discussed below. Three categories of relevant events were distinguished for separate treatment: (i) Market Disruption Event; (ii) Adjustment to Index; and (iii) Correction of Index.

The effect of a Market Disruption Event
"Market Disruption Events" are events that disrupt the underlying market or markets relevant to the Index and make it impractical if not impossible for the Index level on

any such day to reflect accurately the value of the Index. A Market Disruption Event is defined as the occurrence or existence on any Index Business Day during the half hour period that ends at the Valuation Time of any suspension of or limitation imposed on trading on the specified Exchange in securities comprising 20 per cent or more of the level of the Index if the Calculation Agent determines that suspension or limitation to be material. For example, assume that trading in the shares of several of the companies whose shares comprise the Nikkei 225 is suspended. Assume also that, immediately prior to those suspensions, the level of the Nikkei 225 was 17,000. A Market Disruption Event would exist for an OTC option on that Index if (i) the shares of those companies were suspended within the half hour immediately preceding the close of trading on a day that, but for those suspensions, would have been a Valuation Date, and (ii) the total price of the shares of those companies (after application of the appropriate divisor and adjustments) would contribute 3,400 or more to the level of the Index immediately prior to the shares being suspended. If the Index is capitalisation weighted, then the size of a company that has had trading in its shares suspended on the Exchange, and not just the price of those shares immediately prior to their suspension, will be relevant.

Parties may add to the definition of Market Disruption Event suspensions or limitations on specified exchanges in option contracts or futures contracts on the Index. Such an addition might be appropriate for a transaction in which the seller is purchasing option contracts or futures contracts on such exchanges to hedge its obligations under the transaction. Thus the seller of an option on the Nikkei 225 might be hedging in futures contracts on the Nikkei traded on the Singapore International Monetary Exchange or the Chicago Mercantile Exchange. In that case, the parties might agree that a disruption in the trading of Nikkei futures contracts on those exchanges could result in a delay in the valuation for the transaction.

Parties are advised to consider whether certain types of exchange-imposed limitations on trading should be ignored by the Calculation Agent in determining whether a material suspension or material limitation has occurred. For example, certain securities exchanges impose limitations to regulate price movements in individual contracts or securities. These limitations, such as certain maximum intra-day price movement limitations, might be triggered frequently during the course of a trading day. After reviewing the policies of a relevant exchange in respect of such trading limitations, the parties may wish to consider specifying that the Calculation Agent should ignore all or certain of these limitations that imply in a non-discriminatory way to regulate price movements.

If there is a Market Disruption Event on a day that otherwise would be the Valuation Date, then the Valuation Date will roll to the first succeeding Index Business Day on which there is no Market Disruption Event, unless there is a Market Disruption Event on each of the five Index Business Days that immediately follow that first day that would have been a Valuation Date. In that case, that fifth Index Business Day will be the Valuation Date and the Calculation Agent will determine the level of the Index as at the Valuation Time on that Index Business Day in accordance with the formula for and method of calculating the Index last in effect prior to the commencement of the Market Disruption Event. In constructing that level, the Calculation Agent is required to use the exchange-traded price as of the Valuation Time on that Valuation Date of each security comprising the Index unless trading in the relevant security had been materially suspended or materially limited, in which case the Calculation Agent is instructed to use its good faith estimate of the exchange-traded price that would have prevailed but for that suspension or limitation.

The Calculation Agent is required to notify the other party (or the parties in the event the Calculation Agent is a third party) of the existence or occurrence of a Market Disruption Event on any day that would but for the occurrence of a Market Disruption Event have been a Valuation Date.

Other contemplated adjustments

Change in the sponsorship or methodology of the Index may give rise to adjustments to the calculations contemplated by the Confirmation. Not every change in sponsorship or methodology will have this consequence. Each such change will be assessed in the first instance by the Calculation Agent. The Confirmation provides that if the Index is not calculated by the agreed sponsor but is calculated by a successor acceptable to the Calculation Agent or if the Index is replaced by a successor index using the same or a substantially similar formula for and method of calculation as used in the Index, then the Calculation Agent is required to use the Index so calculated and announced.

If, however, there is a material change in the formula for or method of calculating the Index or the sponsor in any other way materially modifies the Index (other than a modification prescribed in the formula or method to maintain the Index in the event of changes in constituent shares and capitalisation and other routine events) or the sponsor fails to calculate and announce the Index, the Calculation Agent is required to calculate the Cash Settlement Amount using, in lieu of the published level for the Index, an Index level determined by it. In making that determination, the Calculation Agent is required to use the formula for and method of calculating the Index last in effect prior to the modification of the Index or the failure of the sponsor to publish the Index, as the case may be, but will use only those securities that comprised the Index prior to that change or that failure.

Taking account of corrections

The Confirmation also provides that, if an Index level used to calculate a Cash Settlement Amount is subsequently corrected, a compensating payment will be made in certain circumstances. The payment will be required if the correction is published within 30 days of the original publication and one of the parties notifies the other of the adjustment within 30 days of publication of the correction. Interest shall be paid on the adjusted difference at a rate equal to the cost of funds of the party receiving the payment.

How to calculate the Cash Settlement Amount

Generally speaking, the "Cash Settlement Amount" is the amount, if any, by which the option exercised is in-the-money based upon the level of the Index at the Valuation Time on the Valuation Date. The Cash Settlement Amount will be determined by the Calculation Agent and will equal the number of options multiplied by the "Strike Price Differential" multiplied by the currency unit of the country in which the Index is compiled. Strike Price Differential means, in the case of a call, the amount by which the Index level exceeds the Strike Price, and, in the case of a put, the amount by which the Strike Price exceeds the Index level. Thus, the buyer of a call receives payment in the event the Index exceeds the Strike Price and nothing otherwise, and the buyer of a put receives a payment in the event the Index level is less than the Strike Price and otherwise receives nothing.

The seller is required to pay the buyer the Cash Settlement Amount three Currency Business Days after the Valuation Date.

As noted in a footnote to the Confirmation, parties may wish to provide details as to how, when and by whom the relevant exchange rate will be determined if a currency conversion is contemplated.

Credit-related provisions

If parties are using the Confirmation other than in connection with the ISDA Master Agreement or any other master agreement, they should consider adding credit-related provisions to the Confirmation. There is no provision in the Confirmation itself for defined events of default, such as cross-default to third-party debt, or for early termination or settlement.

In addition, and in any event, parties using the Confirmation are advised to consider applicable local law issues, regulatory, tax and accounting matters and any other issues not specifically addressed in the Confirmation.

Developments since publication of the Confirmation

The equity products working group has not been idle since the publication of the Confirmation. The group[12] is preparing forms of confirmations for OTC options on shares of a single issuer: one of those forms provides for settlement of the option by physical delivery of shares and the other for cash settlement.

Also on the group's agenda are a form for equity swaps and a booklet of definitions that would include most of the non-economic substantive provisions and definitions presently contained in the Confirmation or contemplated for other equity derivative transactions, including OTC options on shares of a single issuer and artificially created clusters or "baskets" of shares. The definitions booklet would permit a much shorter version confirmation that would incorporate by reference provisions currently set out at length in the Confirmation.

Notes

[3] Reprints of the Confirmation are available, each at US$5 for ISDA members and US$10 for non-members, from the International Swaps and Derivatives Association's New York office at 1270 Avenue of the Americas, Rockefeller Center, Suite 2118, New York, NY 10020-1702 (tel: (212) 332 1200, fax: (212) 332 1212) or London office at 33 King William Street, London EC4 9DU (tel: (071) 283 0918, fax: (071) 860 1150).

[4] ISDA is an international organisation of more than 150 commercial, merchant and investment banks and other institutions. Since its founding in 1985, a primary ISDA purpose has been to promote practices conducive to the efficient conduct of the business of swaps and other derivatives. Outlined below is a chronology of events in the area of documentation that demonstrates ISDA's commitment to achieving this goal:

1992: New *ISDA Master Agreement* introduced. Makes possible documentation of a broad range of derivatives transactions under a single master agreement and promotes the benefits of cross-product netting, which works to reduce risks. ISDA also publishes separate booklets of definitions for foreign exchange and currency option transactions and swaps with US government entities.

1991: *ISDA Definitions* published, covering five new currencies, new floating rate alternatives and new products – commodity swaps, foreign exchange forwards and forward rate agreements.

1990: *Addenda to ISDA Schedules for Options* published, extending documentation under the 1987 ISDA Master to options on swaps ("swaptions").

1989: *Addenda to ISDA Schedules for Interest Rate Caps, Collars, and Floors* published, extending documentation under the 1987 ISDA Master to caps, collars and floors.

1987: *ISDA Interest Rate and Currency Exchange Definitions* published. Providing common language with which to define swap.transactions in 15 currencies.

1987: Standard form contracts – *ISDA Interest Rate Swap Agreement* and *ISDA Interest Rate and Currency Exchange Agreement* – introduced.

1986: *Code of Standard Wording, Assumptions and Provisions for Swaps* updated, offering more thorough coverage for events of default and termination, tax-related issues and cross-border issues, but still limited to US dollar swaps.

1985: *Code of Standard Wording, Assumptions and Provisions for Swaps* introduced. Establishes a common vocabulary for swaps participants to speak the same language in defining the terms for US dollar interest rate swaps.

[5] Active in the working group were representatives from Bankers Trust, Citibank, Crédit Suisse Financial Products, J.P. Morgan, Merrill Lynch, Mitsubishi Finance, Nomura, Paribas Capital Markets, Swiss Bank Corporation and Union Bank of Switzerland, and from Allen & Overy, Linklaters & Paines and Cravath, Swaine & Moore.

[6] Use of the name of a sponsored index could, depending upon the context, give rise to certain licensing issues. The working group decided that it would not be appropriate to take a collective view on these issues given the multiplicity of sponsors and approaches to the subject.

[7] But see the "Developments since publication of the Confirmation" section.

[8] Parties may also specify in the introduction that they are incorporating the 1991 *ISDA Definitions* into the Confirmation. These definitions provide more detail and choice in respect of certain matters covered by the Confirmation, such as business day conventions and the role of the Calculation Agent. Language is included for establishing the presumption that any conflict between the Confirmation and any definition or term incorporated into it will be resolved in favour of the provision that is set out in the Confirmation.

[9] It is possible also to document an "Asian style" option (ie, the option pay-out would be based on an average of the Index level at specified intervals during the relevant period) by specifying that choice and making certain minor modifications to the form.

[10] See note 12 of the Confirmation.

[11] There may be reasons why the parties may require the valuation to be based on the arithmetic mean of levels of the Index either (i) at the Valuation Time on more than one Valuation Date or (ii) at more than one Valuation Time on a single Valuation Date. Averaging may smooth out temporary aberrations in price level. Also, it may be undesirable or impossible to unwind an entire hedge position concurrently with a one-off valuation. Although multiple valuation dates and multiple valuation times are not expressly provided for in the Confirmation, modifications to permit valuation by reference to either or both can be accommodated.

[12] Membership of the working group has been expanded to include representatives from Deutsche Bank, Goldman Sachs and Salomon Brothers.

Appendix to Chapter Eight

Confirmation of OTC equity index option transaction

Heading for Letter[1]

[Letterhead of Party A]

[Date]

Transaction

[Name and Address of Party B]

Heading for Telex[1]

Telex:

Date:

To: [Name and Telex Number of Party B]

From: [Party A]

Re: Option Transaction

Dear

The purpose of this [letter agreement/telex] (this "Confirmation") is to confirm the terms and conditions of the Transaction entered into between us on the Trade Date specified below (the "Transaction"). [This Confirmation constitutes a "Confirmation" as referred to in the ISDA Master Agreement specified below.][1]

[The definitions and provisions contained in the 1991 ISDA Definitions (as published by the International Swap Dealers Association, Inc.) are incorporated into this Confirmation. In the event of any inconsistency between those definitions and provisions and this Confirmation, this Confirmation will govern.][1]

[This Confirmation supplements, forms a part of, and is subject to, the ISDA Master Agreement dated as of [date], as amended and supplemented from time to time (the "Agreement"), between you and us. All provisions contained in the Agreement govern this Confirmation except as expressly modified below.][1]

The terms of the Transaction to which this Confirmation relates are as follows:

General Terms:

Trade Date:	[ ], 199[ ]
Option Style:	[American] [European] Option
Option Type:	[Put] [Call]
Seller:	[Party A] [Party B]
Buyer:	[Party A] [Party B]
Index/Price Option:	[ ]
Number of Options:	[ ][2]
Multiple Exercise:	[Applicable/Inapplicable]
[Minimum Number of Options:][3]	[ ]
[Maximum Number of Options:][3]	[ ]
[Options Must be Exercised in Integral Multiples of:][3]	[ ]
Strike Price:	[ ][4]
Premium:	[ ]
Premium Payment Date:	[ ], subject to adjustment in accordance with the Following Business Day Convention.
Index Business Day:	A day that is a Seller Business Day and is (or, but for the occurrence of a Market Disruption Event, would have been) a trading day on [each of] the Exchange [and [insert relevant Option and Future Exchanges]] other than a day on which trading on [any] such exchange is scheduled to close prior to its regular weekday closing time.
Seller Business Day:	Any day on which commercial banks are open for business (including dealings in foreign exchange and foreign currency deposits)[5] in [ ].[6]
Currency Business Day:	Any day on which commercial banks are open for business (including dealings in foreign exchange and foreign currency deposits) in the principal financial center for the relevant currency.
Exchange:	[ ]
Calculation Agent:	[ ], whose determinations and calculations shall be binding in the absence of manifest error.[7]

Procedure for Exercise:

Exercise Period:	[The Expiration Date][8] [Any Seller Business Day from, and including, [ ] to, but excluding, the Expiration Date between 9:00 a.m. and [4:00 p.m.] (local time in)][9]
Expiration Date:	[ ] or, if that date is not an Index Business Day, the first following day that is an Index Business Day.
[Notice of Exercise and Written Confirmation:][10]	[Applicable, except in the case of automatic exercise.[11] If the notice of exercise is deliv-

Automatic Exercise:	ered after [4:00 p.m.] on a Seller Business Day, then that notice will be deemed delivered on the next following Seller Business Day, if any, in the Exercise Period.][12] [If not previously exercised,][13] an Option shall be deemed automatically exercised on [the Seller Business Day immediately preceding the Expiration Date][13] [the Expiration Date].[14]
Seller's Telephone or Facsimile Number and Contact Details for Purpose of Giving Notice:	[ ]
Exercise Date for an Option:	The Seller Business Day during the Exercise Period on which that Option is or is deemed to be exercised.
Valuation:	
Valuation Time:	At [the close of trading on the Exchange] [:00 a.m./p.m. (local time in)[15]].
Valuation Date [in Respect of Each Exercise Date][16]:	[The Exercise Date][17] [The Index Business Day next following the Exercise Date][18], unless there is a Market Disruption Event on that day. If there is a Market Disruption Event on that day, then the Valuation Date shall be the first succeeding Index Business Day on which there is no Market Disruption Event, unless there is a Market Disruption Event on each of the five Index Business Days immediately following the original date that, but for the Market Disruption Event, would have been the Valuation Date. In that case, (i) that fifth Index Business Day shall be deemed to be the Valuation Date, notwithstanding the Market Disruption Event, and (ii) the Calculation Agent shall determine the level of the Index as of the Valuation Time on that fifth Index Business Day in accordance with (subject to "Adjustment to Index" set forth below) the formula for and method of calculating the Index last in effect prior to the commencement of the Market Disruption Event using the Exchange traded price (or, if trading in the relevant security has been materially suspended or materially limited, its good faith estimate of the Exchange traded price that would have prevailed but for that suspension or limitation) as of the Valuation Time on that fifth Index Business Day of each security comprising the Index.
Market Disruption Event:	The occurrence or existence on any Index Business Day during the one-half hour period that ends at the Valuation Time of

	any suspension of or limitation imposed on trading (by reason of movements in price exceeding limits permitted by the relevant exchange or otherwise)[19] on [(i)] the Exchange in securities that comprise 20% or more of the level of the Index [or (ii) [ ][20] in options contracts on the Index or (iii)[ ][20] in futures contracts on the Index] if, in the determination of the Calculation Agent, such suspension or limitation is material.
	For the purpose of determining whether a Market Disruption Event exists at any time, if trading in a security included in the Index is materially suspended or materially limited at that time, then the relevant percentage contribution of that security to the level of the Index shall be based on a comparison of (i) the portion of the level of the Index attributable to that security relative to (ii) the overall level of the Index, in each case immediately before that suspension or limitation.
	The Calculation Agent shall as soon as reasonably practicable under the circumstances notify the [parties] [other party] of the existence or occurrence of a Market Disruption Event on any day that but for the occurrence or existence of a Market Disruption Event would have been a Valuation Date.
Adjustment to Index:	If the Index is (i) not calculated and announced by the agreed sponsor[21] but is calculated and announced by a successor sponsor acceptable to the Calculation Agent or (ii) replaced by a successor index using, in the determination of the Calculation Agent, the same or a substantially similar formula for and method of calculation as used in the calculation of the Index, then the Index will be deemed to be the index so calculated and announced by that successor sponsor or that successor index, as the case may be.
	If (i) on or prior to any Valuation Date the Index sponsor makes a material change in the formula for or the method of calculating the Index or in any other way materially modifies the Index (other than a modification prescribed in that formula or method to maintain the Index in the event of changes in constituent stock and capitaliza-

	tion and other routine events) or (ii) on any Valuation Date the sponsor fails to calculate and announce the Index, then the Calculation Agent shall calculate the Cash Settlement Amount using, in lieu of a published level for the Index, the level for that Index as at that Valuation Date as determined by the Calculation Agent in accordance with the formula for and method of calculating the Index last in effect prior to that change or failure, but using only those securities that comprised the Index immediately prior to that change or failure (other than those securities that have since ceased to be listed on the Exchange).
Correction of Index:	If the level of the Index published on a given day and used or to be used by the Calculation Agent to determine the Cash Settlement Amount is subsequently corrected and the correction published by the Index sponsor or a successor sponsor within 30 days of the original publication, either party may notify the other party of (i) that correction and (ii) the amount that is payable as a result of that correction. If not later than 30 days after publication of that correction a party gives notice that an amount is so payable, the party that originally either received or retained such amount shall, not later than three Currency Business Days after the effectiveness of that notice, pay to the other party that amount, together with interest on that amount at a rate per annum equal to the cost (without proof or evidence of any actual cost) to the other party (as certified by it) of funding that amount for the period from and including the day on which a payment originally was (or was not) made to but excluding the day of payment of the refund or payment resulting from that correction.
Cash Settlement Terms:	
Cash Settlement:	Applicable; Seller shall pay to Buyer the Cash Settlement Amount, if any, on the Cash Settlement Payment Date for all Options exercised or deemed exercised [in respect of that date].[22]
Cash Settlement Amount:	An amount, as calculated by the Calculation Agent, equal to the [Number of Options][23] [number of Options exercised on the relevant Exercise Date][24] multiplied by the

	Strike Price Differential multiplied by one [ ].[25]
Strike Price Differential:	An amount equal to the greater of (i) the excess, as of the Valuation Time on the [relevant][24] Valuation Date, of [the Strike Price over the level of the Index][26] [the level of the Index over the Strike Price][27] and (ii) zero.
Cash Settlement Payment Date:	Three Currency Business Days (each of which is a Seller Business Day) after the [relevant][28] Valuation Date.
Transfer:	Neither party may transfer any Option, in whole or in part, without the prior written consent of the non-transferring party.

Account Details:
   Payments to Seller:
      Account for payments:
   Payments to Buyer:
      Account for payments:

This Confirmation will be governed by and construed in accordance with the laws of [   ] [(without reference to choice to law doctrine)].[29]

Closing for Letter[30]

Please confirm that the foregoing correctly sets forth the terms of our agreement by executing the copy of this Confirmation enclosed for that purpose and returning it to us or by sending to us a letter or telex substantially similar to this letter, which letter or telex sets forth the material terms of the Transaction to which this Confirmation relates and indicates your agreement to those terms.

                                    Yours sincerely,
                                    [PARTY A]
                                    By: _____
                                        Name:
                                        Title:

Confirmed as of the date
first above written:
[PARTY B]
By: _____
   Name:
   Title:

Closing for Telex[30]

Please confirm that the foregoing correctly sets forth the terms of our agreement by sending to us a letter or telex substantially similar to this telex, which letter or telex sets forth the material terms of the Transaction to which this Confirmation relates and indicates agreement to those terms, or by sending to us a return telex substantially to the following effect:

"Re:

We acknowledge receipt of your telex dated [   ] with respect to the above-referenced Transaction between [Party A] and [Party B] with a Trade Date of [   ] and an Expiration Date of [   ] and confirm that such telex correctly sets forth the terms of our agreement relating to the Transaction described therein. Very truly yours, [Party B], by [specify name and title of authorized officer]."

Yours sincerely,
[PARTY A]
By: _____
Name:
Title:

Notes

[1] Include if applicable.

[2] In addition, include a Multiplier if it is intended that the Cash Settlement Amount will be based on a percentage (eg,. 50% or 200%) of the performance of the Index.

[3] Include if an American style option providing for multiple Exercise Dates.

[4] The parties may insert a number representing an index level as the strike price or a formula from which the strike price will be determined.

[5] If the Seller is not a commercial bank and is located in a city in which commercial bank holidays may differ from local stock exchange holidays, add "and which is a scheduled trading day on local stock exchanges".

[6] Specify city in which Seller is located for the purpose of receiving notices.

[7] If the Calculation Agent is a third party, the parties will want to consider any documentation necessary to confirm its undertaking.

[8] Include if European style option.

[9] Include if American style option. Specify city in which Seller is located for purposes of receiving notices.

[10] Include if American style option.

[11] Alternatively, specify: "Except in the case of automatic exercise, Buyer must deliver irrevocable notice to Seller (which may be delivered orally, including by telephone) of its exercise of any right granted pursuant to an Option during the hours specified above on a Seller Business Day in the Exercise Period. If the notice of exercise is delivered orally, Buyer will execute and deliver a written confirmation confirming the substance of that notice within one Seller Business Day of that notice. Failure to provide that written confirmation will not affect the validity of that oral notice."

[12] If an American style option providing for multiple Exercise Dates, add "Buyer must specify in that notice the Number of Options being exercised on that Exercise Date" and, as a new paragraph, "Buyer may exercise all or less than all the unexercised Options on one or more Seller Business Days during the Exercise Period, but, except in the case of automatic exercise as provided below, on any Seller Business Day may not exercise less than the Minimum

Number of Options or more than the Maximum Number of Options and that number of Options must be an integral multiple of the amount specified above."

[13] Include if American style option.

[14] Include if European style option.

[15] Specify city in which the Exchange is located, if applicable.

[16] Include if multiple exercise American style option.

[17] Include if European style option.

[18] Include if American style option.

[19] Certain exchanges impose different types of limitations on trading to regulate price movements in individual contracts or securities. The parties should consider whether any such limitations should be ignored by the Calculation Agent in determining whether a material suspension or material limitation imposed on trading has occurred (eg, whether only limitations on maximum intra-day price movements should be considered in order to avoid the frequent Market Disruption Events which would otherwise occur on some exchanges).

[20] Specify the relevant exchange, if applicable.

[21] Consideration should be given to whether a sponsor to an Index should be identified as such in the relevant Confirmation.

[22] Include if multiple exercise American style option.

[23] Include if European style option or single exercise American style option.

[24] Include if multiple exercise American style option.

[25] Specify the currency unit of the country in which the Index is compiled or the currency unit to which the underlying values comprising the Index are converted for purposes of compiling the Index (eg, ECU for Eurotrack 200). If a Multiplier has been specified in this Confirmation, add "multiplied by the Multiplier".

If a currency conversion is contemplated, parties may wish to provide for how, when and by whom the relevant exchange rate is to be determined.

[26] If the transaction is a Put Option.

[27] If the transaction is a Call Option.

[28] Include if multiple exercise American style option.

[29] Consider whether any additions or deletions relating to applicable jurisdiction or regulatory, tax, accounting or other requirements should be made in this Confirmation if these are not addressed in a related master agreement.

[30] Include if applicable.

9

Long-term implications

John Watson
Westminster Equity Limited

Introduction

Predicting the future is rightly regarded as an area where angels fear to tread. To mitigate in advance the possible charge of foolishness it may be useful to make explicit what the aims of the activity are and are not.

First, however gratifying it would be, the aim is not to be accurate. A prediction does not lose its value because it subsequently proves not to have been correct. More important are the roles it has to play in preparing people to adjust to change and in providing a framework within which that change can be better understood regardless of the exact form it takes. It is in this spirit that what might otherwise appear as a list of foolhardy predictions is put forward here.

The impact of equity derivatives can be broken usefully into three sectors. First is the part they have to play in bringing about closer integration of the equity market with other major financial markets. Second is their influence on the culture, traditions and structure of the underlying stock market. Finally is their emergence as a new and fast-growing market in their own right.

Other markets, notably the bond and FX markets, are already at an advanced stage in these same processes. Much can be deduced from the changes they have already undergone about the changes likely to be experienced in the stock market. But the uniqueness of the stock market, and its likely reaction to derivatives, must not be underestimated. It has a higher public profile and is more closely regulated than other markets. It has a culture and set of traditions more deeply entrenched than most.

For these reasons change may be slower. It is nonetheless inevitable. It is a matter of time before any remaining Canutes finally disappear beneath the incoming waves.

All interest groups will experience the rising pressure for change. Institutional investors, fund managers, issuers, traders and brokers will all need to adjust themselves to changes in available products and the risks and opportunities offered by them. The industry as a whole will need to evolve a fundamentally different structure. We attempt here to define the forces at work and to anticipate what the emerging structure will look like.

Impact on other financial markets

Acceleration of market integration

The continuing evolution of equity derivatives has some predictable effects on other financial markets. Perhaps the most crucial is the increasing erosion of barriers between those markets.

Consider the effect of the ability to swap an equity portfolio. It is hard to overestimate the potential for fundamental market change from this source. For the first time, a direct comparison can be drawn for example between the economic effect of owning an equity portfolio and that of holding a portfolio of bonds.

Suppose the one-year equity swap market will pay the S&P 500 against Libor flat, and the interest rate swap market will pay Libor flat against T-Bills minus 50 basis points. Hence the swap market as a whole will pay the S&P 500 plus 50 basis points against T-Bills flat. Anyone who continues to hold T-Bills who has access to the swap markets and complete freedom to invest must logically believe therefore that the S&P 500 will underperform T-Bills by 50 basis points over one year.

Any financial instrument which can be swapped into US$ Libor can be compared directly with another. Just as concepts such as yield to maturity or spread to treasuries provided an objective method of establishing the relative value of different instruments in the bond market, swaps for the first time allow an objective measure of relative value between markets.

In this way it could be said that the financial market's "subconscious" view of where the equity market is going relative to other markets is revealed by equity swaps. Furthermore, they provide the means whereby anyone who disagrees with that view can express his disagreement and benefit if he proves to be right.

This is not so clear at present, given that equity swap rates are still largely determined by the costs (and particularly by the treatment of taxation of dividends) of market makers who will hedge their position in the swap using cash or futures markets. The longer-term expectation, however, must be that equity swap rates will be driven by supply and demand from end-users who will use the market to express their views of its valuation relative to other markets. As has been seen already in the case of the futures market, the swap market will tend, longer-term, to lead the cash markets. In the long run the tail may well be expected to wag the dog.

Of course this is oversimplified in taking no account of the value of liquidity (ie, the value of being able to liquidate a position prior to maturity at a lower transaction cost) or of credit considerations. The basic economic equivalence, or rate of exchange, between markets is nonetheless clearly established. If the bridge is not yet built, at least the bridgehead is secured.

The effect of this must be an ever-increasing traffic between the equity market and other financial markets and, as both cause and effect, the traditional users of one market will become increasingly familiar with the others. For financial institutions these developments will demand greater flexibility of structure, particularly with regard to product-related organisational divisions.

The writing is on the wall for the traditional investment banks' dichotomy between fixed interest and equity businesses. Demand will grow for financial institutions and individuals in them who straddle different markets. It is easy to overdramatise, but probably more dangerous to underestimate, the implications of this development. It would not be inappropriate to draw an analogy between the power of swaps to integrate different financial markets, and that of a move to a recognised common currency for settlement on the development of trade.

Impact on the equity market

The erosion of barriers between the equity market and other financial markets will profoundly affect the equity market itself. Given the very particular nature of equity market culture and its long-established traditions, this is probably more true of the equity market than of most others. There will in addition be effects from the advent of derivatives which can be thought of as internal to the equity market.

Impact on market price

The very word "invest" implies that the investor is a buyer. Its near antonym, "divest", implies that the "divestor" is a seller, but of something previously bought. Leaving the issuing companies aside, we can say that through derivatives it is, for the first time, possible to sell the stock market without previously having bought it.

This simple fact has profound consequences which may represent a kernel of truth behind the common fears and suspicions of derivatives. The Japanese authorities' belief that derivatives were responsible for driving down their stock market seems to be a good case in point.

Ignoring the issuer of stock, it can be said that before the advent of derivatives (or at least stock loans and shorting techniques which as previously mentioned are derivatives of a sort), a bearish view on the market had to be expressed by selling stock already held. Unless selling at the top of the market, this would involve pain, ie locking in a loss (or a profit below the highest previous mark to market). The further the market fell the greater the pain. On the other hand, a buyer would naturally be reluctant to sell and miss out on future gains in a rising market. This gave the market an unbalanced tilt in favour of upside moves.

We might try to clarify this as follows. Before derivatives the universe of people who could express a bearish view on a stock was limited to those already holding it, while the universe of those who could express a bullish view on the stock would include this but would extend to all potential stock investors. Now derivatives extend the universe of those who can express a bearish view on a stock beyond those already holding it to those who are able to short it. The development of short funds, which set out explicitly to take outright short positions, is evidence of how far this possibility has already been institutionalised in practice.

It would be foolish to ascribe a historical tendency for stock markets to rise to this upward tilt. What can legitimately be claimed, however, is that the advent of derivatives counterbalances an existing upward tilt of the market. The fallacy behind the Japanese authorities' position was that it assumed that the market had previously been in a state of equilibrium, while derivatives tilted it towards the downside. It can be seen that, in removing an existing tilt, derivatives could be said to provide a more balanced market environment which could be a healthier background for long-term development.

It might be worth adding for the sake of completeness that there may always remain an upward tilt to the market in that there will always be more risks in holding a short compared with a long position. The risk that a stock loan may be called is one. Another is the fact that a short position in stock has unlimited, while a long position has limited, downside. If we accept (as seems by definition true) that a share price cannot fall below zero then an investor with a long position cannot lose more than the original cost of the shares, whereas there is no theoretical limit to how much an investor with a short position could lose. Finally, a long position can be held indefinitely, whereas the concept of a perpetual stock loan seems to be too far into the realms of financial science fiction. The existence of these risks gives grounds to believe that some degree of upward skewing of market forces may be a permanent feature of the market. Hence the advent of derivatives may reduce, but will not remove, the upward tilt in the stock market.

Impact on market volatility

A fear frequently voiced is that the growth of derivative markets will cause volatility in the underlying markets. Is there any substance in this fear?

The crucial question is whether market end-users will be net buyers or sellers of options (volatility). If end-users are natural buyers of volatility then, by definition, market middlemen will be net sellers. Market middlemen will hedge option positions in the underlying market. If they are net sellers of volatility they will tend to sell stock into a weak market and buy stock in a rising market. In spite of their need to experience the lowest possible volatility, their intervention will thus actually magnify whatever volatility already exists in the underlying market. If, on the other hand, end-users become net sellers, and hence middlemen net buyers, the opposite will be true and the growth of the derivative market will reduce market volatility.

What reasons are there to suppose that the balance of end-user interest will be long or short volatility? In general it seems easier to imagine end-users who need protection against high volatility than those who can profit from it. That makes it tempting to think that end-users will be net buyers of options. But end-users generally buy options as directional, not as volatility, positions. This may be the emerging long-term trend but for the immediate future it is less easy to see the balance of demand for equity options.

In commodities it seems more clear cut. The end-user is characteristically a consumer or producer trying to buy protection against excessively high or low prices and is thus a natural buyer of volatility. This is less obviously true of equity derivative markets where there is nothing exactly corresponding to a consumer with his "real" need to buy, nor a producer with his dependence on selling, and where major market end-users will include those selling covered calls against their existing positions in the underlying.

In the heyday of the OTC Nikkei options market, end-users were strong net sellers of volatility, mainly Japanese institutional investors aggressively selling Nikkei puts.

This is not to say that equity market end-users will tend to be net sellers of volatility, only that there are significant forces on the selling side which ought to restrain the growth of volatility in the underlying market. The common fear of derivative-induced volatility in the underlying market does not seem well founded.

If the impact on the direction of volatility is unclear, it does seem clear that, as these processes become more frequent and transparent, volatility will increasingly come to be seen as a tradable commodity in its own right, and studies of the dynamics of volatility and predictions as to its likely future direction will become commonplace. On the back of this, traders who manage short-term positions in volatility are already emerging as a type. A natural development would be volatility funds to offer retail investors a long-term play on the volatility of selected instruments or markets.

Impact on investors

Deeper analysis of view

We have already put forward the view that equity investors, however reluctant or unaware of it they may be at present, are in some way or other already users of equity derivatives. Awareness of this will grow along with increasing familiarity with derivatives. This will, in turn, give rise to a deeper analysis by the investor of his own needs and wants. For example, as he becomes aware that owning a share means being long a call and short a put, he will become aware of the possibility of owning the call without taking the short put position. This will encourage him separately to evaluate the upside and downside in a stock. Eventually he will learn to express his view by selling the put or buying the call and to think of appropriate strike levels, according to how he perceives the relative probability of downside risk and upside potential. The decision may, in the long run, also be dependent on what he thinks of the market's valuation of volatility. All other things being equal, buying the call will be relatively more attractive than selling the put when the volatility implied by their prices is below that which the investor expects in the underlying market during the life of the options.

Polarisation of market view and single stock view
Another fundamental question the traditional stock investor will have to start asking himself is whether his desire to buy a stock comes from a belief that the market as a whole is undervalued, or from a belief that the individual stock is undervalued relative to the market. Greater confidence in analysing his belief into these two components will lead to greater use of index derivatives to express the view or mixture of views he has. He will learn to express a bullish view of the market by buying index futures/calls, selling index puts or receiving the index on a swap, and he will learn to isolate his view of a company's undervaluation relative to the market by offsetting a long position in the company's stock with a short position through index derivatives.

Will derivatives bring more money into the equity market?
There is some reason to believe so. Logically it could be said that it is only possible to have a view on the investment value of a single stock if you have a prior view on that of the whole market. It is utterly pointless to think that Toyota is a buy unless you think the Nikkei is a hold or a buy or at least will not lose value sufficient to wipe out the expected gain on Toyota. In practice all too few investors seem to approach the question so systematically.

Logically, more information is needed to invest in an individual stock than to invest in a market as a whole. This means that more money should be available to be invested in the market as a whole than in individual stocks. Index derivatives, which provide a relatively simple and easy means of investing in the market as a whole, may therefore increase the total amount of money invested in the stock market. The two processes described above for futures and options will ensure that, as long as the derivatives positions taken are themselves bullish, the effect on the underlying market will also be bullish.

The specific impact of the gearing effects of derivatives on the underlying markets is discussed as a separate topic below.

Is it a "zero sum game"?
The question is whether for every winner in the game there must be a loser. Sceptics tend to assume that, if derivative markets are profitable for market middlemen, then the end-user must be a loser. The question is most usually asked of the OTC options markets. Futures and exchange-traded options markets are thought to be more transparent and to have more obvious parallels with the underlying markets.

If this is accurate then there is a long-term inhibiting factor on the growth of the market. If it is not accurate but is believed to be accurate by potential end-users, then it will inhibit market development in the short run.

Consider the case of a market middleman who sells a call option to an end-user and hedges himself by taking a long position in the cash market. The end-user makes money if the market moves up. Who then is losing out? Provided he manages his hedge properly and has not underestimated market volatility, the market middleman ought to make money regardless of which way the market moves, and thus he is not the loser.

It is clear that there is no loser in the derivatives market corresponding to the winner. Is there one in the underlying market? It does not seem to make sense to say that the seller of the long cash position is the loser. The strongest statement that could be made about him is that he incurred an opportunity loss by selling early, but that is a very different matter from an actual loss and in no way acts as a counterbalance to the option buyer's very real profit. That is true also of trading in the underlying market itself, so the most that can be said is that derivatives are no more of a zero sum game than the underlying.

Where is the value added?
The point that the exponent of the "zero sum game theory" of derivatives might be making is that there is no value added by derivatives. If so, it is a bleak outlook indeed for the future development of the market.

In Chapter One, various sources of value added have been discussed in terms of how derivatives satisfy the fundamental needs of end-users. These included execution considerations, protecting end-users against, or enabling them to sell their indifference to, future uncertain events and allowing them to express views of the market which are not efficiently expressed by cash market strategies.

At this stage it is possible to provide a more fundamental answer to the question. We have said that options should be seen as components of cash positions. The options trader (who hedges his position in the cash market) can thus be seen as splitting the cash instrument into its component parts. This creates value in the same way as an oil refiner creates value by splitting crude oil into its more marketable distillates. The value of the sum of its parts may be greater than that of the whole, and the person who splits the whole into its parts provides a valuable service for which he can rightly expect to be paid.

Impact on broking

Traditional research-driven brokerage is set to disappear. It is expensive for a broker to develop, and sometimes difficult to keep, a market-leading research function. It is even more difficult to be repaid for this through brokerage commissions. A customer cannot be compelled to execute transactions with a particular broker regardless of the quality of his research.

As has already been implied, the logical role for microeconomic analysis is in relation to stock picking. This means running alpha funds or spread-trading stocks. There is no similar relationship between microeconomic logic and the promotion of derivative sales.

The research/commission relationship which has been withering on the vine in traditional stock brokerage may therefore be adapted to the alpha or single-stock-related investment and trading businesses but has no identifiable place in mainstream derivatives business. end-users will not buy options or structures from you based on your view of the underlying index, basket of stocks or stock. This battle will have to be fought rather on the grounds of understanding (and perhaps leading) the client's needs, ability to tailor transactions to those needs, credit, execution efficiency, and last but not least, pricing. The main determinant of pricing will be the relative efficiency with which hedging can be executed in the cash markets.

None of these factors can in any obvious way be linked to the strength of the traditional broker's stock analysis function.

On the other hand, a different type of research function which is directly related to derivative sales can be envisaged. The blueprint would be an analyst whose function it is to produce macroeconomic views on the back of which derivative sales/structuring staff offer the products to capture those views most efficiently. Such a function would not only meet a real market need but would be tied in much more safely to the commission income stream and can perhaps succeed in keeping the advice confidential and exclusive. The house offering the structure will naturally tend to promote views which can be expressed by those products it knows it can offer and where it has the inside track in design and pricing.

If a stock analyst succeeds in obliging a client who accepts his recommendation to buy stock through his salesmen, the amount of the transaction is unlikely to be significant compared with that of a potential derivatives transaction. Derivative (particularly index) transactions, can easily exceed $100 million, whereas the total amount of one stock bought on the back of a single recommendation will rarely reach a significant fraction of that amount. If the stock analyst is to have a chance of generating significant amounts of commission it is therefore necessary for him to spread his recommendation around a wide range of, if not all, possible buyers. This makes it practically impossible to create any significant obligation on the part of those buyers to place orders with the analyst's firm.

There are some corresponding difficulties lying in wait for the derivatives analyst. One is that clients are suspicious of structures offered by OTC derivatives houses. This suspicion gives rise to a very understandable desire to have any structured transaction priced by a competing house. A wedge is thus inserted also between the derivatives analyst and the income stream he needs to justify his existence. Nevertheless there remains a stronger rationale for the investment in a derivatives research function than for the traditional company analyst function.

Impact on trading
Index as trading benchmark
Equity index derivatives have prepared the way for a revolution in equity derivatives trading not only in providing a practical means of laying off the market risk in running trading books but also, more fundamentally, in providing a market benchmark against which trading can be carried out more rationally. In this respect, equity trading is set to develop along the path already well trodden by the bond markets.

A good indicator of the state of evolution of any bond market is the ease with which a consensus regarding benchmark issues and the "right" relative value to them of non-benchmark issues can be identified. This is crucial to investor confidence in the market. It also reduces the risk for market makers who can hedge their bond positions with offsetting positions in the benchmark. This means that their exposure can be limited to the "spread", ie to the relative price movement between the bond and the benchmark.

Analogy with the bond market – duration/convexity vs. beta
There is nothing exactly analogous to a government bond in equity markets, but since the development of tradable index derivatives, a similar role is increasingly being

played by stock indices. Bond market trading tools utilised in this process, such as duration and convexity, which provide a rational approach to calculating the amount of benchmark necessary to offset the interest rate exposure in a given bond position, have their equity counterparts in various adaptations of the concept of beta which allows the calculation of the amount of index (and hence the amount of index derivative) necessary to offset the market risk in a stock position.

Just as the bond trader can take the interest rate element out of his original exposure and leave himself with a more benign spread risk, the stock trader will be able to hedge the market risk of his trading book in index derivatives, leaving a position which is exposed only to the relative (beta-weighted) over- or underperformance of individual stocks relative to that of the market. In other words, the trader is left to manage an open position in stock alpha.

In bond trading, managing spread risk has developed into a function quite distinct from that of managing interest rate risk. The former requires an intimate knowledge of individual names and their market perception, whereas the latter requires an overview of the domestic economy of the country whose currency's interest rate is concerned, as well as the international economic background into which it fits. The former implies a micro- whereas the latter implies a macroeconomic perspective.

The importation of these techniques is set to have a profound effect on the organisation of a typical equity trading room and on the expertise demanded from the traders. It is to be hoped that, by applying a greater degree of rationality and specialisation to the risk-taking process, there will also be greater benefits to the end-user in terms of a tighter bid/offer spread.

Directional to volatility risk management
A bank which has sold an option to an end-user without hedging its position has directional exposure. That is to say it will lose money if the market price of the underlying moves in the "wrong" direction. As has already been explained, the bank can, by delta hedging its position, neutralise exposure to the market price at the expense of incurring an exposure to the volatility of that price.

The exposure of a hedged option position to volatility is a complex subject and must take account of the fact that, in extreme market conditions, theoretical option models tend to break down. Furthermore, trading may be suspended making it practically impossible to delta neutralise a position just when it is most essential. There are also crucial differences between the type of volatility experienced. Volatility may be directional, ie trending or mean reverting (tending to fluctuate on either side of a price level without going anywhere). The same statistical volatility can produce dramatically different results for a dynamically hedged portfolio depending on the type of volatility and the price and time intervals adopted for rebalancing the hedge.

At its most basic level, the exposure is fairly simple. Assuming normal market conditions, a net seller of options will profit from low and suffer from high volatility and vice versa. But even at this level, very few financial institutions are presently really comfortable with the risk.

Very few people at senior management levels in banks and investment banks have a sound grasp of what is involved. What limits should be imposed on a volatility book, and how to police those limits, are subjects which require a higher basic understanding of derivatives than is commonly found at upper management levels. Market risk may be second nature to senior investment bankers and credit risk second nature to senior commercial bankers, but volatility risk is a relative novelty to both. The full potential of the market may not begin to be realised until an understanding of volatility risk percolates up to the highest levels of management. Until then financial institutions will be rightly nervous about the size of their exposure to volatility. In the immediate future, market middlemen will gear their business to laying off volatility risk by finding the other side of a trade.

The market will, during this period, tend to act most efficiently as a conduit between end-users with a need to buy volatility and those with a need to sell it. The growth of the market's function as a net buyer or seller of volatility will be limited. This may be no bad thing as it would be worrying to think that powerful houses with the ability to create volatility by impact trading in the cash markets would have a vested interest in doing so as a result of being heavily long volatility through their options books. Well-known incidents along these lines have already occurred. This is a key area which will need to be monitored by market regulators who must be prepared to react with a swift, and perhaps heavy, hand if the existing trickle should develop into a stream.

Volatility forward curve
The volatility manager's desire to minimise his exposure by finding the other side of a trade is, in a crucial way, more problematic than that of the swap or bond book manager. A swap book manager can lay off a four-year swap against a five-year swap leaving himself exposed to the one-year rate four years forward. His break-even one-year rate is a fairly simple arithmetical calculation and he may be able to achieve a reasonable degree of neutrality by duration or convexity hedging.

A volatility manager who tries to cover a short five-year option position by buying a four-year option (even with the same strike) has no simple arithmetical measure of the effective implied volatility at which he owns the forward option and no tools ready to hand with which to neutralise the risk.

A similar situation holds for options of the same maturity with mismatched strikes.

Until the technology becomes better developed and more widely disseminated, volatility managers will not be able to set off their volatility risk with similar looking positions of different maturity and strike. This all points to the option sector of the equity derivative business being more slowly integrated into mainstream business than the futures and swaps sectors, while market middlemen keep their open volatility positions strictly limited.

Impact on blue chip share valuation
There are some interesting implications for the relative valuation of blue chip shares. To the extent that the premium on blue chip shares derives from their use as a vehicle for investors who are bullish on the market but have no views on particular shares, the premium will be eroded as investors learn to use the more efficient route of index derivatives.

To the extent that the premium derives from the liquidity of blue chips and consequent lower transaction costs, it is also due to be eroded by the advance of those index derivatives where efficient markets have developed. It might be said that the premium on blue chip stocks is set to be reduced both by their "market benchmark" premium and at least by part of their liquidity premium, as their function is usurped by index derivatives.

Growth of derivative-related trading in cash markets
Derivative-related trading already accounts for a significant share of the volume of the

more advanced stock markets. The expectation must be that this will increase as end-users take more of their equity exposure through derivatives.

Given that pricing competitiveness will be a critical determinant of market share for equity derivative houses, and given the scale of stock brokerage and bid/offer costs, it is clear that those houses with the strongest stock execution capacity will tend to dominate the equity derivative business in the longer term.

This may be no bad thing in that the benefit of more efficient cash market execution skills will be passed back to the end-user in the form of more competitive derivative pricing. At the same time, those in the best position to execute transactions most efficiently will have the strongest possible incentive to do so.

One structural problem with the stock market is the weakness of the incentive of the agency broker to obtain best execution for his clients. Too often a broker can window-dress his execution through impact trading. Assume that an investor asks a broker to execute a buy programme in a given stock. Assume further that the client measures the performance of the broker each day against closing prices. It is easy for the broker to trade in such a way that he drives the price as far up as possible at the close and so achieves an average buying price through the day which compares favourably with the close. This is one of many examples of inefficiency or malpractice in existing stock market trading. It is one which is set to decline as stock trading houses are forced by derivative price competition to execute their own hedge transactions with the maximum efficiency, and finally forced by the same competition to pass more and more of this efficiency onto the market end-user.

Impact on fund management
The death knell for index tracking
The likely future for index-tracking funds seems predictable enough. Equity index derivatives give investors the ability to track indices with 100 per cent accuracy. The days of fund managers earning high fees for tracking indices with limited accuracy while incurring high transaction costs must surely be numbered. Matching the performance of an index will cease to be a meaningful target and instead will become a hurdle which fund managers will have to overcome before they can expect to earn significant fees.

Strategic to tactical asset allocation
Asset allocation will increasingly become tactical rather than strategic. This phrase, or something like it, is often thrown out in discussions about the impact of derivatives on fund management. What does it mean?

Asset allocation addresses the question of how much of a fund is invested in different markets. The markets may be markets for different product types, eg shares, bonds, commodities, or different markets for the same product type, eg US equity market, Japanese equity market, German equity market. Until now it was necessary for a fund manager to employ specialists in each market in which he intended to invest. Furthermore, the specialist needed infrastructural support such as data supply. This meant that a decision to invest in a new market necessarily involved a long-term commitment and could appropriately be made only at the most senior management level.

Now a fund can dramatically change its allocation among markets without incurring tracking error which would previously have given rise to a need for market specialists. Responsibility for changing allocation within a fund can now be devolved to lower management levels and no longer means changing the structure of the organisation.

The continuing role of stock picking
The traditional market specialist is skilled in taking decisions about relative values of securities within a market, not in assessing the relative value of one market against another. It might seem at first sight as if tactical asset allocation threatens the livelihood of this traditional market specialist or stock picker. This is not necessarily so.

Polarisation of market risk and alpha risk management
Strategic asset allocation may undergo a metamorphosis and re-emerge as addressing, not the question of which markets to be in, but of which markets to manage alpha (or spread) risk in. This does require traditional market specialists and so needs to be treated as a long-term decision, made at the highest levels of management.

It must be understood that the decisions of the tactical asset manager to move out of a particular market have no logical implications for the business of alpha (or spread) risk management within that market. It is now possible for a fund to close down its entire exposure to a market and yet keep the same number of stocks, or even increase the number of stock positions in the market, as long as the market risk in that stock portfolio has been neutralised.

The question of how much of the fund's capital to invest in the over- or underperformance of individual stocks against the market is a matter of, among other things, the fund's strength relative to the competition in picking stocks in that market, not of its perception of the valuation of the market relative to others.

The move from strategic to tactical asset allocation in fund management, and the consequent evolution of fund managers into tactical asset managers and stock pickers, runs exactly parallel to the polarisation of stock traders into market traders and spread traders predicted earlier.

If the mating of the equity and derivative markets gives birth to tactical asset allocation within existing funds, a predictable next generation is global or tactical asset funds. The whole idea of such a fund would be to derive value not from the skill of selecting instruments within a market but from the skill of being in the right market at the right time. It is possible to identify several new products coming onto the market bearing evidence of this progeny.

Securitisation of fund management (replication)
Funds presently requiring active management will be replicated by derivative structures which have no need for active management. The most obvious case is the index-tracking fund already mentioned, but in general, wherever fund managers are following a consistent and systematic policy there is potential for their policy to be replicated by a derivative or combination of derivatives.

In Chapter One it was mentioned that the policies of cyclical and counter-cyclical equity fund managers could be replicated respectively by buying a call and selling a put on the market. It is necessary for such managers to ask themselves what value they are adding by doing this "manually". If they are confident of outperforming the derivative strategy, they should be aware that it is this marginal value that justifies their departure from it. They should be clear about the source of this marginal value and how to obtain the best leverage from it. Where this is a matter of stock picking ability, they should be clear that this has nothing to do with the basic strategy of buying calls or selling puts on the market as a whole, and decisions relating to that should not be allowed to cloud their stock picking decisions.

It is only to be expected that, as time passes, more and more sophisticated fund management strategies will be replicated by new derivative instruments. The derivatives will be made available to retail investors in the form of warrants. It will thus become necessary for fund managers to show how they can add value over and above what could be done by a derivative, in order to avoid their role in the market being usurped by warrants or other securitised derivatives.

Impact of increased gearing

Equity derivatives increase the leverage available to the equity investor. What will happen to the cash that is freed? It is useful to work through some of the implications with some simple models. Suppose equity investors were suddenly converted to using derivatives as a substitute for stock buying.

First, assume that they sell their stock portfolios and replace them by buying futures. If the margin on futures is 15 per cent and they can keep their stock market exposure constant, this will release 85 per cent of their original investment amount. The futures premium would obviously be inflated as a result of their activity and this would be exploited by cash/futures arbitrageurs putting on long stock/short futures positions. The net effect on the stock market might therefore be neutral as the arbitrageurs buy up the stock sold by the original stock investors. This still leaves the original investors with a cash amount equivalent to 85 per cent of the value of their original stock portfolio. Any part of this invested in further purchases of index futures will exert upward pressure on the stock market. The immediate effect will be to raise the futures premium, but this will again feed quickly through to the cash market owing to the activities of cash/futures arbitrageurs.

A rather different scenario can be envisaged if we assume that the original stock investors replace their stock holdings with call options (on exactly the same amount of exactly the same stocks).

The call options will cost a fraction of the value of the underlying stocks (say 20 per cent). The sellers of the options will hedge themselves by taking long positions in the stock, ie by buying back some of the stock sold by the original investors.

Assuming the hedge to be 60 per cent, the net effect on the stock market would be a reduction by 40 per cent of the money invested in the stock market. On the other hand, 80 per cent of the value of the original end-investors' portfolio is now available for investment elsewhere. If they invest all of it in other markets, the net effect on the stock market would be unilaterally bearish. If, on the other hand, they invest all of it in further purchases of calls, the net effect would be an increase in funds coming to the market as the option sellers would hedge their positions by buying a further 48 per cent (60 per cent of 80 per cent) of the original portfolio amount, making their total holding 108 per cent of the end-investors' original total.

The net effect of the end-investors' move from cash to options markets is thus somewhere between a 40 per cent reduction and an 8 per cent increase in the total stockholdings of the end-investors and the option sellers, depending on the amount of released cash invested in taking additional stock market exposure. We shall not attempt to estimate the net final impact on the amount of funds invested in the cash market. Rather we will limit this to a description of the mechanism whereby funds will be redistributed around the market by derivatives.

Likely evolution of the derivatives market

Is there a future?

Before speculating further on the type of future it is worthwhile asking whether there will be a future. There are specific reasons for raising this question. The first is the other side of the coin from the risk to the fund manager that his role may be usurped by derivatives which replicate his fund management strategy. The question raised earlier was: Why should the fund manager's strategy in the cash market not be replicated by a derivative and subsequently securitised? But replication is a symmetrical relationship and it must logically be possible to reverse the question. Why should derivatives offered to the market by the middleman not be replicated by the end-user via cash market trading strategies?

Take the example of an end-user who wants to buy a call. He buys it from an option trader who hedges his position by a (dynamically adjusted) long position in the cash market. If end-users develop sufficient familiarity with derivatives, what is to stop them "making their own"? If the business of delta hedging option positions is a profitable one for the middleman, could the end-user not earn that profit by taking the hedge as a substitute for the option?

The most sophisticated market end-users are already doing this and the trend will continue. There are some reasons to suppose that there are limits to how far it will go. First, a market middleman can potentially harness economies in hedge adjustment transaction costs by his ability to agglomerate a diverse portfolio of options on the same underlying instrument. That is to say, he needs only to hold and adjust the net hedge for the total portfolio, thus reducing his interest rate exposure and potentially reducing transaction costs. An end-user, almost by definition, will not be able to do this. This factor can, by itself, allow the middleman to sell options profitably to the end-user at a cost below that which the end-user could achieve by replicating the hedge.

The second competitive advantage of the market middleman is his inside track on execution in the cash market. If the derivative market middleman is also an active broker/dealer in the cash market, he will be able to cross trades, avoid commissions and potentially get inside the market bid/offer. In general, the further up the information curve he is, the more access he has to deal flow, the more he will be able to cut his transaction costs.

Both these factors relate more directly to the single stock or small-basket sector of the equity derivatives market where transaction costs dominate the economics of a trade. In the stock index derivatives sector, where transaction costs are less significant, the end-user will find it easier to replicate option positions in the cash market rather than buying them from middlemen. It seems therefore that the position of non-index-based market middlemen may be secure for the foreseeable future.

Dependence on new product flow
In Chapter One it was stated that derivatives are subject to the same product life cycle as other financial instruments. This means that the industry, as presently structured, needs a constant flow of new products if it is to support not only exchanges and brokers, but also arbitrageurs and OTC traders. Is there any reason to suppose that the flow of new products will continue, and if so, where is it likely to come from?

Customer demand
At the moment, the initiative in developing the derivative market lies not with the end-users, but with the middlemen. In this respect it is no different from other high-technology industries which must anticipate and, to some extent, create (or at least catalyse) their end-users' future needs. This phenomenon is familiar enough in the software business where the marketing tries to convince people that they need something they cannot yet even understand.

The standard sell must not be "these are your needs – here is the product to satisfy them" but "wouldn't you have these needs if there was a means of satisfying them? Here is a product that provides you with the means".

In the future, end-users may be more proactive in the process of development. For the moment it is market middlemen to whom we must look for the next generation of products. The question is how can they approach this challenging task?

New combinations of existing products
It may be less glamorous to look in this direction for the development of new products, but it would be wrong to underestimate its importance. In the swaps market, the simple idea of combining a swap with a bond (asset), as opposed to a bond liability, gave rise to the asset swap market, a whole new important subsection of the derivative market, and provided the bond market for the first time with a lender of last resort (by creating a ceiling for individual bond yields). Another obvious member of the same family is the swaption, which again is the result of a simple combination of two products but one which has carved itself a formidable niche in the derivatives market.

For a serious product development specialist the construction of a matrix of financial products and systematic exploration of the commercial possibilities of the logical combinations would be a mandatory and productive exercise.

Isolation of new distillates
Going back to the fundamental source of value added from the OTC options business, that is to say its splitting a complex entity (stock) into its component parts (long call and short put), the question is whether or not this splitting could go on indefinitely or whether options themselves already represent the ultimate unsplittable "subatomic particle".

The answer to this is already indicated in Chapter Six where a regular call is said to be equal to a down-and-in call plus a down-and-out call. Splitting a call in this way does not seem to have the same fundamental logic as splitting the underlying into call and put. It seems as if the latter is in some way unique, whereas the former is one of several splits that could be made. Leaving that question aside, there seems no reason to suppose that, for example, the down-and-in call is not itself capable of further analysis. Whether any commercial application can be found for the resulting new products is another question.

Reconfiguration of the defining characteristics
The other major method of developing new products is by reconfiguring the defining characteristics of an existing product. For example, the defining characteristics of an option include: underlying; size; start date; maturity date; exercise date; and strike.

Reconfiguration can involve removal, multiplication or variation. By asking whether we need a maturity date at all we might end up with a perpetual option. By asking whether there must be only one maturity date we might develop an amortising option. By asking whether the maturity date must be fixed, we might develop an option that pays out in terms of extended maturity.

Variation of a defining characteristic begs the question of variation in relation to what. The usual suspect is the level of the underlying market. Strike lookback and cliquet options are obvious examples. But there is no reason for the horizon to be limited to that.

One likely alternative candidate is the volatility of the underlying. As has been said, volatility is one exposure against which the option market middleman cannot neutralise himself. If he is long volatility then he will make excess profits from high market volatility. It would be enormously advantageous to him to be able to give away some of that value in return for protection against low volatility, for example, by linking the strike or maturity of the option to actual market volatility levels.

Some defining characteristics are easier to fit to this pattern than others, but there is a need for the product development specialist to develop the matrix and explore all of the logical possibilities and their possible commercial applications however implausible they may initially appear.

A combination which looks at first sight impossible to create, price or apply in any commercial context, may be your competitor's next flavour of the month. It seems clear enough that the alternatives have not yet been exhausted. Further finds are to be expected before the mine is finally closed down.

Introduction of further fundamental concepts
Just as forwards and futures rely on the fundamental concept of time value of money, options can be said to rely on the additional fundamental concept of volatility. Any equivalent fundamental concept could potentially revolutionise the market and give rise to an entire generation of new products. Are there any candidates?

The most obvious candidate is correlation. Some would question its novelty on the grounds that it is a necessary component of multi-factor interest rate option models. Outperformance and better-of options are clear examples of options involving covariance but they look rather more like a subspecies of existing options (the result of multiplying a defining characteristic – the underlying) rather than a new species in their own right.

It is perhaps too early to say what the long-term impact of correlation on the market development will be. What is clear is that it would be foolish to rule out the possible introduction into the process of further new fundamental concepts and that any which are introduced would be a source of new products.

Conclusion

Time and space have restricted this to a hurried whistle-stop tour around the long-term implications of equity derivatives. Although it is far from comprehensive, at least the scale and some likely directions of change have been signposted.

Not only the equity derivate market itself, but the underlying equity market and other financial markets will feel the force of change. All existing interest groups – investors, borrowers and market professionals – will be affected fundamentally.

The directions of change are so numerous and diverse that it makes no sense to encapsulate them in a short summary. Two themes, however, do seem to justify being singled out.

The first because it is counterintuitive as well as far-reaching in its consequences. That is that the stock market is not the natural habitat for the end-investor. While he might be attached for the moment to the illusion of security offered by familiar names on stock certificates, he will eventually come to understand that shares are effectively closet compound derivative positions which do not exactly address his needs. His needs as more clearly defined will be more efficiently and exactly met by derivative products specifically designed for the purpose. The underlying market will become the rightful domain of the market professional. Competition among those professionals will be expressed not only through the design and introduction of new derivatives, but in the increasing efficiency of hedge execution in the underlying market. The post-glasnost redrawing of borders and resettlement of peoples have their counterparts in restructuring and a potential refugee problem in the post-derivative financial world.

The second major theme is not at all counterintuitive but deserves to be singled out. It emerges in different guises through the range of parties presently interested in the market. That is the polarisation of matters concerning single stocks and those concerning whole markets or indices. This will represent a major decision point both for the various types of institution and for the individuals working in them. Investors will have to choose between alpha funds and asset allocation funds; traders between managing spread risk or market risk; the emerging category of volatility trader between managing single stock volatility and market or industry volatility; the analyst between a micro- and a macro-economic focus.

It might seem as if the major derivative-related changes have already taken place. The opposite may be true. Compared with older, supposedly simpler and more primitive, industries the financial industry is still lamentably backward in its structural evolution. Take the building industry as as example. Specialists within this industry include real estate agents, developers, architects, building surveyors, quantity surveyors, structural engineers, building contractors and myriad categories of sub-contractor. In spite of all the expenditure of capital and effort and in spite of the prevalence of super-qualified "rocket scientists", the derivatives industry has so far struggled to organise itself into: salesmen, traders, "product development guys" and just possibly "structuring guys". It should come as little surprise that there are a few changes on the cards.

10

Glossary

Americus Trust A US alternative to derivative instruments in which a special-purpose trust buys common stock and then sells instruments which entitle the holders to different parts of the future income and growth components of that stock. The trust acts as a depositary for the shares which are exchangeable into a certificate or unit divisible into two parts. (See PRIMES and SCORES.)

Asset swap The generic term for any structure in which an interest-rate or currency swap (qv) is applied to an existing asset, such as a bond, to transform its cash flows. The asset swap market looks for anomalies between bond pricing and the swap curve to generate attractive, synthetic investment opportunities. In practice, the market tends towards the creation of high-quality floating-rate structures for bank investors.

Basis risk The risk that the price of an instrument does not move in exact correlation with the price of another being used as a proxy for it. Often used in the context of the relationship between the price of a derivative instrument (especially futures) and the underlying asset or market. When a portfolio of stock is used as a surrogate for, or is intended to follow, an index, this risk is referred to as tracking (qv) risk.

Beta (β) Beta is a measure of the sensitivity of the price of a stock to moves in the market as a whole.

A high beta stock will be expected to outperform in a rising, and underperform in a falling, market. Statistically it is the covariance between the price of a stock and market level.

BOUNDS A proprietary equity derivative product listed on the Chicago Board Options Exchange (CBOE). The BOUNDS is a long-term option-like product that replicates the return of an option buy-write. (See also PRIME.)

Buy-write An option strategy involving the purchase of the underlying and selling out if the money calls against it.

Calendar spread   A derivatives trade involving combinations of futures or options with different maturities, for example the purchase/sale of a short maturity option and the sale/purchase of a long maturity option. In the simplest version of the trade the options have the same strike price. Such trades allow traders to take views on volatility and on the differing time-decay characteristics of the options.

Call   A call option gives the buyer the right to purchase an underlying instrument at a pre-determined price or level before or at maturity. The higher above this price the underlying rises, the more valuable the call. Buying calls is therefore a bullish strategy.

Cash   In general, the term cash market is synonymous with underlying market. The cash market underlying an interest-rate futures contract would be the relevant bond market; that underlying an equity option would be the relevant stock market. The term is frequently used interchangeably with "spot", particularly in relation to futures markets.

Collar   Also known as a cylinder, a collar is the combination of a call and put (normally the sale of a call and the purchase of a put) which limits exposure to movements in the price of the underlying instrument within a range defined by the strike prices of the call and put. For example, the collar would hedge against a stock index falling below a certain level but would limit an investor's ability to benefit from upward rises. The strike prices of the call and put can be chosen in such a way that the collar hedge involves no upfront payment of premium (a free collar).

Convertible bond   Usually referred to as simply convertibles or converts, convertible bonds are bonds whose principal can, at the holder's option, be redeemed in the issuer's stock at a pre-determined price. In effect, these bonds contain a long-term embedded American-style call option. In exchange for this option, the bondholders typically accept a lower coupon than currently available on straight bonds in the same currency and maturity.

Covered warrants   An option or warrant is covered if it is matched by an offsetting position in either the underlying or in another option or warrant. Like equity warrants (qv), covered warrants are normally long-dated securitised call options. Unlike equity warrants, they are exercisable into existing shares and so do not lead to dilution (qv) of the company's share price. For the life of the warrant the issuer holds "cover" in the form of shares or options/warrants on the shares to ensure its obligations in the event of exercise. Such warrants are issued by financial institutions unrelated to the company but are also issued by institutional holders of the shares who wish to enhance the yield on their portfolio by taking in option premium.

Delta   The delta of an option is a measure of the amount the option price will change for a unit change in the underlying asset. A stock option with a delta of 0.65 will be expected to move 65 cents in price for every $1 move in the price of the underlying stock. The delta of an option increases as the option goes more in-the-money and decreases as it goes further out-of-the-money. Delta is also affected by the time remaining before expiry.

The measure, derived from options pricing models, also gives the ratio of options to stock that needs to be held to create a portfolio that is riskless for small changes in the price of the underlying. A delta of 0.65 means that such a portfolio could be constructed by going long options on 100 shares and short 65 shares. The concept that positions can be hedged by combining underlying instruments and derivatives in delta-related ratios is at the heart of the risk management of derivatives.

Dilution   The effect on the earnings per share, and so share price, of existing shares of issuing new stock via, for example, secondary market issues, the exercise of convertibles (qv) or warrants (qv).

Future   A futures contract is a form of forward contract that obliges the holder to take delivery of/deliver a specified quantity of an asset at a fixed price on a fixed date in the future. Anyone long futures is contracted to buy the underlying asset, anyone short futures has to deliver the asset. Contracts need not be held to maturity but may be closed by selling a long position or buying back a short position. Although physical delivery is still required in some financial futures contracts, many are now cash-settled. Instead of delivering the underlying asset, the buyer (seller) of the contract receives (pays) the difference between the contract price and the underlying price.

Futures contracts are exchange-traded and standardise the quantity of the underlying asset to be delivered per contract, the minimum price movement for the contract, and the period of the contract. Futures contracts are normally traded in a cycle of March, June, September and December deliveries/settlements. Thus, to maintain an exposure to a market for longer than three months, users have to renew or roll-over their futures positions.

Futures are used to hedge against or speculate on movements in these underlying markets. Financial futures contracts are available on equity indices, exchange rates and interest rates. So, for example, an investor wishing to speculate on a rise in the FTSE-100 stock index could buy a contract on Liffe for a sterling price around 25 times the level of the index (because the Liffe contract specifies £25 per index point). If the index rises, the contract will rise in value accordingly. Currency futures are priced in terms of their underlying exchange rate. So, a September 1993 sterling/dollar contract quoted at 1.4350 means that that the futures market will sell sterling for dollars at a rate of 1.4350.

Gamma   The amount by which the delta (qv) of an option changes for a unit change in the price of the underlying asset. Most strategies for hedging options positions are based at least partly on the concept of delta neutrality – that is immunising the option portfolio against small changes in the price of the underlying asset. Gamma is an important concept in the process of delta hedging because it is a measure of how quickly a position can move from being delta neutral to becoming a bullish or bearish price trade.

Hedge   To protect an existing position against price movement by buying or selling fully or partially offsetting positions in either the cash or derivatives markets.

In-the-money   An option is said to be in the money if it has intrinsic value (qv). A call is in the money if the price of the underlying asset is above the exercise price. A put is in the money if the asset price is below the exercise price. In general, an option is in the money if exercising it would produce a profit at present market levels, ie if it has intrinsic value (qv).

Intrinsic value   The profit that would be realised if an option were immediately exercised – the greater of the difference between the exercise price of the option and the price of the underlying and zero.

LEAPS   A proprietary product listed on the Chicago Board Options Exchange, introduced in 1990. LEAPS are long-term (three to five year) equity options available as both puts and calls (qv) on individual stocks and on selected indices. (See also SCORES.)

Margin   The amount of money, or other acceptable security, that must be deposited against futures positions (and some options positions) to cover book losses in the position arising from adverse price changes in the contract. Initial margins are increased or reduced depending on movements in position values. Such increases or decreases are sometimes referred to as variation margin.

Margin back option/warrant   Options/securitised options which guarantee the option buyer a payout at maturity at least equal to the premium (qv).

Option   The right to buy (call) or sell (put) a specific quantity of a specific asset at a pre-determined level (the strike or exercise price) at or before a future date. Options exerciseable only on maturity are known as European-style; those exerciseable at any time during their life are known as American-style. Unlike a futures contract, the buyer is under no obligation to exercise his right to buy or sell. If the cost of exercising the options would be greater than the cost of executing the trade in the underlying market, the option is allowed to expire worthless. This limits the maximum potential loss of the holder to the initial cost of the option (the premium). The seller (writer) of an option, however, is obliged to fulfil his side of the bargain if the holder exercises. His potential losses are therefore unlimited.

The price of an option (the subject of many option pricing theories and models) is typically viewed as consisting of two parts: intrinsic value (qv) and time value (qv). The latter, the value the market attributes to the probability of profitable exercise before the option expires, depends on the underlying asset price, the exercise price, the time to expiration, interest rates, and on the expected volatility of the price of the underlying asset. The more volatile the price, the more likely it is to breach the strike of the option profitably. This dependence on volatility lies at the heart of options pricing models and at the heart of much options trading. Options are not simply tools for hedging against or speculating on price movements in the underlying asset, a call being used to go long and a put to go short, they can be used to construct price-neutral trades whose pay-off is independent of the level but dependent on the volatility of the price of the underlying.

Exchange-traded financial options are available on most major stock indices, long- and short-term interest rates and exchange rates. A flourishing over-the-counter market also exists in which options with customised maturities and strike prices can be purchased. As well as options with simple strike price and pay-off characteristics, a number of so-called exotic structures are available which give buyers the average or even the highest price of the underlying over a given period, or which give exposure to a basket of underlying assets unavailable in the cash markets.

Options are highly-leveraged instruments. For a small upfront premium, exposure can be gained to large positions in the underlying asset. Their prices tend therefore to be more volatile than the underlying.

Put/Call parity   The proposition that, ignoring interest rates, the price of a put option is equal to the value of a call option with the same exercise price and time to expiration and a short position in the stock. An arbitrage possibility exists if this is not the case, although this is limited in practice by transaction costs.

Path-dependent options   A class of options where the pay-off is a function of the path followed by the underlying price during the options' life rather than the underlying price at exercise or maturity. The most common types are Asian or average options, where the pay-off is the difference between the strike and the average price of the underlying asset rather than its price on a specific date; lookback options, whose pay-off is the difference between the strike and the best possible price achieved over the lifetime of the option; cumulative options, whose pay-off is a function of cumulative movements in the underlying; and options whose strike price is set on maturity and is related to the path of the underlying price.

Program trading   In the context of derivatives, "program trading" refers to arbitrage trading between equity cash and futures markets. At its simplest, it involves going long one market and short the other to exploit anomalies in pricing in the futures markets. More generally, the term refers to any trading of large "baskets" of stock, especially that involving the highly computerised exploitation of anomalies between cash and derivatives markets.

Put   A put option is the right without obligation to sell the underlying asset at a pre-determined price.

PRIMES   One of the two units created by Americus Trusts (qv). The acronym stands for "prescribed right to income and maximum equity". Equivalent to an out-of-the-money European buy-write entitling the holder to all the income and some appreciation from the underlying shares.

Quanto   Quanto options are options where the notional principal of all or part of the transaction is unknown (hence the name, which means "how much?"). This condition occurs most commonly in instruments which contain embedded currency exposures, for example equity index swaps (qv) which give investors exposure to a foreign market but which are denominated in the investor's local currency.

For example, a US investor may wish to receive the Nikkei stock index and pay US dollar Libor but, because he does not wish to take a view on the yen/dollar exchange rate, he needs to have the Nikkei return dollar neutralised. If the Nikkei increases in value by 10 per cent over the life of the transaction, the investor will expect to receive a 10 per cent return in dollar terms on the Nikkei side of the swap.

Range forward   Synonym for zero-cost collar (qv) – an options position involving the purchase of a call option and the sale of a put option with exercise prices chosen so that the premium paid for the call is cancelled by that received for the put. The position removes all the downside exposure beyond a pre-determined point determined by the exercise price of the call option and pays for this by eliminating all the upside exposure beyond a point determined by the strike price of the put.

SCORES   Acronym for special claim on residual equity. Equivalent to a long-term

European-style warrant entitling the holder to all the appreciation in price of the underlying security above a pre-determined strike price.

Spot   The spot price of an asset is the current price in the cash market.

Strike   The price of the underlying asset at which the holder of an option can exercise it.

Swap   In the context of equity derivatives, the term swap normally refers to equity-index-linked swaps. These are agreements to exchange a payment stream that mimics the return of a specified equity index or basket for a payment stream based on a (usually) short-term interest rate index such as three-month Libor. Just as with interest rate swaps, the payments are based on a notional principal amount but no principal amounts are exchanged. The index-return payment is typically the total rate of return (dividend return plus price return) plus or minus a fixed spread, and the floating-rate payment is typically Libor flat. The payment streams may be denominated either in the same currency or in different currencies, and the index-return payment may be hedged into a currency other than that in which the index would naturally be in. For example, an investor can choose to receive returns based on the performance of the German DAX index denominated in dollars.

Swaption   An option which gives the holder the right to enter into a swap at a future date. A payer swaption is the right to pay Libor in exchange for an equity index return. If the index rises above the swaption strike price, the purchaser would exercise the option, locking in the outperformance of the equity index over Libor. A receiver swaption is the right to receive Libor under the swap. If the index return falls below the swaption strike price, the purchaser would exercise the option, locking in the outperformance of Libor. Such swaptions can be used in the monetisation of the value of options embedded in index-linked bonds.

Systematic risk   An alternative term for market risk. The risk common to all securities of the same type. In the case of equities it is the risk that a particular stock position will lose value through the stock price moving in line with the market as a whole. (See Beta.)

Time value   The value of an option deriving from the probability of its moving into or further into the money in the time remaining to expiry. Time value can be thought of as the theoretical fair value of an option less its intrinsic value.

Tracking   In the context of passive portfolio management (indexing) the matching of the returns of a portfolio of shares to those of an equity index. Tracking risk is the risk that the fund fails to match the performance of the index. The amount by which it fails to match the index is known as "tracking error".

Volatility   The amount by which the price of an asset fluctuates over a given period. Normally measured by the annualised standard deviation of daily price changes. When pricing options, traders use historical volatility – the volatility of the asset over a chosen period of time in the past – to estimate future volatility during the life of the option which is input into an options pricing model to estimate the fair price of the option. As an alternative, the option valuation model can be solved in reverse by inputing the market prices to determine the volatility implied by the price. The implied volatility, compared with historical volatility, is often used as a general measure of whether an option is cheap or expensive. In many exchange-traded and some OTC markets, option prices are quoted not in cash terms but in terms of the volatility implied in their pricing.

Warrant   A long-dated, securitised option usually listed in a recognised exchange. Warrants are now available on stock indices, baskets and single stocks as well as currencies and interest rates. Equity warrants are normally simple American call options on the stock of a single company. The issuer (writer) of the option is the company itself which will issue new shares in the event of exercise, unlike the case of covered warrants (qv), where exercise of the option will be satisfied by the delivery of existing shares. Hence equity warrants give rise to stock dilution (qv), whereas covered warrants do not.